AF335174

DEVELOPMENT IN AN INSECURE AND GENDERED WORLD

Gender in a Global/Local World

Series Editors: Jane Parpart, Pauline Gardiner Barber
and Marianne H. Marchand

Gender in a Global/Local World critically explores the uneven and often contradictory ways in which global processes and local identities come together. Much has been and is being written about globalization and responses to it but rarely from a critical, historical, gendered perspective. Yet, these processes are profoundly gendered albeit in different ways in particular contexts and times. The changes in social, cultural, economic and political institutions and practices alter the conditions under which women and men make and remake their lives. New spaces have been created – economic, political, social – and previously silent voices are being heard. North-South dichotomies are being undermined as increasing numbers of people and communities are exposed to international processes through migration, travel, and communication, even as marginalization and poverty intensify for many in all parts of the world. The series features monographs and collections which explore the tensions in a 'global/local world', and includes contributions from all disciplines in recognition that no single approach can capture these complex processes.

Forthcoming titles in this series

**Politicization of Sexual Violence
From Abolitionism to Peacekeeping**
Carol Harrington
ISBN 978-0-7546-7458-0

**Contours of Citizenship
Women, Diversity and Practices of Citizenship**
Edited by Margaret Abraham, Esther Ngan-ling Chow,
Laura Maratou-Alipranti and Evangelia Tastsoglou
ISBN 978-0-7546-7779-6

Previous titles are also listed at the back of the book

Development in an Insecure and Gendered World

The Relevance of the Millennium Goals

Edited by
JACQUELINE LECKIE
University of Otago, New Zealand

ASHGATE

Published by
Ashgate Publishing Limited
Wey Court East
Union Road
Farnham
Surrey, GU9 7PT
England

Ashgate Publishing Company
Suite 420
101 Cherry Street
Burlington
VT 05401-4405
USA

www.ashgate.com

British Library Cataloguing in Publication Data
Development in an insecure and gendered world : the
  relevance of the millennium goals. -- (Gender in a
  global/local world)
  1. Social policy. 2. Economic development--Social aspects.
  3. Women--Social conditions--21st century. 4. Women--
  Economic conditions--21st century.
  I. Series II. Leckie, Jacqueline.
  305.3'09051-dc22

Library of Congress Cataloging-in-Publication Data
Development in an insecure and gendered world : the relevance of the millennium goals /
edited by Jacqueline Leckie.
     p. cm. -- (Gender in a global/local world)
  Includes index.
  ISBN 978-0-7546-7691-1 (hardback) -- ISBN 978-0-7546-9388-8 (ebook)
  1. Women in development--Developing countries. I. Leckie, Jacqueline.

  HQ1240.5.D44D46 2009
  305.4209172'4--dc22
                                                                    2009031262

ISBN   9780754676911 (hbk)
ISBN   9780754693888 (ebk)

Printed and bound in Great Britain by
MPG Books Group, UK

Contents

PART I   INTRODUCTION

**PART II   BEYOND BARE LIFE TO RECONSIDERING
             EMPOWERMENT**

PART III   LOCALIZING DEVELOPMENT IN AN INSECURE WORLD

PART IV   REFLECTIONS

List of Figures and Tables

List of Abbreviations

ACP	African, Caribbean and Pacific Group of States
ADB	Asian Development Bank
ASEAN	Association of South East Asian Nations
AusAID	Australian Government's Overseas Aid Programme
BRA	Bougainville Revolutionary Army
BWPF	Bougainville Women for Peace and Freedom
CCF	Citizens' Constitutional Forum (Fiji)
CEDAW	Convention on the Elimination of all Forms of Discrimination Against Women
CEDAWSEAP	Convention on the Elimination of all Forms of Discrimination Against Women Southeast Asia Programme
CIDA	Canadian International Development Agency
CROP	Council of Regional Organizations in the Pacific
DAWN	Development Alternatives with Women for a New Era
ECOSOC	United Nations Economic and Social Council
EPAs	Economic Partnership Agreements
EU	European Union
GATT	General Agreement on Tariffs and Trade
GDP	Gross Domestic Product
GLBT	Gay, Lesbian, Bisexual and Transgender
GNI	Gross National Income
GT	Gross Tonnes
IGO	International Governmental Organizations
ILO	International Labour Organisation
IMF	International Monetary Fund
IPC	International Poverty Center
LPEM–UI	Institute of Economic and Social Research, University of Indonesia
MDGs	Millennium Development Goals
MMAF	Ministry of Marine Affairs and Fisheries (Indonesia)
NCDs	Non Communicable Diseases
NGO	Non Governmental Organization
ODA	Official Development Assistance
OECD	Organisation for Economic Cooperation and Development
OWAAMV	Okinawa Women Act Against Military Violence
PACER	Pacific Agreement on Closer Economic Relations
PACFAW	Pacific Foundation for the Advancement of Women

PIANGO	Pacific Island Association of NGOs
PICs	Pacific Island Countries
PICTs	Pacific Island Countries and Territories
PICTA	Pacific Island Countries Trade Agreement
PNGDF	Papua New Guinea Defence Forces
PPA	Pacific Platform for Action on the Advancement of Women and Gender Equality
PPP	Public Private Partnerships
PRAN	Pacific Regional Assistance for Nauru
PRSPs	Poverty Reduction Strategy Papers
PWB	Pacific Women's Bureau
RAMSI	Regional Assistance Mission to Solomon Islands
SEWA	Self–Employed Women's Association
SPARTECA	South Pacific Trade and Economic Cooperation Agreement
SPC	Secretariat of the Pacific Community
STIs	Sexually Transmitted Infections
TCF	Textiles, Clothing and Footwear
UN	United Nations
UNDP	United Nations Development Programme
UNFPA	United Nations Fund for Population Activities
UNICEF	United Nations International Children's Fund
UNIFEM	United Nations Development Fund for Women
UNRISD	United Nations Research Institute for Social Development
UNSC	United Nations Security Council
VAT	Value Added Tax
WHO	World Health Organization
WPS	Women, Peace and Security
WSF	World Social Forum
ZANU–PF	Zimbabwe African National Unity–Patriotic Front

List of Contributors

Ronni Alexander is a peace activist and Professor of Transnational Relations at the Graduate School of International Cooperation Studies, Kobe University. She has been in Japan since 1977, teaching at Kobe University since 1989. Her research interests centre on what makes living things secure, and include such topics as gender, HIV, sexuality, development and nuclear issues, with a focus on the Pacific Island States. Recent work also emphasizes peace education. In 2006, she began the Popoki Peace Project, a grass roots peace education endeavour based on her books *Popoki, What Color is Peace?* (2007) and *Popoki, What Color is Friendship?* (2009) to encourage critical thinking, creative expression and action for peace.

A. Haroon Akram–Lodhi is Professor of International Development Studies at Trent University, Peterborough, Canada and has recently co–edited *Peasants and Globalization: Political Economy, Rural Transformation and the Agrarian Question* as well as *Land, Poverty and Livelihoods: Perspectives from Developing and Transition Countries.* His principal research interest is in gender relations and the political economy of agrarian change, with special reference to Asia.

María Angélica Arce Mora was Ambassador of Mexico in New Zealand during 2004–2009. She joined the Mexico Foreign Service in 1981 and holds an MA in International Relations from the National Autonomous University of Mexico. Her diplomatic career has included postings to the Permanent Mission of Mexico to the United Nations in New York, where she became highly experienced in matters relating to disarmament and international security. Arce Mora has previoualy held posts at the Embassy of Mexico in Sweden and at the Permanent Mission of Mexico to the International Organizations in Geneva. She has also served at the Ministry of Foreign Relations in Mexico as Director for International Organizations and as Deputy Director for Canada.

Jenny Bryant–Tokalau is the Coordinator of Pacific Studies at Te Tumu – School of Maori, Pacific and Indigenous Studies, University of Otago and formerly a Senior Lecturer in the Department of Anthropology there. As former Associate Professor of Geography at the University of the South Pacific (Fiji), and Sustainable Development Adviser, as well as Head of the Global Environment Facility unit for UNDP in Suva, she has authored a number of publications and reports on poverty and development. Research interests include poverty, inequality and environment linkages in the Pacific, and issues of environmental governance. She is a member of the Governing Board, Commonwealth Human Ecology Council, London, and until recently a member of the Scientific Committee for Comparative Research on Poverty, International Social Science Council. She serves on the Editorial Boards of *Fijian Studies* and *The Environmentalist*. Current research includes poverty and environmental governance in the Pacific; Fijian *qoliqoli* legislation and the urban poor; Urban housing and poverty in the Pacific. Jenny is currently completing a film project on Making Poverty History; global poverty strategies and their appropriateness to the Pacific. Recent publications include J. Bryant–Tokalau and I. Frazer (eds) *Redefining the Pacific? Regionalism, Past, Present and Future* (Ashgate 2006).

Phil Goff has extensive academic and political expertise in international relations. He has held the portfolios of Minister of Foreign Affairs and Trade, Minister of Justice Minister of Defence, Minister of Trade, Minister for Disarmament and Arms Control, Minister of Corrections, Minister of Pacific Island Affairs and Associate Minister of Finance. Goff's academic career includes lecturing in political studies at Auckland University and Auckland Institute of Technology. He graduated with a MA (Hons) in Political Studies from Oxford University in 1979. In 2009 he was leader of the New Zealand Labour Party and Leader of the Opposition.

Helen Hintjens is a Senior Lecturer in Development and Social Justice at the Institute of Social Studies in The Hague. She works mainly on genocide and post–genocide politics in Rwanda and the Great Lakes, having recently published a chapter on 'Political Identities in post–Genocide Rwanda' in a major volume edited by Phil Clark and Zachary Kaufman, *After Genocide. Transitional Justice, Post–Conflict Reconstruction, and Reconciliation in Rwanda and Beyond* (Columbia University Press 2009). She has worked on post–colonial relations in connection with refugee and immigration rights in Europe. She has published articles on the global social justice movement, on immigration advocacy, on post–genocide Rwanda, and conflict and environment in the Great Lakes, as well as on gender and rights–based approaches. Until 2005, she worked at the former Centre for Development Studies at Swansea University in Wales.

Jane Kelsey is a Professor of Law at the University of Auckland. She specializes in the political economy of international law and policy, with particular reference to international economic regulation. Since 2000 she has been working on the implications for the Pacific Islands of trade negotiations at the WTO, and with the European Union, Australia and New Zealand. She is the author of numerous books and reports on the neoliberal restructuring of New Zealand economic and social life since 1984 and on the economic, social, cultural and political impacts of globalization, especially free trade and investment agreements. These include: *International Economic Regulation* (2002), *Reclaiming the Future. New Zealand in the Global Economy* (1999), *The New Zealand Experiment. A World*

Model for Structural Adjustment? (1995), *Rolling Back the State. Privatisation of Power in Aotearoa/New Zealand* (1993), *A Question of Honour? Labour and the Treaty 1984–1989* (1990).

Jacqueline Leckie is an Associate Professor at the University of Otago in the Department of Anthropology, Gender and Sociology. She has taught and published extensively on issues relating to gender, ethnicity, migration, mental health, and work, within the Asia Pacific region. She has taught history at the University of the South Pacific in Fiji and at Kenyatta University in Nairobi. In 2007 she wrote *Indian Settlers. The Story of a New Zealand South Asian Community* (Otago University Press). She previously wrote *To Labour with the State: The Fiji Public Service Association* and co–authored *Labour in the South Pacific*. Leckie is Vice–President of the Pacific History Association and Chairperson of the Editorial Board of *Sites: A Journal of Social Anthropology and Cultural Studies*. Current projects include co–editing two books: *Decentering Asia* and *Localising Asia in Aotearoa*, and research projects on the historical construction of mental illness in Fiji, and South Asian identities in New Zealand.

Jane L. Parpart is Visiting Professor, Centre for Gender and Development Studies, University of West Indies, St. Augustine, Trinidad and Tobago; Professor Emeritus, Dalhousie University (International Development Studies, Gender Studies and History); and Visiting Professor at Stellenbosch University (South Africa) and Aalborg University (Denmark). She has written extensively on gender and development, feminist theory and development and African history with a focus on Southern Africa. She is a co–editor of *Rethinking Empowerment* (2002), *Gender, Conflict and Peacekeeping* (2005) and *The Practical Imperialist* (2006) as well as the forthcoming *Rethinking the Man Question in International Relations* (2008). She is currently working on empowerment and gender in an increasingly insecure world; the legacies of violence; gender, care–giving and HIV/AIDS and a study of the urban elite in Bulawayo, Zimbabwe (the latter two with Miriam Grant).

Vijay Naidu was born in Fiji and educated there and in the United Kingdom. He is Professor and Director of Development Studies at the University of the South Pacific. He held a similar position at Victoria University of Wellington (2003–2006). He has written on aid, migration, ethnicity, higher education, electoral politics, land tenure, the state, poverty and security. Naidu is on the editorial board of a number of journals and is a regular reviewer of papers on Pacific issues. He is actively involved in the civil society movement as a member of the Citizens' Constitutional Forum and the Fiji Human Rights Group and has ties with the Council of International Development (CID), Pacific Cooperation Foundation, Save the Children Fund, NZ Law Commission and New Zealand Human Rights Commission. He is also the Co–Chair of Aotearoa New Zealand International Development Network (DEVNET).

Budy Resosudarmo is a Fellow at the Economics Division of the Research School of Pacific and Asian Studies, Australian National University (ANU). His research interests include determining the economic impact of environmental policies, analysing the impact of fiscal decentralization on regional economies, and understanding the impact of corruption and illegal activities on the economy and on natural resource endowment. He has published papers in scientific journals such as *Economic Record*, *Ecological Economics* and *Bulletin of Indonesian Economic Studies*, and edited, *The Politics and Economics of Indonesia's Natural Resources* (ISEAS 2005). Before joining ANU, he was a lecturer at the Graduate Program in Economics, University of Indonesia, and a researcher at the Indonesian Agency for the Assessment and Application of Technology. Resosudarmo received his PhD degree in development economics from Cornell University.

Christine Sylvester is Professor of International Relations and Development at Lancaster University. Prior to that she was at the National Centre for Development Studies at the Australian National University and the Institute of Social Studies, den Hague. She has two books on Zimbabwe, two on feminist international relations, with *Art/Museums: International Relations Where We Least Expect It* due in 2008. Pieces related to this chapter on pernicious biopolitics appear in *Third World Quarterly*, *The Geographical Journal*, *Postcolonial Studies*, *Alternatives* and the *International Feminist Journal of Politics*.

Terence Wood works for the Development Resource Centre, a Wellington based Non Governmental Organization. He is also works part time at Victoria University. He completed his Masters thesis in 2004; this research involved assessing experiments in participatory democracy.

Series Editors' Preface

Does flawed global development policy translate into policy failure? Need it be so? Challenging conventional discourses on human (in)security and gendered development, this timely collection, the 16th in our series, sheds new light on the prospectus and progress of millennium development goals established for the year 2015. We are particularly pleased that *Development in an Insecure and Gendered World* contains cutting–edge new theoretical chapters, previously unpublished, and yet it also links theory to practice, policy, and particular places around the Pacific.

Editor Jacqueline Leckie introduces the volume by inviting readers to share an interrogation of the 'madness of development'. She begins by mapping the contours of the book's emergent critiques about overly restrictive notions of human security and global development. The exercise in critical assessment is rendered all the more urgent by such catastrophic environmental and social disasters as the 2004 tsunami which cut a swath of destruction through South and Southeast Asia. This is the context on the minds of some contributors to the volume who gathered at the Otago Foreign Policy School in New Zealand a little over one year later, to begin the initial conversations that led to the production of this book. As Leckie explains, the debates explored in various chapters expose how mainstream approaches to human security seem unable or unwilling to accommodate gendered violence, arguing instead for broadening policies and practices without losing sight of other forms of inequality. Global development agendas are seen as similarly restrictive. Hence contributions broach important critiques about gender mainstreaming and other now taken–for–granted approaches to human development, empowerment being one particularly important example. But the debate here over the contemporary relevance of development agendas and approaches also presents an array of voices (theorists, activists, and policy makers, all with innovative ideas to share) and a range of cases from around the world. We highly recommend *Development in an Insecure and Gendered World* to a wide readership interested in understanding how to engage with contemporary approaches to development in these times of heightened global economic distress, when development spending and the circumstances of aid recipients have all but disappeared from view.

Pauline Gardiner Barber
Marianne Marchand
Jane Parpart

Acknowledgements

This book originated from the 40th Otago Foreign Policy School in 2005 that considered 'Human Security and Development. Meeting the Millennium Development Goals?' The theme was considered timely as that year marked the United Nations' 60th anniversary. I codirected this School with Jenny Bryant–Tokalau and Paul Hansen who were a great pleasure to work with. We could not have realized the success of the event without our Coordinator, Julie Wilson, and other members of the Academic Committee of the Otago School, who provided us with necessary advice and support, including Robert Patman, Philip Nel, Ian Frazer, Louis Leland, Rob Rabel, David MacDonald, Giora Shapira, Betty Mason, Stephen Haigh and Bill Harris.

I can now confess that one of my motives for accepting being a Director of the Otago School was to inject a gendered perspective and introduce a little anthropology. We achieved this through attracting several prominent female speakers. This book has resulted from my concern to link development, international relations and gender. Diverse perspectives on this were aired at the conference. I thank all the presenters but especially those who have been able to contribute chapters relevant to the themes of this collection. The later contribution of chapters from authors who did not attend the School has really strengthened this book. I am especially indebted to suggestions and support for this publication from Jenny Bryant–Tokalau, Haroon Akram–Lodhi, Pauline Gardiner, Jane Parpart and Claire Slatter. Ashgate Publishing has been great to work with, especially Margaret Younger and Emily Jarvis.

The codirectors of the 40th Otago Foreign School acknowledge the sponsorship and support that has been vital to this publication. We thank the following based in Wellington, New Zealand: Asia New Zealand Foundation, Australian High Commission, Canadian High Commission, Embassy of France, Embassy of Japan, Embassy of Mexico, Embassy of the United States of America, Royal Netherlands Embassy, Ministry of Foreign Affairs and Trade (New Zealand), New Zealand Agency for International Development, The Peace and Disarmament Trust. In Dunedin, New Zealand, we are grateful to the Division of Humanities, University of Otago, the Department of Anthropology, Gender and Sociology, University of Otago, and Vincent George House of Travel.

As editor I was awarded an University of Otago Research Grant – enabling the assistance of Karin Reid, Marsa Dodson and Stephanie Dobson. Loving support came from my partner Graham and our young daughter Tara. I really value our conversations about many of the issues covered in this collection.

It is to the young and the communities who suffer and survive within an insecure and gendered world that this book is dedicated. We have a tiny window into this with Sreedevi's poems. Thank you, Sreedevi and thank you, Jubilee Rajiah for allowing me to reproduce how the human spirit endures.

PART I
Introduction

Chapter 1

Development, Gender and Security in a New Millennium

Jacqueline Leckie

Offering
Tied from the roof rafters
    The child you rocked in the hammock
To save this precious child
    You were thrown high on the roof top
You gave up your life

Your body the Tsunami carried
    On its shoulders
As you saved the child you bore
    On your shoulders
And you lost your life

To all women
    Her life was an offering
To the tsunami
    Her life was an offering
My verses all
    To this mother an offering.

(Sreedevi 2005)

Sreedevi's poem 'Offering' is both a dedication and a poignant opening to this publication. It evokes the sacrifice people make during catastrophic and unpredictable disasters to secure the survival of their loved ones and the sustainability of their communities. This poem was written by a grieving and traumatized young survivor from the 'Boxing Day Tsunami' of 26 December 2004 in South India. Sixteen months later, in the midst of a snowy winter in southern New Zealand, Jubliee Rajiah recited Sreedevi's poem to delegates at the 40th University of Otago Foreign Policy School.[1] This book emanates from

---

1 I codirected the 2005 Otago Foreign Policy School 'Human Security and Development: Meeting the Millennium Development Goals?' with Jenny Bryant–Tokalau and Paul Hansen. As elaborated in Bryant–Tokalau's chapter, Dr Rajiah, a psychiatrist,

this meeting that focused on Human Security and the Millennium Development Goals (MDGs). These once confident goals were contested especially when several speakers brought gender to the fore. Conventional concepts of security were also disrupted with attention to gendered violence, as well as a broader and more inclusive rendering of human development, considering, for example, food, environmental, economic and reproductive security. The Otago Foreign Policy School was a microcosm of divergent perspectives on the MDGs being voiced by 2005. These ranged from official governmental endorsement, outlined here in Phil Goff's (New Zealand's former Minister of Foreign Affairs and Trade)[2] and María Angélica Arce Mora's (then Mexico's Ambassador to New Zealand) chapters, to the critiques and increasing disillusionment of the project by expressed by academics, non governmental workers and others. The later inclusion of other contributors is indicative of the mounting divergence over the rationale and feasibility of the MDGs. The result is this collection that considers development in an insecure and gendered world.

Speakers at the Otago Foreign Policy School also discussed if the MDGs would be attained by 2015. Already by 2005 serious critiques had emerged of not only the MDG blueprint of mainstream development but also whether the goals were 'on track'. Four years later, writing this introduction during the 2009 global economic recession, earlier scepticism about the discourse, outcomes and possibilities of this global development plan is warranted. However as addressed in several chapters in Part III of this book ('Localizing Development in an Insecure World'), the MDGs, or a global strategy to broad based development, still matter to many in the 'lesser developed regions.'[3]

Sreedevi's other poems, reproduced in Jenny Bryant–Tokalau's concluding chapter, also question the politics and practices of well–meaning development aid and the role of Non Governmental Organizations (NGOs). Sreedevi was frustrated

---

worked in five coastal villages in southeast India. She encouraged young survivors of the tsunami to write poems as part of their recovery after the disaster. The poems reproduced here have been translated from Tamil.

2   Goff was also Minister of Justice, and Minister of Pacific Island Affairs. His chapter is an indication of the international perspective and pivotal role New Zealand had on security and development in 2005. Goff is now the leader of the Opposition and the New Zealand Labour Party.

3   The discourse of development remains problematic. Arturo Escobar's (1995) foundational work interrogated the making and implications of the discursive binary, development/underdevelopment. 'Development' both as discourse and practice was reconsidered in *Development* by renowned experts and practitioners (Alloo, Antrobus, Berg, Emmerij, Escobar, Esteva, Horn, Kerr, Kothari, Mahfouz, Moseley, Mumtaz, Mwapachu, Okello, Raghuram and Rice 2007). Most 'development experts' now reject the concept of the Third World. Just as that concept could imply derogatory categorizations, so too can the designation of 'South' for less developed regions. We now take pride here in the 'South' Pacific of our colonial nomenclature but also recognize that between and within the 'North/South' development divide there are many inconsistencies of wealth and resources.

by international and national aid agencies to respond and manage disasters such as the 2004 tsunami. This critique extends to the paradoxes of international development and human security in an insecure world. Her village in southeast coastal India, along with millions of others throughout South and Southeast Asia, and communities in the Indian Ocean, were decimated when people elsewhere were recovering and cleaning up after the excesses of Christmas celebrations. If a traumatized young woman can discern such ironies of development why do think–tanks and higher level agencies often fail to do so?

Sreedevi's poems speak to people's pain, struggles and survival in a gendered world, a theme that runs through several of the contributions in this book. She also articulates another aim of this collection, to address empowerment and development in an insecure world. Her poems relate to not only the subjectivity of empowerment but also that of development and international relations. Christine Sylvester's chapter alerts us to how subjectivity, expressed through poems, novels, or memoirs reveals the inconsistencies and 'madness' of development, or as Jane Parpart coined at the Otago School, development as 'fantasyland'. A striking contradiction that emerges from these chapters is how to reconcile an imagined world that can be developed in a world where the realities of war and gendered violence are all too prevalent.

The interrogation of the 'madness of development' is critical to issues that weave through this book. We explicitly address the contradictions within mainstream solutions in development. Although the United Nations has, especially through the MDGs, focused on global programmes of development and security, as investigated in Part II of this collection ('Beyond Bare Life to Reconsidering Empowerment'), these have continued to be denied by many postcolonial regimes. Sylvester (page 46) observes that, 'for some, it is better to die from the very things the UN seeks to eradicate than die at the hands of one's own "developmental" government.' Parpart's chapter goes on to explore how the literatures of (a) gender, empowerment and development and (b) war and conflict generally do not speak to each other. Such divides are investigated in several case studies in this volume, especially in Part III, 'Localizing Development in an Insecure World.' Ronni Alexander's chapter especially traces the gaps between discourse and practice surrounding gender, empowerment, development and conflict in the Pacific. She alerts us to communities where gendered and environmental security has been threatened by US security within military bases in Okinawa and Guam. Alexander's chapter speaks to the place of NGOs and social movements in a brutal, insecure and gendered world. The possibilities of these movements are explored in Helen Hintjens' chapter on gender justice movements as a challenge to insecurity and the quantitative targets of the MDGs.

But first we need to consider the historical context and further critiques of the MDGs, as a contemporary global development paradigm. The contradictions of development in an insecure world dominated by neoliberal economics are then addressed in several of the book's chapters. This introduction briefly considers violence and development in the 'new wars' including the exigencies of 'bare life.'

We know that gender matters here but can this be reinstated through an emphasis on empowerment and gender mainstreaming? This takes us back to retracing concepts of security where we argue that a gendered perspective broadens conventional parameters to a more inclusive approach, including environmental security. Within both the general chapters and the case studies, gender issues remain crucial to a broader rights approach that does not loose sight of other collective inequalities.

MDGs in the dawn of a new millennium

Sreedevi's poems were written in the aftermath of the new millennium that had heralded the MDGs. These emerged from the Millennium Declaration adopted by the United Nations General Assembly in 2000 that became the primary global development framework within the United Nations (UN) system.[4] The MDGs identified specific targets that should be achieved to surmount and eradicate key problems in human development by 2015. Table 1.1 lists the ambitious aims of the MDGs while a more complete list, including the targets, are in Table 4.1 within A. Haroon Akram–Lodhi's chapter.

Table 1.1   The Millennium Development Goals

Goal 1	Eradicate extreme poverty and hunger
Goal 2	Achieve universal primary education
Goal 3	Promote gender equality and empowerment
Goal 4	Reduce child mortality
Goal 5	Improve maternal heath
Goal 6	Combat HIV/AIDS, malaria and other diseases
Goal 7	Ensure environmental sustainability
Goal 8	Develop a global partnership for development

The first seven goals targeted nations of the global 'South' while MDG 8 pinpointed issues of trade and aid that were inclusive of the 'North' as partners. This collection does not address all of the MDGs but several chapters focus on gender issues especially problematic for women. MDG 3 is most relevant and contentious, as it aims to promote gender equality and empower women. We argue that this should not be isolated from the other MDGs, as these affect women. Gender is central to the discourse and implementation of the MDGs in the context of human security (and insecurity).

---

4   Ashwani Saith (2006, 1169–1170) provides a useful synopsis of the origins of the MDGs.

When the MDGs were interrogated at the 2005 Otago Foreign Policy School, it was clear that criticism about these goals had set in. By 2005 UN Secretary General Kofi Annan was concerned at the lack of progress towards attaining the MDGs (Annan 2005; UN Millennium Project 2005). So too was his successor Ban Ki–moon who called for an 'aggressive push' towards attaining the anti–poverty targets world leaders had pledged to achieve by 2015.[5] This was in response to the 2008 United Nations Millennium Development Goals Report that alerted the detrimental impact that high food and fuel prices and the global economic slowdown would have on progress towards the MDGs (United Nations 2008). As detailed in Terence Wood and Vijay Naidu's chapter, the critiques embraced both the scope and bias of the original MDGs, as well as their monitoring and progress. The goals were ironically considered both too broad and too narrow in scope (e.g., Saith 2006). However Vandemoortele (2008) points out that there does not have to be an all encompassing global strategy for the MDGs because not all nations have been held responsible to the commitments that emanated from various UN conferences during the 1990s (Barton 2005a, 78).

Others have questioned the base line and monitoring of the goals or what Thomas Pogge in his 2005 address to the Otago Foreign Policy School referred to as 'statistical gimmicks'. He critiqued the narrowness of the ambitious first MDG (see Pogge 2004) by challenging the official statistics that linked this worthy goal to halve extreme poverty by 2015. The World Bank placed US$1.08 per day in purchasing power parity terms as the most basic poverty line, lumping those below to be in 'extreme poverty'. Pogge argued that this negated that the poorest spend around 80 per cent of their income on food – rendering any universal 'consumption basket' – as meaningless. He also presented statistical evidence to question the base lines from which poverty measurements are tabulated and compared. This manipulation has lead to a huge distortion of progress primarily because poverty levels have been set too low. Vandmoortele's (2008) analysis also begins by locating MDGs from a base of 1990 from which targets are projected over a 25–year period. This contrasts the lack of implementation since 2000 against 1990–2000 achievements. However as Raghuram (2008, 242) cites, Vandmoortele 'defends global target setting and suggests that though the target is entirely achievable, but rarely met, it is still the *raison d'etre* for the realization of several important targets.' This is indicative of official optimism for the framework of the MDGs, as outlined in the chapters by Goff and Arce Mora.

This book addresses some of the most trenchant criticisms of the MDGs – development, security and gender (see also Henry 2007). A growing body of work by academics, practitioners and participants have demonstrated the shortcomings of development, including the MDGs, to address the viability of human security in a gendered world; referred to earlier as the 'fantasyland' of idealistic development.

5　<http://www.endpoverty2015.org/english/news/ban-urges-urgent-action-millennium-goals/11/sep/08>, accessed 3 February 2009.

A human rights framework has been notably absent in the MDGs despite this being key to the Millennium Declaration. For Carol Barton (2005b), this contradiction is especially striking given the questions about the viability of combining human development goals and a neoliberal agenda (see also Gold 2005). In a recent review of the discourse on the MDGs, Shobha Raghuram (2008, 244) suggests a critique of the MDGs should not be about the '…targets but about the bigger silence on democracy, social justice and citizenship, which are vital for providing for the conditions of a social environment in which these goals may be set.'

Akram–Lodhi's and Hintjens' chapters echo Saith's (2006) assessment of the MDGs as highly instrumentalist and limited in the context of the global economy. Akram–Lodhi strongly contests the 'florid rhetoric' of the MDGs that lack an intellectual foundation, calling for 'a humane, democratic, alternative and socially–embedded development paradigm that highlights the agency–led systemic changes necessary to achieve human security' (see page 76). Referencing Long and Long's (1992) foundational work, Akram–Lodhi identifies the contradiction between agency and structure as lying at 'the heart of the conundrum that is the MDGs.' Likewise, Parpart's chapter interrogates similar contradictions in gender mainstreaming and empowerment.

Ironically although this collection explicitly critiques the MDGs from a gender perspective, Akram–Lodhi (pages 81–82) reminds us that, 'gender equality is neither a necessary or sufficient condition for the fulfilment of the MDGs; the fulfilment of the MDGs is quite consistent with increased gender inequality.' Similarly, Wood and Naidu caution against rejecting the MDGs because of the shortcomings in addressing gender and development.

Despite their optimism, Wood and Naidu echo other concerns that earlier UN global commitments on gender were not reflected in the MDGs; specifically Goal 3 on gender equality and the empowerment of women. Eileen Kelly's address to the 2005 Otago Foreign Policy School profiled this silence within the MDGs.[6] The absence of goals towards achieving universal access to quality sexual and reproductive health by 2015 was a glaring omission in the health and poverty aims of the Goals (see also Antrobus 2003; Wood and Naidu, page 149). Instead Kelly argued, that components of the 1994 Cairo International Conference on Population and Development's definition of reproductive health were distributed blandly among various other MDGs: particularly Goals 5 and 6 on maternal health and HIV/AIDS. Kelly argued that this circumvented global agendas concerning sexuality. This was considered necessary if nations with different religious, cultural or moral views on reproductive security and development were to accept the MDGs (for example, with programmes addressing women's control over their fertility). Arce Mora touched on these impediments in her address to the 2005 Otago Foreign Policy School (and here in Chapter 11), noting that although by

---

6   Titled, 'The MDGs and Poverty – How Can Civil Society Make a Difference?' Kelly was Manager, Family Planning International Development.

then Mexico had made considerable progress in meeting the MDGs, both child and maternal mortality remained serious problems.

By 2006, a new target to 'Achieve, by 2015, universal access to reproductive health' was added to MDG 5. Nevertheless the continued fundamental issue of achieving any consensus on global reproductive rights and development does not augur well for feminist visions of development. The chapters that address this issue in this volume do not adopt a universal feminist development model but lean towards a more nuanced approach to development and empowerment.

Violence and development: New wars and 'bare life'

Another glaring weakness of the MDGs was the absence of measures towards reducing human conflict and war, essential to enhancing human security and development. The limitations of development in an insecure world are confronted particularly in Part II of this book, reflective also of Mary Kaldor's (1999) analysis of the differences between 'new wars' and 'old wars' (also Duffield 2001, 2007; Munkler 2005). 'New wars' allow one soldier to kill many more civilians than before, thereby reversing the proportion of military to civilian deaths. Several military forces today are not regular forces but are assembled from children and mercenaries. The chapters in Part II by Sylvester and Parpart and in Part III by Alexander address how gender permeates the new wars, both through violence against women and also with women's violent engagement in wars such as the 1994 Rwandan genocide. Parpart questions whether this is 'empowerment' for women. In her address at the Otago School she urged feminists to confront women's complicity in militarization and to 'look the dark side in the face' (see Sjoberg and Gentry 2007). The new wars have socialized people into accepting different levels of violence that perpetuate violence and insecurity.[7] Hoogensen and Rottem reiterate this cycle that links war and global violence with domestic and gendered violence. If the latter is overlooked in the bigger stakes of international security it,

---

7   This can begin with the seemingly innocuous such as a cheap packaged starchy snack, 'Rambos', that was released in Fiji in 1989, two years after the Pacific's first military coup d'etat. Not only did the slogan 'Rambos – Fiji's newest snack food hero' reference the fictional cult figure played by Sylvester Stallone but Rambo was also a nickname given to Colonel Sitiveni Rabuka after he had staged the 1987 coup. The snack was marketed at children with the packet portraying three menacing 'warriors', one carrying an automatic rifle, another brandishing a bow and arrow and a third wielding a sword. Rambos' promotion included an 'assault course' for children to test those 'tough enough' to complete it. This coincided with the huge burgeoning of military infrastructure when Fiji was subjected to military rule until the mid 1990s. Danone Snacks in Malaysia produces Rambos snacks.

> ...prevents us from fully understanding the causes of the latter. Recognizing the nature and causes of these different levels of violence allows us to work with, and cooperate on, these securities before they develop into the sort of atrocities that are often the primary focus of the human security agenda. A broadened understanding of security can work towards prevention (Hoogensen and Rottem 2004, 169).

Barton (2005a, 77) has also addressed how political–religious fundamentalisms, neoliberalism, and militarism, war and similar interventions are interlinked forces that have intensified in recent years. Duffield (2007, 1–31) documents the long genealogy behind this and among which (following Agamben 2005), the contemporary intensification is a return to a liberal problematic of security. This has severely undermined women's rights and jeopardized women's lives. In recent decades, many mainstream and alternative global development agencies have identified violence and specifically gendered violence as a development issue (e.g., Jacobsen 1993; WHO 2005). Arce Mora's case study indicates how gender insecurity remains a problem on Mexico's borders while Alexander's chapter focuses on gendered violence in the Pacific in the context of war and militarization. She argues that the latter is promoted through neoliberal strategies for development, which glorify consumption while simultaneously destroying traditional livelihoods. Alexander employs the concept of cultural governance, which emphasizes 'gender' to ironically create both spaces for resistance to violence and recreate the militarized culture of violence in the region. This 'double edged sword' relates to gender mainstreaming and empowerment as expanded in Parpart's chapter.

Sylvester chillingly depicts that a goal of the new wars is not necessarily control of land but over bodies. Her chapter focuses on postcolonial transitions in parts of Africa where the state actively injures or kills local citizens in the name of justice and development. Using Zimbabwe and Rwanda as cases of such transitions, and drawing on selected development and postcolonial writings, Sylvester positions these examples of the 'bare life' camp biopolitics articulated by Giorgio Agamben (1998). This is beyond negotiation, and at its most extreme, is the concentration camp. The 'camp' is not just physical but a zone of indistinction where people are made to disappear. This is 'bare life', where the individual is *homo sacer* and submitted to the sovereign's state of exception. People exist as beings but the state denies them any political significance because *homo sacer* is a non–person. Sylvester outlines this scenario in Zimbabwe, where the state has excluded an increasing number of citizens from rights, a biopolitical war against 'enemy bodies.' She suggests that states that employ this enter into the terrain of fascism, a form of political economy that has been neglected in development studies and by international agencies, notably the UN. Since it is unlikely that any development goals can be achieved in the context of pernicious biopolitics, so it is problematic that the MDGs ignore such threatening issues of personal security – the injury, suffering and genocide of local governments against their citizens. Sylvester (page 38) emphasizes the contradictory connections between security, gender and development within the biopolitics of postcolonial states:

> African women's legs bowed out under the weight of water pots on their heads, flies hovering around children's faces undeterred by the listless hosts, men drinking themselves into oblivion at 10 am. Roadsides hold the remains of rusted technologies of development. Hospitals can be places no one should be allowed to enter. Death can arrive swiftly and early – through AIDS, civil violence, or something as relatively curable as diarrhoea. These biopolitical horrors stand side–by–side, incongruously, with clear markers of development achievement: a new school in a village, a dredged port, posters informing people of how to avoid contracting HIV, clinics for pregnant women, literacy classes for adults. The picture is crowded with inconsistent objects that beckon our attention.

Sylvester (page 37) cites Ravij Patel and Philip McMichael's (2004) who identified 'patterns associated with European colonial–development projects to moments of a postcolonial state under economic and political pressure.' She asks how can we help women, implement development in an insecure world when the 'pernicious state' fails to protect its citizens? This can range from direct violence to prohibiting access to relief aid. A recent case in 2008 was after cyclone Nargis decimated coastal Myanmar when tens of thousands of lives were probably lost because of the junta's prolonged delays in granting visas to relief workers and accepting foreign aid.[8]

Non state actors

The ambivalent role of non state actors, specifically NGOs, in doing development in an insecure world requires elaboration. NGOs can be caught in contradictions when operating within the 'liberal problematic of governance' (Duffield 2007, 34). Hintjens outlines the dilemma of the United Nations Development Fund for Women (UNIFEM) in trying to endorse small governmental steps towards improving women's conditions while simultaneously supporting more proactive programmes from non state actors. Wood and Naidu's chapter also addresses the ambivalent relationship between the state and civil society in development in the Pacific. More invidiously the conundrum of when non state actors work within repressive regimes can be extended to the 'entitlement of exception' (Agamben 2005). Duffield (2007, 51) asserts that NGOs, especially in emergency intervention, do decide the point of exception and exercise a sovereign power over life – as in whether or not to direct aid into feeding a starving child (who may die) or helping a poor child (with better chances of survival

---

8   For a timeline of the delays and frustrations in providing aid to Myanmar see <http://www.siiaonline.org/?q=programmes/insights/myanmar-cyclone-nargis-timeline>, accessed 2 February 2009.

but at what cost?) 'NGOs have shown a tenacious ability to accommodate despotic rule as a necessary price of betterment' (Duffield 2007, 44). Duffield (2007, 33) has trenchantly questioned the growth and bureaucratization of the NGO movement within the liberal problematic of security: '…it has internationalized and deepened its institutional reach through the expediency of permanent emergency'. NGOs justify working within illiberal regimes by arguing that 'the alleviation of poverty must come before politics, reduced to a life of exception, if they [the poor] are to helped' (Duffield 2007, 44).

However NGOs and social movements occupy many different spaces and positions within the neoliberal world. Claire Slatter, a NGO activist based in Fiji,[9] articulated this diversity in her summation at the 2005 Otago FPS. As Slatter explained elsewhere:

> In the current new world order of neo–liberalism, civil society organisations have emerged as an important countervailing force to the power of multilateral institutions and transnational corporations, and as watchdogs on states. The global movement against neo–liberalism and its manifestation in economic and trade liberalisation is an unprecedented international resistance movement comprising a broad range of civil society organisations, social movements, development NGOs and public interest groups opposed to the ideological, economic and political forces that have been reshaping the world in the past 16 or so years with devastating impacts on the lives of millions of people, and the environment (Slatter 2006, 23).

Mary Kaldor, Helmut Anheier and Marlies Glasius (2003, 4) stress global civil society's role in fostering human development, as an 'answer to war' but do not see this as a magical solution or alternative to war. The UN Millennium Project identified civil society's 'watchdog role' in ensuring the MDGs were on track,

> In every country [Civil Society Organisations – CSOs] can focus public attention on the Goals and the actions under way – or not under way – to achieve them. CSOs drive broad–based mobilization and create grassroots demand that can hold leaders accountable and can help place the Goals at the heart of national debates (UN Millennium Project 2005).

With hindsight this appears overly optimistic. The paradoxes faced and produced by non state actors and social movements, operating within a neoliberal world, and at times fascistic regimes are interrogated in Hintjens' chapter.

---

9   Slatter is a founding member and former General Coordinator of Development Alternatives with Women for a New Era (DAWN), and a founder member of the Citizens' Constitutional Forum in Fiji. She has a background in the anti–nuclear, women's, trade union and democracy movements in Fiji.

Empowerment and gender mainstreaming

The advocacy of the MDGs by global development agencies and by implication endorsement by NGO 'watchdogs' is a form of development mainstreaming. The cooption and commodification of 'Making Poverty History', such as during New York Fashion Week, (see Figure 1.1) or as Saith, referring to the Monterrey Consensus (2006, 1170), '...embedded the MDG implementation process within mainstream neoliberal strategic and policy framework'.[10]

G–STAR and MDG: A unique collaboration between the United Nations Millennium Campaign and international denim brand G–Star Raw sets out to raise awareness for the eight Millennium Development Goals (MDGs) during New York Fashion Week.

Actors Alan Cumming and Heather Graham will lend their support to draw attention to the commitments made by world leaders to achieve the MDGs and end extreme poverty by 2015. The platform will be the G–Star Raw Spring/Summer 2009 runway show. Following the runway show both actors will curate the first New York edition of the global G–Star Raw Night series, on behalf of the UN Millennium Campaign.

Performers will get total creative freedom to bring their talents to highlighting the MDGs in an original and pure form. Uniquely designed MDG–themed decor will decorate the venue and there will be a dedicated MDG Room where, guests will be able to take action by sending digital messages of support for the MDGs to Heads of State (YouTube 2008).

Figure 1.1   Mainstreaming the MDGs at New York Fashion Week

Several authors in this book question gender mainstreaming. This development strategy was affirmed at the 1995 Beijing UN Conference on women and endorsed by the UN and other key development agencies. Parpart builds upon earlier work (Parpart, Rai and Staudt 2002) to directly challenge mainstream notions of gender empowerment. Akram–Lodhi engages with this, advocating the need to deepen efforts at gender mainstreaming into international institutions, bilateral donor agencies and partners.

Gender and empowerment have become identified with agency, voice and the ability to transform society. Whether analyzing empowerment from a critical alternative or a more mainstream perspective, the literature on empowerment, particularly gendered empowerment, tends to assume that institutions, structures

---

10   When US President George Bush announced US support for the MDGs in 2002. Saith (2006, 1171) discusses the '...new raft of public–private partnerships (PPPs) on a widening and increasingly intimate relationship between the UN and business.'

and even attitudes and practices can be transformed to create a gender equitable world (see also Bessis 2001). The practice of gender mainstreaming has become a technical 'fix' that should guarantee women's empowerment. Hilary Charlesworth (2005a, 2) (who presented at the 2005 Otago Foreign Policy School) also questioned 'the rather bland, bureaucratic acceptance of the method of gender mainstreaming in international institutions...to suggest that it detracts attention from the ways that sexed and gendered inequalities are woven into the international system.' Mainstreaming has, according to Charlesworth, 'effectively drowned out the project of equality between women and men.'

Chapters here by Akram–Lodhi, Hintjens, Kelsey, Parpart, Wood and Naidu address the contradictions of development and empowerment, including those for women, within the dominant macroeconomic framework. Akram–Lodhi, Wood and Naidu highlight women's 'time poverty.' Akram–Lodhi (page 85) endorses the significance of development goals such as MDG 2 to achieve universal primary education, but argues that 'improved training and education for females...may not obviate labour market discrimination or the time poverty that results in underutilised human resources, lesser incomes, and poverty.' Along with Wood and Naidu, Akram–Lodhi calls for a reconceptualization of how the 'care economy' and other social assets ironically generate 'macroeconomic processes that foster discriminatory outcomes that are wholly inconsistent with MDG 3' (Akram–Lodhi, page 85; also Elson and Çağatay 2000; Kurian 2006; Truong 2006; Truong, Wieringa and Chhachhi 2006, xx–xix; van Staveren 2001). Akram–Lodhi also introduces gendered time as a missing premise in macroeconomic analysis of the MDGs.

Barton (2005a, 79–80) has also questioned how women's empowerment translates into the MDGs and the Task Force that expanded the scope of Goal 3 to affirm the human rights framework along with government commitments to CEDAW and those made at the Beijing and Cairo UN women's conferences. The Task Force's proposals reintegrated goals on reproductive rights, violence, and women's unpaid labour, labour market discrimination and property rights. Barton (2005a, 79) reiterated the MDG Task Force's 'call for meeting goals through "fundamental transformation in the distribution of power, opportunities and outcomes for both men and women."'

Gender mainstreaming in development ignores the limits placed on agency and social transformation by inequality, violence and conflict, particularly for women. Alexander's chapter further illustrates this through case studies of conflict in the Pacific. She questions the liberal feminist approach of international security and development communities, presented in Resolution 1325, that aimed to promote gender mainstreaming (see also Charlesworth 2005a; Shepherd 2008). Although the ultimate goal of gender mainstreaming is to include women as actors with equal opportunities to men's, 'in practice, however, it often entails merely the addition of numbers of women, without concomitant changes in patriarchal social structures' (Alexander, page 135), and may conversely reinforce the reproduction of traditional gender roles and inequalities, perpetuating and violence justified on cultural grounds. Bryant–

Tokalau cites Ruth Pearson (2005, 169–170) that although gender is now mainstreamed, there is little evidence that gender is acknowledged in practice. As a result many MDG targets will not be realized, as shown for example with the statistics on access to fresh water. Gender mainstreaming has too often produced 'an inherent teleology of approach' (Shepherd 2008, 168).

Parpart makes a strong plea for gender equality and empowerment to be rethought as conventional practices have both underestimated the deeply held and intractable impediments to gender transformation and failed to acknowledge the courage and empowerment of people who struggle to survive in desperate circumstances. She rejects the binary of empowerment and disempowerment to advocate a more nuanced notion of empowerment, to foster more critical assessment of the obstacles to gendered empowerment while encouraging scholars, policy makers and practitioners to recognize, analyze and support the many ways empowerment occurs in an increasingly insecure and often violent world. For many women silent and secret strategies can empower their lives; 'partial, incomplete, tentative and sometimes barely voiced' (Parpart 2009; also McKenzie Aucoin 2008). Parpart reminded participants at the Otago Foreign Policy School of agency, the power of emotion, silence and secrecy even within 'the camp' (also Parpart 2009).

From security to human security to human insecurity

This book considers gender and development in the context of human security and human insecurity. David Roberts (2008, 5–6) identified Critical Security Studies as reflecting 'a growing consensus relating to a relationship between development and security, especially when security was defined in terms of the environment, natural resources and poverty.' Human insecurity are 'avoidable civilian deaths…that could have been avoided and not caused by guns, bombs or machetes' or what he identifies as a 'problem of good intentions having lethal unintended consequences which are then ignored or denied' (Roberts 2008, 5). This is pertinent to gender and development, especially when considering the shortcomings of the MDGs. The reduction and elimination of conflict is pivotal to achieving the MDGs but reasons for failures to meet these, notably in sub–Saharan Africa and the Pacific, fall within a broader concept of human insecurity. This collection stresses that gender insecurity has exacerbated in an increasing insecure world, with gloomy prospects for development.

Feminist critiques of international relations and security studies were crucial in the development of post–realist security studies that widened the subject from that of state actors, the economy and the military (Roberts 2008, 159–163). Part II of this book builds upon a feminist critique of international relations and foreign policy that one of the authors, Sylvester (2002), explores in her 'Unfinished Journey' through *Feminist International Relations*. This also examines foundational works in feminist international relations; principally Jean Bethke Elshtain (1987), Cynthia Enloe

(1989) and J. Ann Tickner (1992).[11] Tickner was as an early advocate of the need to eliminate unequal power hierarchies, including gender, to attain human security:

> …attempts to alleviate these military, economic and ecological insecurities cannot be completely successful until the hierarchical social relations, including gender relations, intrinsic to each of these domains are recognized and substantially altered…the achievement of peace, economic justice, and ecological sustainability is inseparable from overcoming social relations of domination and subordination; genuine security requires not only the absence of war but also the elimination of unjust social relations, including unequal gender relations (Tickner 1992, 128).

In a later publication Tickner further developed the link between feminist revisions of international relations and security/insecurity:

> Whereas conventional security studies has tended to look at causes and consequences of wars from a top–down, or structural, perspective, feminists have generally taken a bottom–up approach, analyzing the impact of war at the microlevel. By so doing, as well as adopting gender as a category of analysis, feminists believe they can tell us something new about the causes of war that is missing from both conventional and critical perspectives. By crossing what many feminists believe to be mutually constitutive levels of analysis, we get a better understanding of the interrelationship between all forms of violence and the extent to which unjust social relations, including gender hierarchies, contribute to insecurity, broadly defines (Tickner 2001, 48–49).

Sylvester has reemphasized the feminist input into broadening state centred security to human security:

> IR generally poses international relations in abstract and unitary terms, while feminists are mostly attuned to the social relations of the international… Feminists tend to see aspects of sociality – positive or negative in their outcomes for women and other groups in the international system – as the reality of international relations. Just as neorealists see very little (and then often irritable) sociality in an anarchic system (Sylvester 2002, 10; also Blanchard 2003).

Specifically, mainstream concepts of security have overlooked everyday security issues faced by women, especially gendered violence, which are linked to gender

---

11   There is now substantial feminist analysis of international relations. Youngs (2004) provides an excellent survey of this while Grant (1991) traces the origins of gender bias in international relations. On feminist theory and international relations see also (Pettman 1996; Steans 1998; Steans 2006; Sylvester 1994; 2002).

inequalities. This is detailed in Alexander's chapter while globally Gillian Youngs (2004, 83) and the collection edited by Thang–Dam Truong, Saskia Wieringa and Amrita Chhachhi (2006) have surveyed how traditional parameters of security have neglected the impact of war, military occupation, militarization, migration (including forced migration), human trafficking, sexual and other forms of slavery on women and children – serious issues that link gender with development and security.

Hilary Charlesworth's address on 'Sex, Gender, War and International Law' at the 2005 Otago Foreign Policy School echoed Enloe's (1989, 133) earlier question of 'Where are the women?' in academic and media accounts of war. Charlesworth outlined how women's voices and experiences were mostly excluded from representations of the war in Iraq (Charlesworth 2005b), with the exception of Condaleeza Rice, former Head of the United States National Security Council. In her 2005 presentation at Otago Charlesworth depicted the war against terror after '9/11' (terrorist attacks in the US on 11 September 2001) as 'a men–only event': 'Women's voices and experiences are regarded as especially unimportant when issues of homeland security, war, and retribution are at stake'. According to Charlesworth, the absence of women's voices in the formation of international law skews its development and undermines its legitimacy.

Although several of the chapters in this collection critique international relations and security studies through a feminist lens and question the possibilities of development in an insecure and gendered world, they and others recognize shifts in mainstream policy and practice that have disrupted conventional militarized concepts of security. Indeed UN proclamations concerning this originated after World War II but it was the 1994 United Nations Development Programme's *Human Development Report* which explicitly identified human security as pivotal to development, defining human security as 'freedom from fear, freedom from want' (UNDP 1994: 23–24).

UN General Secretary, Kofi Annan endorsed these aims in the 2000 UN Millennium Report:[12] '..."human security" can no longer be understood in purely military terms. Rather, it must encompass economic development, social justice, environmental protection, democratization, disarmament and respect for human rights and the rule of law.' This laid the foundations of the MDGs and indicated a mainstream shift that 'No longer focused on the negative "absence of threat" approach, human security speaks to 'enabling, making something possible' and 'making each secure in the other' (Hoogensen and Rottem 2004, 157 citing McSweeney 1999: 14–15). Mainstream development embraced,

> A broader definition of security, trickling up and out to policymakers and community action, allows for deeper and more effective exploration of the insecurities articulated by diverse identities – including through gender – regarding famine, disease, the sex trade, environmental degradation, oppression and, among many other things, war (Hoogensen and Rottem 2004, 169).

---

12   Available at <http://www.un.org/millennium/sg/report/full.htm>.

Global mainstream concepts of security were further widened in 2000 when United Nations Security Council Resolution 1325 was passed. This broadened the notion of security to address gender issues in conflict areas by recognizing women's key role in peace–building and conflict resolution and the differential effects of conflict on women and men. Shepherd (2008) has linked this with development through a discursive deconstruction of 1325. She illustrates how such discourse is simultaneously descriptive, constitutive and proscriptive of development. Alexander 's chapter also critiques the implementation of UN 1325, to reiterate how, especially in the Pacific, cultural governance interferes with gender mainstreaming and other initiatives for women.

Environmental security

Corpses

We dug and dug to get the bodies
Why dig to bury again?
What sin did we do?
That you should so hunger for our lives
You have made us stand
    In the streets to eat
Though we are homeless
    We still depend on you for our livelihood.
We cannot see God
But we can see you
You have sent us away to God
We can't even find the bodies
    And we toss and weep
The waves auctioned death
Now the ocean is still.
              (Sreedevi 2005)

A poem by Sreedevi, written in the aftermath of the 2004 'Boxing Day Tsunami', opened this chapter. We return to another poem by Sreedevi, 'Corpses', which evokes how environmental security is fundamental to human security. Military and civilian conflict decimate but so too do environmental disasters, that may also be consequences of human conflict (see Roberts 2008). For Sreedevi the ocean is as omnipresent as God but 'We cannot see God/But we can see you'. Ecological security is political (Tickner 1992), and pertinent to Angelica Arce Mora's assessment of Mexico's implementation of the UN Millennium Declaration. She notes that for many years state economic policies have overridden environmental issues and that environmental sustainability was not on the national agenda until the 2001–2006 National Development Plan was adopted, Environment issues there also link with security and gender. For example, water is a national security issue in Mexico but also has direct implications in millions of women's lives. The links between environmental and human security (and development) and the political context are explicitly investigated in Budy Resosudarmo's chapter on the environment and development in the world's largest archipelago, Indonesia. It is rich in natural resources but still confronts extreme poverty and hunger and a seriously uncertain future of environmental sustainability. This has not augured well for Indonesia meeting the MDGs but a change in political direction with the fall of President Soeharto in 1998 provided the opportunity for Indonesia to quickly instigate *'reformasi'*. This aimed to replace previous authoritarian rule with more democratic governance. A key means of achieving this was through shifting from a highly centralized towards a more decentralized system of government. Resosudarmo remains gloomy about the impact of these radical changes that have instead created an environment of political uncertainty, inconsistent laws and regulations, weak law enforcement, a weak governmental system and insecurity of land tenure. These all have gendered implications. Resosudarmo's study of environmental security in Indonesia under the *Reformasi* era highlights the contradictions of environmental reform aimed at promoting sustainability and democratic governance when corruption and competition between interest groups remains rife.

Feminist dilemmas: Rights and development in a neoliberal world

While human security has become more central to both development studies and international relations, there remains the question of human rights. Nira Yuval–Davis (2006, 1) suggests that human security has to some extent become a substitute for human rights – gaining currency after the post–cold war era and especially post 9–11. This 'reflected the growing unease not only with the spread of ethnic conflicts and wars but also with the growing poverty and inequity under [sic] neo–liberal globalised market.' Yuval–Davis indicates that the shift from human rights to human security was influenced by the capabilities approach (Sen (1981, 1992; Nussbaum and Sen, 1993; Nussbaum, 2000) that 'rejects the discourse of rights and entitlements as well as of general measures of opulence, such as GNP per capita, and instead focuses on the ways people positioned in all groups in society are capable to achieve quality of life in terms of achievement and freedom. It argues that resources have no value in themselves apart from their role in promoting human functioning' (Yuval–Davis 2006, 2). Is the discourse of human security more open to cultural relativity than that of the more universalistic human rights? (see Yuval–Davis 2006; also Sen 2000). Global feminist organizations such as DAWN and the Women's International Coalition for Economic Justice advocate that human security should be integrated with rights, gender and development. As Hintjens outlines here, feminists have also reaffirmed linkages with broader social movements and with human rights activists of all genders. Hintjens interrogates examples ranging from inductive 'top–down' agendas, as in CEDAW to deductive, 'bottom–up' strategies such as the Self Employed Women's

Association (SEWA). Thang–Dam Truong, Saskia Wieringa and Amrita Chhachhi (2006, xxii) argue: 'When grounded in realities of deprivation for which a politics of social transformation is required, an interpretative approach to human security can contribute to redressive action more properly suited to the context in which rights are claimed.'

However Barton has identified the persistent divide between people working on gender justice issues, such as sexual and reproductive health, violence, GLBT (Gay, Lesbian, Bisexual and Transgender) rights, and women's control over their bodies, and those in development and economic justice. This gap remains despite the Cairo International Conference on Population and Development and the Beijing Fourth World Conference on Women that linked agendas of rights and development with feminist development networks.

> While feminist economists and economic justice activists have worked hard to develop a feminist macro–economic analysis over the past 20 years addressing debt, structural adjustment, trade, neo–colonialism, and the current neo–liberal model from a feminist perspective, this is often still marginalized from what is considered a 'feminist' agenda. At the same time, women working in the development arena have too often failed to name issues of violence, sexual and reproductive health, and sexual rights as critical issues in addressing women's poverty, as well as factors feeding the ascendancy of right–wing political forces that advance both the neo-liberal agenda and war (Barton 2005a, 75).

Neoliberalism's failure for women, and the direct links to insecurity echoes through many of our chapters. Akram–Lodhi critiques neoliberalism through the concept of 'feminist development economics'. He echoes earlier links between human rights, gender justice, and the MDGs with insecurity (Neuhold 2005). Wendy Harcourt connected this with patriarchal relations:

> …we cannot pretend government keep to promises if there is international pressure to spend money else where – such as the military on top of the pressure to enter the world market etc. Nor can we deliver health and education services if there is on–going conflict which is destroying those services…Gender is about power relations, so in terms of security we are speaking about hierarchical patriarchal relations where masculine orders determine behaviour which condone violence and rape as a weapon of war (Harcourt 2005, 23–4).

Harcourt is suggestive of the need to interrogate gender as a crucial component of identity and security in non state views of security, to consider how 'identity shapes individual and collective security needs' (Hoogensen and Rottem 2004, 156), and development. Identity is also embodied and human (in)security and informs this, as discussed in Part I of this book. Truong, Wieringa and Chhachhi (2006, xviii) also emphasized:

> S/he is not just an abstract construct of the 'person' as a bearer of rights, but also
> a body inscribed with cultural mores that shape their mode of being and relating,
> and a socially–embedded actor whose pursuit of rights and responsibilities in
> everyday life requires flexible structures of negotiation and resolution of tensions.
> Security of existence entails security of identity and a sense of belonging.

At the Otago Foreign Policy School, Parpart highlighted the silence in the MDGs on masculinity and patriarchy in her critique of gender mainstreaming and conventional models of development through women's empowerment (see also Henry 2007; Jones 2006; Parpart and Zalewski 2008).

Pacific peoples in an insecure and gendered world

A deliberate decision was made to include several chapters that embrace the Pacific region. Despite constituting the largest space on the globe (albeit water not land),[13] Pacific nations and cultures are invariably absent from the international literature on issues of gender, security and development. Here we offer four chapters on the Pacific. This includes Goff's keynote address to the Otago Foreign Policy School. He outlined the New Zealand government's contribution in 2005 to regional and global development and security. The MDGs are addressed here as an external issue as part of New Zealand's external aid and not as a domestic issue.

Alexander's chapter considers examples from the Pacific that apply several of the global and theoretical issues presented by Sylvester and Parpart. This addresses the intersection of militarization, gendered violence and resistance within gendered and militarized spaces. Although the numbers involved, for example, in the decade of armed conflict on Bougainville Island, may have been much smaller than genocide elsewhere, the parallels of gendered violence and implications for human security and development are striking. Alexander also reminds us of the negative implications for those societies and environments affected by military bases in the Pacific, such as Okinawa and Guam. She coins such militarization as 'costly development' for women and human security. This chapter also critiques gender mainstreaming from a Pacific institution, the Pacific Women's Bureau. Its monitoring of the implementation of the Pacific Platform for Action on the Advancement of Women and Gender Equality and the MDGs poses

---

13   Epeli Hau'ofa's (1993) paper is foundational to rethinking representations of the Pacific or Oceania as an inclusive 'sea of islands' rather than a Eurocentric gaze of 'islands in a far off sea.' He stressed the spiritual, historic and contemporary linkages between the many cultures in the region. See Bryant–Tokalau and Frazer (2006) for a collection on Pacific regionalism. Anne–Marie Hilsdon, Martha Macintyre, Vera Mackie and Maila Stivens (2000) compiled a collection on gender politics and human rights in the Asia Pacific region while more recently M. Anne Brown's (2007) collection interrogated security, development and conflict management in the Pacific.

the contradiction of providing a political space for the promotion of women 'while at the same time subjects all women to the gender mainstreaming lens invoked by the international development/human security community' (page 121).

Wood and Naidu's chapter opens with the contradictory representation of the Pacific as a predictably marketed touristic idyll and that of an unpredictable arc of crises (Fry 1997) that threaten development and human security in the region. Although their examination of the strengths and weaknesses of the implementation of MDGs within Pacific Island Countries (PICs) is not optimistic, they present the key impediments of conflict and gender issues as challenges (see also Huffer 2006).[14] The authors argue that better human development and security outcomes in the Pacific are feasible not only through changes within the Pacific Island countries but are also possible with changes in how the 'regional powers' interact with the PICs. Their chapter advocates that nations such as New Zealand and Australia should cease acting only in self interest within areas such as trade agreements. Along with other chapters, Wood and Naidu reiterate a more pragmatic, people–centred approach to development instead of practices being dictated by economic ideology. This is expanded in Jane Kelsey's chapter that asks who is setting the 'trade driven development' agenda of a proposed 'Pacific Economic Community'. This model has become so pervasive that it excludes examination of the economic, social and political consequences for PICs and their people. Kelsey interrogates food, employment and temporary migration, to reveal the tensions between trade liberalization and people centred development, and the contradictions that are embedded in the MDGs.

Conclusion: Offering and survival in a global world

Globally, millions of people in very basic ways, daily and persistently, against huge odds, aim for personal and collective security. Despite publicized attention to international agreements and the quieter sharing of human values, there is not always consensus on the meaning and priorities of security, who sets this agenda and what the desired outcomes are. Moreover individual security requires the guarantee of collective rights. This is especially pertinent to the interrogation of human and gender rights that runs through this book. It is imperative that collective rights and needs are not lost sight of in the project of securing gender rights.

This chapter began with a young woman's grief in the aftermath of a catastrophic environmental disaster. Sreedevi recognized the power of nature but she was far less accepting of the destructiveness and wastefulness caused by human power. Her grief evoked anger – not just from personal loss and insecurity – but also from the frustration at the delivery of relief and development aid. Likewise, such

---

14   Elise Huffer originally presented this at the 2005 Otago Foreign Policy School, as 'Human Security, Development and the Millennium Development Goals in Oceania. How do they fit into the Pacific Plan?'

anger and disappointment, has emerged from many of the intended recipients of the MDGs. The vision of the MDGs to 'make poverty history' and secure basic measures of development by 2015 was based upon ostensibly achievable goals. Although many contributions in this book are optimistic about the rationale of the MDGs, and applaud the goals that have been reached, they are equally cautious. Some contributors are not simply hesitant about this global development agenda but see the goals as unachievable not only within the timeframe but also because, as Akram–Lodhi (page 72) assesses, of a flawed '…analytical framework that is used to drive the policies and programmes designed to achieve the MDGs and hence enhance human security offer only a partial transcript of actually–existing social and economic processes.'

This book covers extreme contexts of violent and gendered insecurity, from the horrors of Kigali on the African continent to those on the island of Bougainville in the Pacific. Too often in academic discourse and global development and security policy the island states outside the major continents are neglected. We only offer selected case studies but hope this will heighten awareness that life threatening and livelihood issues of development, gender and insecurity are as applicable to the islands of Pacific and Asia as they are to centres of conflict that have attracted global attention or condemnation. Human insecurity extends from cosy homes to the camps of 'bare life.' These may as Alexander argues, constitute a form of gendered structural violence, but only under certain circumstances result in direct violence.

We aim within the general chapters of Part II and addressing specific contexts in Part III, to highlight significant gaps in the development and security literature. Gender is a vital link between development, conflict and human security. This is not only through how this speaks to women's continued subordination and threat of violence (despite gender mainstreaming in development) but also provides a lens for a broader and equitable conception of development. Several writers in this collection critique the shortcomings of MDG 3 to promote gender equality and empower women, not only because of this Goal's limited targets but also because it can be argued that the aims are at odds with other MDGs, such as MDG 10 to develop a global partnership for development. Even in countries with high rates of female political participation, such as New Zealand, women's incomes still lag behind men's and many women face appalling rates of gendered violence.[15]

We emphasize the interweaving of regional and global crises and the impact of this on community development and security. Resoduarmo reminds us of the 1997 Asian economic crisis that affected global markets that subsequently compromized Indonesia's development goals, including those aimed at more

---

15   The New Zealand Council of Trade Unions (2007) reported a gender pay gap of around 14 per cent for women, while Heather Henare, Chief Executive of the National Collective of Independent Women's Refuges (2008) stated that 'the scale of family violence in New Zealand is at an epidemic level' (see also Fanslow and Robinson 2004). See Human Rights Commission (2008) for a census of women's participation.

democratic outcomes. This points to the entanglement of regional, global and local interests during the financial, fuel and food crises of 2008–2009. Bryant–Tokalau paints a gloomy prognosis in the final chapter. The current economic recession has compromized the possibility of halving those living in sub–Saharan Africa on less than $1 per day while millions others face severe poverty there and in South Asia (United Nations 2008).

The already tenuous commitment of aid donor countries to overseas development has come under more intense review with the impact of the recession. Most countries whether donors or recipients of aid face drastic declining exports and employment redundancies. The decline in external remittances from overseas kin is already impacting upon communities in the Pacific Islands. Internal economic support systems within developing countries will also be eroded. Current economic realities depressingly contradict the cautious optimism of some of our book's contributors for a global consensus on attaining the MDGs and the alleviation of poverty.

The gendered impact of the 2009 recession is still unravelling. Dame Carol Kidu, Papua New Guinea's only female parliamentarian (and Minister for Community Development), asked how this recession will impact upon women in the subsistence and semi–subsistence sector, especially as many families depend upon internal remittances to pay for basic costs such as education, health and 'cultural obligations.'[16] This does not even address other basic needs such as food, housing, water or sanitation.

Sreedevi survived the 2004 tsunami that devastated her family, community, region and thousands elsewhere. The mother is both the victim of the disaster but also the saviour of a child in the poem 'Offering'. Countless other women and men have faced similar choices about life and death within immediate disaster or daily survival.[17] They also agonize over decisions in more enduring situations – such as food, work, income, education, health, environment – as addressed in the MDGs. We retain optimism in people's empowerment as they encounter such challenges but as the following chapters indicate, this is within a gendered and insecure world.

References

Agamben, G. (1998), *Homo Sacer: Sovereign Power and Bare Life,* trans. Heller–Roazen, D. (Stanford: Stanford University Press).

---

16   Interview with Kidu, Radio New Zealand National, 22 March 2009, following presentation of a paper, at 'Eliminating World Poverty: Global Goals and Regional Progress', 20–21 March 2009, Institute of Policy Studies, Victoria University of Wellington.

17   As this book was going to press, Pacific peoples were mourning the deaths of at least 189 loved ones after a devastating earthquake and tsunami hit American Samoa, Samoa and Tonga on 30 September 2009. The tragedy decimated several villages and alerted the Pacific region to the environmental insecurity of small island states.

—— (2005), *State of Exception,* trans. Attell, K. (Chicago: University of Chicago Press).

Alloo, F., Antrobus, P., Berg, R., Emmerij, L., Escobar, A., Esteva, G., Horn, J., Kerr, J., Kothari, S., Mahfouz, A., Moseley, S., Mumtaz, K., Mwapachu, J., Okello, D., Raghuram, S., and Rice, A.E. (2007), 'Reflections on 50 years of Development', *Development* 50, 4–32.

Annan, K. (2005), *In Larger Freedom: Towards Development, Security and Human Rights for All. Report of the Secretary–General* (New York: United Nations Publications).

Antrobus, P. (2003), 'Presentation to Working Group on the Millennium Development Goals and Gender Equality', UNDP Caribbean Regional Millennium Development Goals Conference, Barbados, 7–9 July 2003.

Barton, C. (2005a), 'Integrating Feminist Agendas: Gender Justice and Economic Justice', *Development* 48, 75–84.

—— (2005b), 'Women's Movements and Gender Perspectives on the Millennium Development Goals', in *Civil Society Perspectives on the Millennium Development Goals* (United Nations Development Program Civil Society Unit), 1–27, <http://www.choike.org/documentos/mdgs_cso_barton.pdf>, accessed 30 October 2009.

Bessis, S. (2001), 'The World Bank and Women: "Instrumental Feminism"' in S. Perry and C. Schenck (eds), *Eye to Eye: Woman Practising Development Across Cultures* (London/New York: Zed), 11–24.

Blanchard, E. (2003) 'Gender, International Relations, and the Development of Feminist Security Theory', *Signs: Journal of Women in Culture and Society* 23:4, 1289–1312.

Brown, A.M. (ed.) (2007), *Security and Development in the Pacific Islands: Social Resilience in Emerging States* (Boulder, London: Lynne Rienner).

Bryant–Tokalau, J. and Frazer, I. (eds) (2006), *Redefining the Pacific? Regionalism Past, Present and Future* (Aldershot, Burlington: Ashgate).

Charlesworth, H. (2005a), 'Not Waving but Drowning: Gender Mainstreaming and Human Rights in the United Nations', *Harvard Human Rights Journal* 18, 1–18.

—— (2005b), 'The Missing Voice: Women and the War in Iraq', *Oregon Review of International Law* 7, 5–27.

Duffield, M. (2001), *Global Governance and the New Wars. The Merging of Development and Security* (London, New York: Zed Books).

—— (2007), *Development, Security and Unending War* (Cambridge: Polity).

Elshtain, J.B. (1987), *Women and War* (Brighton: Harvester).

Elson, D. and Çağatay, N. (2000), 'The Social Content of Macroeconomic Policies', *World Development* 28:7, 1347–1364.

Enloe, C. (1989), *Bananas, Beaches and Bases: Making Feminist Sense of International Politics* (London: Pandora Press).

Escobar, A. (1995), *Encountering Development: The Making and Unmaking of the Third World* (Princeton: Princeton University Press).

Fanslow, J. and Robinson, E. (2004), 'Violence against Women in New Zealand: Prevalence and Health Consequences', *New Zealand Medical Journal* 117:1206, 12 < http://www.nzma.org.nz/journal/117-1206/1173/>, accessed 17 August 2007.

Fry, G. (1997), 'Framing the Islands: Knowledge and Power in Changing Australian Images of the "South Pacific"', *Contemporary Pacific* 9: 2, 305–344.

Gold, L. (2005), 'More Than a Numbers Game: Ensuring That the Millennium Development Goals Address Structural Injustice', *Center Focus* 168, September.

Grant, R. (1991), 'The Sources of Gender Bias in International Relations Theory', in R. Grant and K. Newland (eds), *Gender and International Relations* (Bloomington: Indiana University Press), 8–26.

Harcourt, W. (ed.) (2005), 'Report on the NCDO–SID–WIDE International Workshop on the Millennium Development Goals, Gender Equality and Human Security', 18 May, Royal Tropical Institute, The Netherlands.

Hau'ofa, E. (1993), 'Our Sea of Islands', in. E. Waddell, V. Naidu, and E. Hau'ofa (eds), *A New Oceania. Rediscovering Our Sea of Islands* (Suva: The University of the South Pacific and Beake House), 2–14.

Henry, M. (2007), 'Conflict, Gender, Security and Development', *Security and Development* 7:1, 61–84.

Hilsdon, A., Macintyre, M., Mackie, V. and Stivens, M. (eds) (2000), *Human Rights and Gender Politics: Asia–Pacific Perspectives* (London, New York: Routledge).

Hoogensen, G. and Rottem, S.V. (2004), 'Gender Identity and the Subject of Security', *Security Dialogue* 35, 155–171.

Huffer, E. (2006), 'The Pacific Plan: A Political and Cultural Critique', in Bryant–Tokalau, J. and Frazer, I. (eds), *Redefining the Pacific? Regionalism Past, Present and Future* (Aldershot, Burlington: Ashgate), 157–174.

Human Rights Commission (2008), *New Zealand Census of Women's Participation* (Wellington: Human Rights Commission), <http://www.neon.org.nz/documents/HR%20Women_screen.pdf>, accessed 30 October 2009.

Jacobsen, R. (1993) 'Domestic Violence as a Development Issue' *Gender and Development* 1, 37–39.

Jones, A. (2006), *Men of the Global South: A Reader* (London: Zed Books).

Kaldor, M. (1999), *New and Old Wars: Organized Violence in a Global Era* (Cambridge: Polity Press).

Kaldor, M., Anheier, H. and Glasius, M. (eds) (2003), *Global Civil Society. An Answer to War* (London: Sage Publications).

Kurian, R. (2006), 'The Globalisation of Domestic Care Services' in Truong, T., Wieringa, S. and Chhachhi, A. (eds), *Engendering Human Security. Feminist Perspectives* (London: Zed Books), 147–168.

Long, N. and Long, A. (eds) (1992), *Battlefields of Knowledge: The Interlocking of Theory and Practice in Development Research* (London: Routledge).

McKenzie Aucoin, P. (2008), '"The Story that Came to Me": Gender, Power and Life History Narratives – Reflections on the Ethics of Ethnography in Fiji', in Lal, B.V. and Luker, V. (eds), *Telling Pacific Lives. Prisms of Process* (Canberra: ANU E–Press), 85–92.

Munkler, H. (2005), *The New Wars* (Cambridge: Polity Press).

National Collective of Independent Women's Refuges (2008) 'Family Violence Figures a Massive Challenge,' 1 April, <http://www.womensrefuge.org.nz/index.cfm>.

Neuhold, B. (February 2005), 'Focus on Human Rights and Gender Justice: Linking the MDGs with CEDAW and the Beijing Platform for Action', Policy Paper for Beijing+10 and MDG+5 Reviews (WIDE: Austria).

New Zealand Council of Trade Unions (2007), 'Gender Pay Gap Persists: 14 per cent in Latest Stats out Today', 4 October, <http://union.org.nz/news/2007/gender-pay-gap-persists-14-per-cent-in-latest-stats-out-today>, accessed 24 March 2009.

Nussbaum, M. (2000), *Women and Human Development: The Capabilities Approach* (Cambridge, New York: Cambridge University Press).

Nussbaum, M. and Sen, A. (eds) (1993), *The Quality of Life* (Oxford: Oxford University Press).

Parpart, J. (2009), 'Choosing Silence' in Ryan–Flood, R. and Gill, R. (eds), *Secrecy and Silence in the Research Process: Feminist Reflections* (London: Routledge).

Parpart, J., Rai, S.M. and Staudt, K. (eds) (2002), *Rethinking Empowerment: Gender and Development in a Global/Local World* (London, New York: Routledge).

Parpart, J. and Zalewski, M. (eds) (2008), *Rethinking the Man Question. Sex, Gender and Violence in International Relations* (London: Zed Books).

Patel, R. and McMichael, P. (2004), 'Third Worldism and the Lineages of Global Fascism: The Regrouping of the Global South in the Neoliberal Era', *Third World Quarterly* 25:1, 231–54.

Pearson, R. (2005), 'The Rise and Rise of Gender and Development', in Kothari, U. (ed.), *A Radical History of Development Studies: Individuals, Institutions and Ideologies* (London: Zed Books), 157–179.

Pettman, J.J. (1996), *Worlding Women: A Feminist International Politics* (London, New York: Routledge).

Pogge, T. (2004), 'The First United Nations Millennium Development Goal: A Cause for Celebration?' *Journal of Human Development* 5:3, 377–397.

Raghuram, S. (2008), 'The MDGs in a World of Multiplying Inequalities and Differentiating Complexities', *Development* 51:2, 241–244.

Roberts, D. (2008), *Human Insecurity: Global Structures of Violence* (London, New York: Zed Books).

Saith, A. (2006), 'From Universal Values to Millennium Development Goals: Lost in Translation', *Development and Change* 37:6, 1167–99.

Sen, A. (1981), Poverty *and Famine* (Oxford: Clarence Press).

—— (1992), *Inequality Re–examined* (Oxford: Clarence Press).

—— (2000), 'Why Human Security', Presentation at the *International Symposium on 'Human Security'*, hosted by the Japan Ministry of Foreign Affairs. Tokyo: Takanawa Prince Hotel, available at <http://www.humansecurity-chs.org/doc/Sen2000.pdf>.

Shepherd, L.J. (2008), *Gender, Violence and Security. Discourse as Practice* (London, New York: Zed Books).

Sjoberg, L. and Gentry, C.E. (2007), *Mothers, Monsters, Whores: Women's Violence in Global Politics* (London: Zed Books).

Slatter, C. (2006) 'Treading Water in Rapids? Non–Governmental Organisations and Resistance to Neo–Liberalism in Pacific Island States', in S. Firth (ed.), *Globalisation and Governance in the Pacific Islands* (Canberra: ANU E Press), 23–42.

Steans, J. (1998), *Gender and International Relations: An Introduction* (New Brunswick: Rutgers University Press).

——— (2006), *Gender and International Relations: Issues, Debates and Future Directions* 2nd Edition. (Cambridge: Polity Press).

Sylvester, C. (1994), *Feminist Theory and International Relations in a Postmodern Era* (Cambridge, MA: Cambridge University Press).

——— (2002), *Feminist International Relations: An Unfinished Journey* (Cambridge, New York: Cambridge University Press).

Tickner, J.A. (1992), *Gender in International Relations: Feminist Perspectives on Achieving Global Security* (New York: Columbia University Press).

——— (2001), *Gendering World Politics: Issues and Approaches in the Post–Cold War Era* (New York: Columbia University Press).

Truong, T. S. (2006), 'From State Duty to Women's Virtue: Care Under Liberalisation in Vietnam', in Truong, T., Wieringa, S. and Chhachhi, A. (eds), *Engendering Human Security. Feminist Perspectives* (London: Zed Books), 169–188.

Truong, T., Wieringa, S. and Chhachhi, A. (eds) (2006), *Engendering Human Security. Feminist Perspectives* (London: Zed Books).

UN Millennium Project. (2005), *Investing in Development. A Practical Plan to Achieve the Millennium Development Goals* (New York, London: Earthscan).

UNDP (1994), *Human Development Report* (New York, London: Oxford University Press).

United Nations (2008), *The Millennium Development Goals Report 2008* (New York: United Nations), <http://www.undp.org/publications/MDG_Report_2008_En.pdf> accessed 8 May 2009.

van Staveren, I. (2001), *The Values of Economics: An Aristotelian Perspective Edition* (London, New York: Routledge).

Vandemoortele, J. (2008), 'Making Sense of the MDGs', *Development: Gender and Fisheries* 51:2, 220–227.

WHO (2005), WHO *Multi-country Study on Women's Health And Domestic Violence Against Women: Initial Results on Prevalence, Health Outcomes and Women's Responses* (Geneva: WHO).

Youngs, G. (2004), 'Feminist International Relations: A Contradiction in Terms? Or Why Women and Gender are Essential to Understanding the World "We" Live In', *International Affairs* 80:1, 75–87.

Yuval–Davis, N. (2006), '"Human security" and the Gendered Politics of Belonging,' Symposium, University of Warwick, 22 March. *Justice, Equality and Dependency in the 'Postsocialist' Condition* (updated 2006), <http://www2.warwick.ac.uk/fac/soc/sociology/gender/news/pastevents/symposium/yuval>, accessed 2 September 2008.

YouTube (2008), 'MDGs on the New York Fashionweek' 17 September, <http:www.youtube.com/watch?v=aJDQ5K4jtcw>.

PART II
Beyond Bare Life
To Reconsidering Empowerment

Chapter 2

Bare Life as a
Development/Postcolonial Problematic[1]

Christine Sylvester

Finding useful intersections of development studies and postcolonial studies can be a challenge. Development studies is an applied field of social science – managerial in thrust, practical in orientation, and in thrall historically to economic theories and technologies. It aims to develop theory and practice that can assist countries of the so–called Third World in achieving economic targets and higher, sustainable standards of living. Postcolonial studies is not an applied field. Associated with the humanities, and often based in academic departments of language, history, and cultural studies, it reexamines a long historical, cultural, and spatial record in which colonies and post colonies appear as (problematic) children of European history. Postcolonial theory also looks at interpenetrating hybridities that all of us experience as a result of the world–historical experience of colonialism, while development theory creates spaces between places deemed developed and those deemed less developed. Everyday lives feature in the novels, films, and testimonials that postcolonial studies examines, whereas development studies generally conceives of the Third World as a problematic of progress that can be arrayed well in statistical terms.

A small body of work is starting to compare and contrast the 'disparate tales of the Third World' (Sylvester 1999) that flow out of these two separate traditions. Some of it discusses how indigenous knowledges appear in and could better influence development thinking (Briggs and Sharp 2004), and some probes the ways subalterns can, and cannot, speak to be heard by development experts (Kapoor 2004; from Spivak 1988). Crossover work in development studies considers how novels and travel tales can infuse development practice with a keener sense of local texture and dailiness (e.g., Chan 2005, Sylvester 2000b, 2004). Within an incipient search for meaningful interdisciplinarities in works that examine the Third World in very different ways, I want to raise a topic that a combination of approaches enables us to apprehend – pernicious, bare life biopolitics that could be termed

---

1   This chapter was originally published as Christine Sylvester, (2006) 'Bare Life as a Development/postcolonial problematic', *The Geographical Journal* 172: 1, 66–77. Reproduced with permission of Blackwell Publishing Ltd. A version of this was presented to the University of Otago Foreign Policy School, Dunedin, New Zealand, 26 June 2005, as 'Security and Development in a Time of Bare Life?'

fascism. The topic arises from observing recent postcolonial transitions in Africa, where some states inflict pernicious injury, suffering, death, and even genocide on portions of their own citizenry in the name of development. While development studies can neglect focused study of such regimes, there is no similar neglect in postcolonial works, in which the many dimensions of bare life development with a fascist edge become clearer.

The essay begins with a foray into political philosophy. The French sociologist and philosopher Michel Foucault (for example, 1980a) was one of the first to draw attention to body facets of politics in his studies of sexuality, security and governmentality. More recently, Giorgio Agamben (1998) has interwoven the biological with the political in ways that push Foucauldian thought into dark spaces. Agamben writes about the politics of sovereign exception that enables, in the extreme, the state construction of bare life zones of indistinction for '*homo sacer*' – those who can be killed but whose deaths are not seen as sacrifices. His work is central to understanding historical and contemporary bare life forms, albeit he draws examples largely from European circumstances.

Two development–oriented specialists, Rajeev Patel and Philip McMichael (2004), extend Agamben's work to Third World contexts. They argue that development activities of today continue a colonial, capitalist, biopolitical project that has always carried latent traits of global fascism. Colonial governance worked, to the degree it did, by managing and controlling bodies. That project has not ended, they claim, but rather has been carried into postcolonial state dynamics. One might say that the postcolonial condition is not adequately 'post' – it retains the sovereign exception and thereby keeps assigning statuses that are despised, dispossessed and, as Agamben would describe these, 'bare'.

Aspects of the fascist experience also emerge in essays, films, testimonials, and fictional literatures that depict everyday forms of pernicious biopolitics in postcolonial settings. The focus here is on experiences depicted in novels by Chenjerai Hove (1988), the late Yvonne Vera (1994) and Gil Courtemanche (2003); these revolve around Zimbabwe in recent years and Rwanda in the mid–1990s. Rwanda is identified with a genocidal campaign against Tutsis and moderate Hutus, which took place in 1994 as the world looked on. Zimbabwe's pernicious biopolitics is not at this extreme. The government has, however, unravelled 20 years of development over the past five years to the point where the country now has the highest rate of child deaths in the world (*The Guardian* 2005, 10), the fourth highest level of HIV/AIDS (24 per cent of the total population), alarming cases of malnutrition, and a political climate of racial scapegoating, routine political violence by parastatal groups, and limitations on all forms of opposition. A combination of approaches brings these problems of bare life into focus.

Agamben on pernicious biopolitics

Agamben theorizes that sovereign states exempt themselves, or make themselves exceptions to, their own laws against killing and their own (usually) constitutionally proclaimed standards of justice. In the name of the state, people can be killed by the state through capital punishment, death in detention, death by torture, or death through war. Death in a war context is thought to be sacrificial, which means that such deaths can be honoured and memorialized.[2] In the case of capital punishment, death occurs at state hands after a criminal trial finds an individual guilty of a heinous crime; this exception to the state prohibition against killing is lawful in some polities. People tortured in prison, gathered into asylum facilities, exterminated in camps, or made to disappear by the state are in the category of the *'homo sacer'*. They are killed or severely mistreated by sovereign states without public acknowledgement or eulogy, in circumstances that fall outside the usual arenas of state exception taking. That is to say, such deaths are neither sacrifices to and for the state nor cases of permissible state punishment by homicide. Entirely excluded from a community of rights, the *homo sacer* enters a 'zone of indistinction between sacrifice and homicide' (Agamben 1998, 83), a 'camp' of bare life existence without hope of justice, where individual life–taking follows no logic. Among all the variants of pernicious biopolitics of this sort, Agamben calls Auschwitz 'the pure space of exception' (1998, 134).

Agamben argues that contemporary politics is still captured by the sovereign exception and the bare life it can exact. In the democratic west the realm of bare life was originally situated at the margins of the political order. Gradually, it has come 'to coincide with the political realm, and exclusion and inclusion, outside and inside, *bios* and *zoe*, right and fact…a zone of irreducible indistinction'. Gradually, that is, democracy and totalitarianism have been converging around an inner solidarity of the sovereign exception: life is valuable – '[t]oday politics knows no value (and, consequently, no nonvalue) other than life' (1998, 10) – and yet the state may except itself from the preservation of life. To Agamben, 'until the contradictions that this fact implies are dissolved, Nazism and fascism – which transformed the decision on bare life into the supreme political principle – will remain stubbornly with us' (1998, 10).[3]

---

2   Not all would agree with this view. Veronique Pin–Fat and Maria Stern (2005) argue that soldiers are actually not sacrificed in war but are among the *homo sacer*.

3   Agamben is not alone in this view. Paul Virilio argues in *Art and Fear* that contemporary art and the contemporary art museum have taken on the pitiless aesthetic and creepy ambient murmuring of a fascist prison camp. He writes: 'When I visited the Museum at AUSCHWITZ, I stood in front of the display cases. What I saw there were images from contemporary art and I found that absolutely terrifying. Looking at the exhibits of suitcases, prosthetics, children's toys…*I suddenly had the impression I was in a museum of contemporary art*. I took the train back, telling myself that they had won!' (2003, 28, emphasis in original). Zygmunt Bauman connects Agamben's ideas to what he calls the

Indeed, if we believe that democracy has banished bare life, we need only think of the current situation of prisoners in international and national wars on terror, who inhabit zones of indistinction in political camps or jails set up by democracies. These prisoners are excluded from society and its democratic laws and rights by democratic states. Their bodies are often forced into nakedness and subjected to humiliating tortures and ghastly living conditions; frequently we are not sure who the dead among them are. Several United States (US) courts have pronounced these practices 'in discord with fundamental principles of American jurisprudence' (Diken and Laustsen 2005, 29; also Butler 2003), which means they operate in an expanded realm of sovereign exception. In this regard, it is noteworthy that Achille Mbembe (2003, 19) calls the 'intimate, lurid, and leisurely forms of cruelty' evident today, examples of necropolitics.

Agamben (1998, 167) mentions 'the *campos de concentraciones* created by the Spanish in Cuba in 1896 to suppress the popular insurrection of the colony...the "concentration camps" into which the English herded the Boers toward the start of the century'. He reminds us that the first concentration camps in Germany were set up by Social Democratic governments in 1923, for communists and later for Eastern European refugees (these were not extermination camps); the Nazi's described their death camps in state documents as exceptional. There is nothing historically new about a pernicious camp politics. What is new is the sneaky normalization of such logics after their apparent defeat, militarily and judicially, in and following World War II. It is not easy to refigure spaces of pure exception once they enter political practice. Like rhizomes, the exceptions can proliferate until they 'begin to overcome the rule' (1998, 168–9).[4] To Agamben, we have identified victims of European fascism and condemned that era's fascist forms, but we have not defeated its attitudes and technologies. Patel and McMichael provide some reasons why this can be so, focusing on places far from Europe and its historical fascist period.

The long biopolitical development era

In common with several critics of development thinking (for example, Escobar 1995; Crush 1996; Nederveen Pieterse 2000), Patel and McMichael (2004) imply

---

wasting of lives; however, he views wasting in general as 'an inescapable side–effect of *order–building* (each order casts some parts of the extant population as "out of place", "unfit", or "undesirable") and of *economic progress* (that cannot proceed without degrading and devaluing the previously effective modes of "making a living" and therefore cannot but deprive their practitioners of their livelihood)' (2004, 5, emphasis in original).

4   Bulent Diken and Carsten Bagge Lausten (2005) argue that the camp has become the prototypical social unit of contemporary western life. It can be a jail or detention centre run by the state as well as a gated residential community, sex tour, or party zone, where participants choose to 'liberate' themselves from messy urban life, acceptable sex partners, or general social decorum. Today, exception and norm have become indiscernible.

that a large geospatial pattern of pernicious biopolitics emerged around state building in Europe and capitalist colonialism elsewhere. Colonial practice clearly relied on biopolitics. Local people were routinely made to cover their bodies, subject their bodies to hygiene, fill their bodies with western knowledge, move their bodies to different lands, use their bodies for slave and wage labour, and fight other bodies in the name of the colonizing state. Bodies that seemed too 'other' to fit on the approved colonized/development line could suffer assault and death through holocausts of the sort Australians conducted in Tasmania, the cavalry led in the US West, and the Spanish and Portuguese unleashed in the American colonies (Davis 2001; Stannard 1992). Both the 'normal' and the abjecting forms of development relied on and exemplified a 'deployment of disciplinary technologies at the level of the individual' (Patel and McMichael 2004, 234). Indeed, Patel and McMichael argue that 'development was integral to colonialism' (2004, 237), and both were body disciplining.

Development thinking and practice, they remind us, was not confined to the colonies. In Europe, capitalist development also featured body regimes to regulate citizenship, marriage, education, health, sport, and labour, often on the basis of 'rules' about what was appropriate for one's race, class, and/or gender. 'For the first time in history, no doubt', Foucault (1980b, 142) noted, 'biological existence was reflected in political existence', with the sovereign state controlling bodies as a way of achieving hegemony. Normal biopolitics became extreme at several points in European history, not least during the global economic crisis of the 1930s, when Germany, in particular, was 'forced to structurally adjust by the League of Nations powers as a consequence of the collapse of the gold–sterling regime' (Patel and McMichael 2004, 234). Fascism emerged there around the 'manoeuvring of elites and a populist appeal by the Nazi party to regenerate an idealized national culture through selective mobilization based on ethnic and racial intolerance, and dedicated to reconstructing modernity via state technologies of control' (2004, 234–5). If the impetus was economic, as Patel and McMichael claim, the solution was political – unifying and purifying citizens, workers, family, military and national culture by policing bodies and exterminating or brutalizing those designated as contaminants.

Patel and McMichael do not 'claim that the tendencies at work from the early days of the development project replicate the features of mid–1930s and 1940s Germany, Italy and Japan' (2004, 233). What they maintain is that the biopolitics of our time and place resonate latently with past capitalist crises as well as with contemporary currents that globalize the commodity form, glorify the market, and assault organized labour, peasant cultures, and public goods. Having cut their teeth on colonial biopolitics, the development project, and, one might add, violent decolonization in many locations, postcolonial elites are familiar with the sovereign exception and subsume it into statecraft. The development conditionalities they face are very real in a world of unequal statuses – this cannot be denied. International political economy can become the stage, though, on which exceptional local policies are defended as normal by those who see themselves as 'sinned against and unsinning, demonizing – correctly – the imperial apparatuses of control without implicating themselves in its functioning' (2004, 236). Ongoing development challenges simultaneously empower that ontological attitude and conjure up a host of colonial/imperial demons to exorcise.

The Dutch Development Minister, Agnes van Ardenne, and Ugandan President Yoweri Museveni recently exchanged words that exemplify the pattern. She charged the president with planning to retain power by amending the constitution to allow unlimited terms of office, and warned him that donors would not support such efforts. The president retorted, seemingly asymmetrically, that Uganda donates its raw materials to the West, which are processed for profit overseas (*Hague Times* 2005, 1). The confrontation is typical: sinned against by the imperial apparatus of uneven development, Museveni implies that a postcolonial head of state cannot be a sinner. For her part, van Ardenne tries to ward off Museveni's anticipated sins without implicating her own state's colonial– development sins of the past and present.[5]

Or consider Zimbabwe. The state–led era of socialism proclaimed in the 1980s gave way to a structural adjustment political economy in the 1990s and then to failed development under increasingly authoritarian politics (see early treatments in Mandaza 1986; Moyo 1999). Elements of pernicious biopolitics were evident through all the transitions, inherited from the colonial era and the armed struggle and amplified by challenges of postcolonial development. The ZANU–PF (Zimbabwe African National Unity–Patriotic Front) government was clearly ill at ease with the give and take of democratic politics, to the point where it sent troops into the south of the country only a few years after independence to punish a popular rival movement. It was intermittently critical of whites, of women in the cities, of journalists, donors and former colonial countries (Sylvester 1991, 2000b). The authoritarian system with fascist undertones, however, emerged only after 2000, when we might say that the ZANU–PF state stopped worrying about maintaining a legitimate sphere of politics and turned exceptions into the rule (see Raftopolous and Campagnon 2003).

Pressured to deliver more than it would (not more than it could), ageing state elites created a twisted version of the anti–colonial struggle as the purest biopolitical moment of Zimbabwean history (Sylvester 2003). Within that story, they could resurrect themselves as young militants through the parastital militias of youth calling themselves, impossibly, 'war veterans'. These irregular forces occupied EuroZimbabwean farms and forced owners off without compensation. They broadened the list of sinners to include black farm workers, who were driven from their homes for the crime of having laboured for white bodies. Homosexuals

---

5 Museveni did persuade the Ugandan parliament to vote overwhelmingly to end the constitutional restrictions on presidential terms. Opposition leader Kizza Besigye was then arrested on charges of treason and rape, prompting another round of criticisms from European governments and further ripostes from Museveni that he is doing nothing wrong: countries with colonial histories are the ones with sins on their plates.

came under state pressure. Courts scaled back the inheritance rights for women that the regime had once touted. Urban ZANU–PF youth turned physically on opposition party members and the government tossed foreign journalists bodily out of the country under the tag of being British agents. This war against enemy bodies of Zimbabwe also killed foreign investment, donor aid, agriculture, most industry and tourism.

Ignoring its 20 years of power, decisions, and policies, the ZANU–PF government accepted no blame for Zimbabwe's harsh turn, even as it widened the circle of exception to exclude more and more Zimbabweans from rights. The sinners are always elsewhere, with the latest being urban dwellers, whose supposed sin of supporting opposition parties electorally resulted in the burning and bulldozing of market stalls and homes. The state as camp commandant then dumped many in re–education camps or in rural areas. Zimbabwe, says the Minister for National Security, Didymus Mutasa, 'would be better off with only 6 million [people], with our own people who support the liberation struggle' (Lamb 2005, 22). Zimbabweans will be ZANU–PF bodies or else. That is the 'rule'.

Echoes of an earlier development era in Europe, with its even harsher scapegoating biopolitics, are discernible in this case; but Zimbabweanists are reluctant to say so openly. We avoid giving the devil his due by continuing to refer to the government as authoritarian or neoauthoritarian (e.g., Darnolf and Laakso 2003; Raftopolous and Campagnon 2003) or totalitarian (Chan 2005). In an era of so–called democratic transitions, development can look away from cases that frustrate expectations (Way 2005). Patel and McMichael force us to push the envelope in the context of Third World transitions from colonial to postcolonial pernicious regimes. They provide a basis for thinking about a genus of politics that combines and extends patterns associated with European colonial development projects to moments of a postcolonial state under economic and political pressure. We might call that pernicious bare life biopolitics, 'fascism'.

Putting together what Agamben is saying with Patel's and McMichael's ideas, when the colonized territory becomes a sovereign state, it takes on the normal state entitlement of exception. That is, it takes up the 'right' to create a range of people that can be killed by the state for a variety of exceptional reasons. When the reasons proliferate and the exceptions grow in pernicious effect, an international community of wink–wink states endeavours to look the other way; or it complains feebly. Local populations experiencing a creeping collapse of recognizable politics can eventually take the increasing exceptions as either inescapable or nearly normal.[6] Agamben enables us to consider that fascism is always already latently present in the sovereign exception, not just in economic conditions associated with capitalism and colonialism. Patel and McMichael help us see that elites armed with inherited biopolitical tools continue the pattern as a matter of anticolonial

---

6   This is the only way I can make sense of Zimbabwe today. The Mugabe government has considerable power to intimidate people, but this is also a society that has experience in overturning an offensive system.

revenge and response to real and manufactured postcolonial development crises. The circle of sinners to rout gets wider and wider as the 'unsinning' elites define more spaces and statuses for themselves. And then the tables can turn, with the unsinning becoming *homo sacer* later, in a vicious and overwhelming biopolitics.

Postcolonial images of biopolitics and development

Additional insights into contemporary pernicious biopolitics come from an unlikely source for development analysis – essays, novels, films, and poetry depicting postcolonial fascist practices. Arundhati Roy (2002, 18) has recently said that '[f]ascism is about the slow, steady infiltration of all the instruments of state power…the slow erosion of civil liberties [and] unspectacular day–to–day injustices'. It is about ordinary people losing control over their lives and then 'being made to feel proud of something'. Writing much earlier, Frantz Fanon (1967, 132, 138) named the postcolonial state as progenitor of a local fascism. He said it is usually economically powerless and 'unable to bring about the existence of coherent social relations', so it 'makes a display, it jostles people and bullies them, thus intimating to the citizen that he is in continual danger'. Gil Courtemanche looks fascism in the face and names it in 1994 Rwanda in his novel, *A Sunday at the Pool in Kigali* (2003). By contrast, development analysts often cannot speak the word 'fascism' without coughing into their handkerchiefs.

Like many development specialists, I have seen some of the harshness of daily life in postcolonial contexts – African women's legs bowed out under the weight of water pots on their heads, flies hovering around children's faces undeterred by the listless hosts, men drinking themselves into oblivion at 10 am. Roadsides hold the remains of rusted technologies of development. Hospitals can be places no one should be allowed to enter. Death can arrive swiftly and early – through AIDS, civil violence, or something as relatively curable as diarrhoea. These biopolitical horrors stand side–by–side, incongruously, with clear markers of development achievement: a new school in a village, a dredged port, posters informing people of how to avoid contracting HIV, clinics for pregnant women, literacy classes for adults. The picture is crowded with inconsistent objects that beckon our attention.

Professionals engaging development problems often work from a laudable sense of urgency and impatience, but many with the greatest resources are tangled in an economic paradigm of development. Structural adjustment might work reasonably well (maybe, perhaps) when applied to stable, seasoned, democratic societies that have the economic capacity to manage change and absorb negative externalities. To prescribe it for countries that lack similar capacities can be inappropriate at best or a recipe for biopolitical tragedy – thus deepening the urgency. As Britain today pushes a new programme of aid to Africa, its advocates can seem unaware that if local elites direct aid in ways that benefit projects of hegemony or their bellies (see Bayart 1993), development can be stymied and local people gravely injured. Postcolonial fiction writers have fewer illusions. Their vantage points on the postcolonial development situation are close range rather than remote and abstract. The politics they record is messy, often nasty. Even those who do not live in the societies they depict – and there are many of these – often produce work that emphasizes the complex humanity of local people, often poor people, as against development reports that provide cases, numbers, needs, and theorizations of always deferred human capabilities.

Consider two short fictional scenes that portray commercial farm sites in pre–2000 Zimbabwe. In *Without a Name*, the late Yvonne Vera evokes an entire biopolitical economy with a few words:

> At the end of the day Mazvita felt weak, felt faint and frantic from the tobacco smell which spread toward her, like decay. The tobacco rose from inside her. The air was mouldy. Dark and wet. She turned her eyes towards the asbestos roof where the air hung downward like soot. It choked her, that smell (1994, 22).

Vera is describing the after–effects of a normal day of work on a commercial farm in Zimbabwe. Chenjerai Hove gives those types of words accompanying sounds in his novel about commercial farm workers, *Bones*:

> Marita, listen to Manyepo shouting at the other women who have not finished weeding their daily portion. The words you used to say were that the women will one day break their backs weeding the fields of the white man. Things are still as they were when your feet walked here, Marita. These women will not have any back to use for playing with their husbands, you used to say, Marita…You women over there, stop gossiping about the latest love potions and get on with the work (Hove 1988, 16–17).

Should such scenes sound contrived or inspired by a gender–aware political correctness, consider the words authored by a woman commercial farm worker in the 1990s, who speaks to me while she labours:

> Farm managers try to get around minimum wage stipulations by increasing quotas on contract workers and paying them less if they can't do it. It's difficult to make a quota because it's too big and because a lot of the maize is rotten and has to be thrown away [before we pack it]. To make ten bags, you have to hire your friends to help you. The problem is that if you do not do ten bags, you're only paid forty cents per bag completed. Many days we work all day from 6:00 to 12:00 and from 1:30 to 5:00 and only complete one bag. On those days, we only make forty cents (see Sylvester 2000b).

The fictional Mazvita ends up killing her baby in a moment of emotional and physical breakdown – 'madness' – after she has been betrayed by her man and has further 'lost her capacity for dream' (Vera 1994, 35–6) in the city, with its 'offerings and denials, its testimonies and silences' (1994, 56–7). She descends into abjectness, as 'no one cast her a pitiful glance. She was not there at all' (1994, 46). The women I interviewed on commercial farms in the late 1980s and early 1990s carry on working as casuals on mostly white–owned properties. Ten years later, no one casts them pitiful looks either, as their jobs disappear in a biopolitical rage directed first at their employers and then at them. Manyepo is not the problem then: these workers face the postcolonial developmental state, highly privileged over the years in the pantheons of development aid, and 'war veterans' who claim to have fought on behalf of that state–to–be against oppressor Rhodesians/British. A new biopolitics commandeers land, drives off owners and the workers, and effectively takes the country out of large scale food production.

Development experts recognize this type of display when they see it, but also have difficulty reading themselves and their activities into communities displaying themselves like this (Sylvester 2002, 224–41). Development missions carried out by democratic western states, and local programmes that install pernicious biopolitics, can share a territory that is not usually named. Agamben (1998, 134) calls it 'humanitarianism separated from politics'. Perhaps it is more accurate to call it humanitarianism absorbed into biopolitics. Agamben says: 'The "imploring eyes" of the Rwandan child, whose photograph is shown to obtain money but who "is now becoming more and more difficult to find alive", may well be the most telling contemporary cipher of the bare life that humanitarian organizations, in perfect symmetry with state power, need' (1998, 134–5). That view of development practices has some empirical base. Philip Roessler (2005, 224) finds that the rise of violent irregular units (for example, informal militias, paramilitaries, vigilantes, and warlords) in Kenya and Rwanda relates to pressures development agencies put on the states and their elites to install democracy. He says pointedly: 'Unfortunately, the international community, particularly western donors, was an unwitting accomplice in driving Rwanda and Kenya to communalize their repression and turn to marauding militias and other irregulars to maintain their ever precarious privileged position. This privatization of repression had devastating consequences for democracy and the protection of human rights, ironically the very two issues the international community felt its external conditionalities and pressure would promote'.[7]

When Museveni, once touted as a promising democratic leader for an African renaissance, mystifies development experts by playing with the 'rule' of democracy, a Dutch Development minister plays the part of not–seeing Dutch complicities in a script of exception that repeats the colonial–development/postcolonial–development drama over and over. When Zimbabwe's Robert Mugabe (or Idi Amin earlier in Uganda or 'Emperor' Bokassa of the Central African Republic in the 1980s) turns on citizens in the name of proper development, we decry his behaviour, impose punishments, and often refuse further development aid until

---

7   Mark Duffield offers the related idea that efforts to use aid networks as levers for social change in Third World countries result most often only in new rounds 'of agency reinvention and repackaging…[which] leaves underlying assumptions and relations unchallenged…deepening normalization of violence around us' (2002, 1068).

the biopolitics change – as if we were not complicit in those. From Agamben's perspective, bare life biopolitics provides moral humanitarians with something to rescue 'in perfect symmetry with state power'.

This point can be missed by those who hope the pernicious biopolitics of Rwanda, Zimbabwe, Uganda, Cambodia, Bosnia, Chechnya, Burma, and Pakistan will prove fleeting in a world increasingly bound to neoliberalizing norms of globalization. When Richard Sandbrook and David Romano (2004) compare how Egypt and Mauritius responded to the structural adjustment medicine dolled out under neoliberal globalization regimes, they find uneven outcomes that give little cause for optimism. 'Mauritius', they conclude, 'has deftly navigated the maelstrom of globalization by achieving growth with considerable equity and genuine democracy, whereas Egypt has followed a path characterized by belated and partial liberalization, irregular growth, the rise of new inequalities and insecurities, repression, and violent Islamist movements. If Mauritius is globalization's prodigy, Egypt is one of globalization's bastards' (2004, 1009). The difference between the two postcolonial countries lies in what the authors regard as Mauritius's 'peculiar' colonial experience. The more usual outcome of interaction between the local and international financial institutions is along the lines of the Egyptian case.

If we are to look the bare life problematic in the eye as a matter of human security and development, we must look at ourselves looking at and aiding others. Courtemanche's *A Sunday at the Pool in Kigali* puts this challenge across especially well. The novel depicts the build up to the 1994 genocide in Rwanda from the vantage point of an expatriate development worker and his local friends. Events filter through white man's eyes, but the novel does not flinch before an extreme biopolitics, which the United Nations (UN) Security Council, neighbouring states, and former colonial powers chose to not–reckon with. Its *faux* eyewitness story thinly fictionalizes events, atrocities, and traumas that appear now in various public records (for example, Africa Rights 1995). By storifying genocidal facts, victims, and perpetrators, Courtemanche enables us to see interchangeable sinners and sinned behaving both true to form and in ways we might not expect in zones of indistinction.

Looking pernicious biopolitics in the eye: A Sunday at the pool in Kigali

Courtemanche's (2003, preface) characters, all of whom 'existed in reality', form three identity and corporeal groups. There are western embassy and military personnel, clerics, and development/aid workers, all of whom are temporarily posted in Rwanda and have the connections necessary to exit the country if they wish. Rwandans are more permanently on site as hotel workers, militants, AIDS sufferers, taxi drivers, prostitutes, lovers, wives, and families. The Rwandan state and its parastital militias form a third, shadowy group of characters, whose pernicious biopolitics is arterial and capillary.

The westerners in the novel come across as mostly opportunistic and narcissistically biopolitical. There in a helping capacity of some sort, Courtemanche helps the reader appreciate the other things that can inspire them, like status, sex, and bodily comforts. There is a certain detached recklessness to their lives, a certain complacency mixed with an apprehension and exceptionalism that regularly compromises ethics. Courtemanche has little sympathy for the diplomatic community in Kigali, particularly the French, Belgians and Canadians. Their hard drinking white bodies gather around the swimming pool at the Mille Collines Hotel, or at a local golf course, and imbibe the desires and ambitions associated with a B film along with their French food and wine. They mythologize the (often brutal) sex they have or want to have with locals. They make a lot of noise. Some (e.g., Belgian soldiers) come across as yobs and others epitomize a certain dull–eyed western ineffectuality: Courtemanche paints Romeo Dallaire, the Canadian commander of UN peacekeeping troops, as a 'miracle of mimesis, a perfect incarnation of his country…[u]nassuming, apprehensive, ineloquent and naïve…' (Courtemanche 2003, 12). 'He is not yet used to this peace that kills on a daily basis' (2003, 14).[8] At least the General is polite. Most others are guilty in Courtemanche's eyes of every colonial trope in the imperial book of manners.

The Rwandans are no angels themselves. They make the best of the veneered but harsh colonial–postcolonial development environment – entrepreneurially, resignedly, violently, enthusiastically, cynically and opportunistically. They are savvier than their many temporary friends and do 'concealment and ambiguity with awesome skill' (2003, 10). Most interesting is the intricate ethnic game some among them play. In an environment where a particular ethnicity is good one day and bad the next, one response is to turn oneself into whatever seems to be privileged at the moment. Alternatively, one can try to lose ethnic identification and find some zone of distinction, some place of safe citizenship that will safeguard the body against the biopolitics of the present moment and the turnabout biopolitics of the future. A central character, Gentille, clings to the idea that love with a westerner can confound local–colonial development biopolitics, even though she thinks love is an unnecessary western emotion that is its own form of excess. The personal collapses into the political through the body, though, and no camouflage really works. Everyone sits anxiously in the forecourts of fascism, trying to ignore the scent of extermination. Yet Courtemanche shows people living daily life as though nothing was amiss. No matter that trucks of youths brandishing machetes

---

8   Courtemanche (2005, 11) now says that his presentation of Dallaire is harsh. On learning the General tried to commit suicide after leaving Rwanda, 'I frantically crossed out several paragraphs of my novel. I was caught up by his tragic humanity and I felt guilty for criticizing a man who sought oblivion in death for his own failure. This man had paid too dear a price'. Indeed, Dallaire's 'failure' in Rwanda is open to interpretation. In the film *Hotel Rwanda*, he is shown using a tiny contingent of UN forces to stand down extreme militants on more than one occasion. See Dallaire's (2004) memoirs.

cut down people at random and leave them by the side of the road to be found anew every morning. Life continues.

The Rwandan state has a virulent voice in the novel but little in the way of corporeal presence. 'It' consists mostly of disembodied voices – radio broadcasts that call for the demise of the Tutsi 'cockroaches'. We see a soldier or two and a few tanks guarding the presidential palace or encircling 'the obligatory symbols of decolonization: Constitution Square, Development Avenue, Boulevard of the Republic, Justice Avenue…' (2003, 2). The key players of state are not–state, which is to say they are paramilitary extremists, who simultaneously plan genocide against the minority Tutsi population – and tell everyone about it well in advance, as though advertizing an upcoming social event – and plan a secret coup d'etat against their own Hutu head of state, which they can blame on the Tutsis. Circa 1994, structural adjustment programmes that contribute to high levels of indebtedness today do not yet heavily weigh down the Rwandan state. Its sovereignty lodges in Foucauldian governmentalities of bodily control that make the exception the rule. It is a governmentality of hate and retribution rather than one of institutions and laws.

The narrator of the novel is a Canadian film maker, Valcourt, who has been in Rwanda for some time awaiting funding to make a documentary on AIDS (one–third of Rwandan adults were HIV/AIDS positive in 1994). He is a quiet observer and a sinner in his own ways: 'Valcourt pooh–poohed racist theories that claimed to deduce a person's origin from the shape of a nose or a forehead, or the slenderness of a body. But, unwittingly [he was] a prisoner of these stereotypes himself' (2003, 31). Endlessly, and with barely suppressed adolescent desire, he fixates on the breasts of a very much younger hotel waitress. He assumes, by her body appearance alone, that she is (always already) Tutsi. He goes on living at the hotel, sitting at the pool, noting the buffoons around him with one eye and the signs of death with the other. Like other humanitarians in Rwanda, he claims exception and powerlessness in the face of what becomes an unmistakeable genocide. It is not that he is 'an accomplice; his presence here did not indicate his approval or even his indifference. Much as he might like to be a general, he was only a solitary onlooker, and he could act only as such, a man alone' (2003, 108). One of his Rwandan friends reminds him of the 'true story' of his kind – that it was white colonials, Belgians, who started 'a kind of Nazism here' (2003, 108) by energetically rewarding the Tutsis for their 'white' looks. Yet Valcourt never seems to worry that he will be sinned against for the crimes committed in the past by his body lookalikes. His job – and it is a classic – is to protect Gentille's body from her own society.

Bare life as life

One of Valcourt's friends, Méthode, experiences bare life most acutely, presciently, and complexly. He is 32 years old, militant in his Tutsi identity, and also experiencing the last stages of AIDS. As other forms of corporeal violence swirl around him, Méthode acts as though he wants 'to die clean, drunk, stuffed with food and in front of the television' (2003, 41). He says he prefers to die 'before the Holocaust' comes to Rwanda, but not before he can read up about that other Holocaust in Europe. He marvels at that one's cold and scientific technologies, calling it 'a terrifying masterpiece of efficiency and organization. A monstrosity of Western civilization. The original sin of the Whites' (2003, 41). There will be a different holocaust in Rwanda, he surmizes. It will be 'the barbarian Holocaust, the cataclysm of the poor, the triumph of machete and club...dirty, ugly, lots of severed arms and legs, women with bellies ripped, children with feet cut off, so these Tutsi cockroaches could never again walk and fight' (2003, 41–2). Although international biopolitics keeps the best AIDS drugs for itself and not for people like Méthode, he considers it a relief to die from a body–destroying disease rather than by the chop of a triumphant machete.

At the end, Méthode has sex for the last time with a willing partner his friends have summoned, gets shot full of morphine by a Canadian development worker, upends a bottle of whiskey, and asks Valcourt to film his parting soliloquy. He dies, 'fulfilled, if only through his eyes' (2003, 45). He has made his choices, as he sees them, and has lived his life well, even in his double zone of indistinction as an AIDS victim and an ethnic victim. And he insists that he is the one choosing and cleverly defying the machete and club. His mode of departing in celebratory style – emphasizing the body as vessel of pleasure and choice – momentarily reminds us that bare life is life. One who is in it as *homo sacer* may try to control death by rewriting its script, substituting another biopolitics of exception for the one that was to be his fate. This particular *homo sacer* refuses the state's fascist machetes and accepts pernicious international epidemiology. The trade–off is far from ideal.[9]

The characters in Kigali never escape what film director, Raoul Peck (cited in MacNab 2005, 9), calls a monster slowly conjured into being. Speaking of decisions he made in filming Sometimes in April, one of the three films made recently on the Rwandan genocide,[10] Peck claims that just about everyone in a community gearing up for genocide is complicit in creating it:

> You look aside the first time when someone is slapped in public. You don't say anything. The next day, they kill him in front of you and you don't say anything. Then, on the third day, they can come and take your wife and rape your wife. And then it's too late for you to do anything. That is how the monster arrives. It starts with little things.

Wrapped up in and overcome by the small to enormous biopolitics of genocide, no one can experience a 'normal' death and no one can claim to be a mere bystander or

---

9   For another recent fictional account of bare life as life, this one set in a European concentration camp and later away from it, see Imre Kertesz's novel *Fatelessness* (2004).

10   The other films are *Hotel Rwanda* and *Shooting Dogs*.

observer. A character in Courtemanche's (2003, 86) novel remarks that development experts 'discuss life and death like great philosophers. We just talk about people who are living and dying'. He tells Valcourt to 'leave us to die peacefully alive' (2003, 82). It can all be indistinct in this zone of creeping bare life.

We 'great philosophers' see the genocide coming but act as though we cannot see death. One of Courtemanche's Rwandan characters asks: 'Monsieur Valcourt, don't people die in your country… (2003, 79–80) [or is it that you all] die by accident, because life hasn't been generous and leaves you like an unfaithful wife' (2003, 86)? The UN in particular has the information about local deaths required to evaluate what is going on in Rwanda, but it is wrapped up in the cloak of exceptionality woven by its member states. An intricate tale of precolonial, colonial, and development biopolitics combusts while international relations carefully weighs the political merits of humanitarian intervention and passes this one by. A resigned consent of silence bows to the sovereign exception of violent politics and bare life in a country that ranks low on international security agendas.

Rwandan women rank even lower than Rwanda. They are raped by genocidal forces or treated as 'rape bait' sex objects by international helpers. They are politicized biological specimens, routinely insulted, routinely subjected to sexualized injuries by the agents of genocide, such as lobbed off breasts, and then routinely left to die (this was Gentille's fate).[11] Sometimes small girls are spared, with the intent of humiliating and torturing them when they are older, for the enhanced sexual pleasure of the attacker. More often the fate of girls depends on the perceived identities and politics of their families. Attempting to place a girl at an orphanage run by Belgian nuns, Valcourt confronts a Belgian mother superior who informs him:

> that hers was an establishment of excellent reputation on which hundreds of future Belgian parents were depending for the adoption of children that were sound in body and mind…The little girl sleeping in Gentille's arms did not appear to have the necessary endowments. If her parents were killed at a roadblock it was no doubt because they were doing something wrong. And when there's something criminal in the parents, there's often some in the children (Courtemanche 2003, 105–6).

Biopolitics all the way down.

At the very bottom, bare in all ways, are the sick. Touring a hospital with the latest Canadian Embassy staff member, Valcourt describes the ultimate zone of indistinction, a 'final solution' camp. Consisting of about thirty low buildings separated by grassed spaces and asphalt paths, it features people wearing long

---

11   It was only when an unprecedented number of babies were born nine months after the genocide in Rwanda began that the UN's fact finding mission noted systematic sexual violence against women. See Gallagher (1997).

white coats and gurneys pushed at breakneck speeds. But there is nowhere to go there, no place where it is remotely possible to help bodies on gurneys. The hospital shelves hold no antibiotics or even aspirin. What they have in ample supply is some antifungal ointment sent by a donor country and bottles of Geritol, marketed in the west as a treatment for 'iron poor blood'. The hospital emergency ward consists of three beds with soiled sheets, bloodstained floors and a bedpan of urine. In the next room, male and female nurses gather around a table drinking coffee from an espresso machine. Pavillion B has only 68 beds for 153 patients. 'How many with AIDS, Bernadette?' 'About a hundred' (2003, 126).

When Patel and McMichael speak of global fascism, they hint at an idea that Agamben's work makes plain and that postcolonial 'fictions' about Rwanda sum up: in response to a variety of challenges, violence of the sort witnessed during World War II repeats in Rwanda, its in–securing as repetitive as poverty, as elusive as universal primary education and gender equality and maternal health, and as crushing as child mortality and HIV/AIDS. The horror thought that comes from considering Méthode's 'fictive' choices is this: for some, it is better to die from the very things the UN seeks to eradicate than die at the hands of one's own 'developmental' government.

The bare life development/postcolonial problematic

Bare life, *homo sacer*, camps, and elements of fascism: these are spaces many do not want to enter. We see that reluctance in the distancing behaviours international agencies took from Rwanda circa 1994 and from Nazi camps during World War II. We peer into the dragon's mouth after some time has passed, but not at the time the fire breath first sends out its stink. To take up the challenge quicker requires tools to name and respond to pernicious biopolitics as the expected local and international relations that Agamben, Patel and McMichael, and writers of postcolonial scenes chronicle. Between regimes in Europe that invented fascism (but not camps) and later regimes located elsewhere, the resonances of fascism linger, stoked by international indifference and/or by international involvement. Perhaps Patel and McMichael are right in insisting that fascism is now in the fabric of international political economy. Many actions we abhor may not be exceptions so much as the rule.

We must sort out important conceptual issues, though, something Patel and McMichael begin but do not satisfactorily carry out. What is fascism today? Where is it? Of what does it consist? What are its varieties? Does 'it' exist or would another concept, a broader register perhaps, better serve the study of pernicious biopolitics? How do its exceptionalities unfold in various places? How do we identify and study the often latent, sometimes all too apparent, fascist conditions evident today while maintaining historical and cultural specificities, safeguarding wounded sensibilities, and drawing conceptual parameters around fascist camps and other zones of indistinction? And how do we speak critically of fascism, bare life, and pernicious biopolitics in Third World contexts today without inadvertently feeding the neoconservative effort to force regime change abroad through military means? Should we not also avoid pinning a complex problematic on one international or local tendency alone, such as colonization or globalization? Sandbrook and Romano (2004, 1028) suggest that globalization in particular must not be demonized without careful study of individual cases, even though its darker scenario 'will more often prevail than the sanguine neoliberal scenario'.

The need for comparative case study also underlies Stephen Chan's (2005, 370) sense that the violence unleashed against white farmers, black commercial farm workers, and Zimbabweans who support the opposition is a limited violence – '[w]e are not talking of the terrors of war in Liberia'. Chan goes on, though: 'Having said that, both the means and ends partake in a rationality that is simultaneously cold–blooded and ruthless, and full of the talk of a yet–to–be– completed liberation' (2005, 370). It is that local talk that can uncork the adrenaline and glorify an armed struggle now sufficiently in the past to be unknown by today's youth. It is that kind of talk that unsettles, combined with the discipline, nerve, and intensity of the ZANU–PF machine in insisting that the fascists are racially marked capitalist farmers, global financial institutions, British, and local sinners of various sorts. Although Zimbabwe today is not genocidal Rwanda of 1994, the state brings global fascist histories home through biopolitics that deliver pain to the very Zimbabweans it once endeavoured to rescue. Overwhelmingly, it is the black subaltern there who cannot speak (out) and increasingly cannot eat. How do we help her when the pernicious state would like to harm her and increasingly prohibits even NGOs from getting close to her?

Rwanda presents a different/similar picture. The state in 1994 wants to give the impression that a wave of violence by the dominant ethnic Hutu against the minority Tutsi, who can be killed and not sacrificed, is the consequence of Belgian colonial favouritism, unfair peace accords, poverty, and, importantly, the characteristics of the Tutsi population. The state orchestrates, commands, and controls the forces of genocide so effectively that humanitarian agencies inside and outside Rwanda are caught flatfooted. In hindsight, perhaps we are overly accustomed to taking our gated–community exceptions to put our bodies in spaces of such stark violence. We can become morally inert, mobbing the first planes out as the relief workers arrive. It is telling that the immediate biopolitics of genocide subsides in Rwanda only when rebel Tutsi forces move up from the Congo and drive out the sinners – to become sinners themselves in different ways in an ongoing story that development efforts have not resolved.

The novelist of postcolonial bare life may not stick around either; or s/he might not have been witness to the events portrayed – Courtemanche was not in Rwanda in April 1994, for example. But s/he can conjure a vivid sense of people in the midst of a specific crisis, and, if there, can recall and write down details, make composite pictures, and put memories in situ. Development texts too often assume that technologies of development lie outside politics (or should), and/or that conflict is temporary (or should be). The rendered stories of life on the ground convey relentless experiences of bare lives in conflict and in pain, reasoning through and trying to bargain with various biopolitics of death, taking small pleasures in the midst of the horrors of extermination (see other examples in Orford 2003). Where development often does not stick, stories about 'it' and its follies stick to the gut and the brain, because they force the coolly distant development expert to the inside of a maelstrom, where we can watch ourselves fleeing the scene for another hotel pool in a less scary space.[12] Sinners and the unsinning come at us – indeed become us – at the uncomfortably close range that should be the usual vantage point of international assistance.

There are many sovereign exceptions a variety of state agents can and do grant themselves/ourselves routinely, with horrible consequences for local development and for humanitarian/human outcomes. There are also brutal local transitions that defy any sense that the world is moving in generally democratic directions. It is important to follow bare life politics into its hideouts, and into our texts and toolboxes as well, searching with undeflecting and nuancing eyes. That is the promise of development studies working with postcolonial studies and other bodies of thought: together we can see and address more of the troubling biopolitics of our times.

References

African Rights (1995), *Rwanda: Death, Despair and Defiance* (London: African Rights).

Agamben, G. (1998), *Homo Sacer: Sovereign Power and Bare Life*, Heller–Roazen, D. trans. (Stanford: Stanford University Press).

Bauman, Z. (2004), *Wasted Lives: Modernity and its Outcasts* (Cambridge: Polity).

Bayart, J.F. (1993), *The State in Africa: The Politics of the Belly* (New York: Longman).

Briggs, J. and Sharp, J. (2004), 'Indigenous Knowledges and Development: A Postcolonial Caution', *Third World Quarterly* 25, 661–76.

Butler, J. (2003), *Precarious Life: The Powers of Mourning and Violence* (London: Verso).

Chan, S. (2005), 'The Memory of Violence: Trauma in the Writings of Alexander Kanengoni and Yvonne Vera and the Idea of Unreconciled Citizenship in Zimbabwe', *Third World Quarterly* 26:2, 369–382.

Courtemanche, G. (2003), *A Sunday at the Pool in Kigali* (London: Canongate).

—— (2005), 'The Nightmare Diaries', *Guardian Review*: 23 April, 11.

Crush, J. (1996), *Power of Development* (London: Routledge).

---

12   I do not place myself outside this unflattering picture of development experts. See Sylvester (2000a) for an autobiographical glimpse.

Dallaire, R. (2004), *Shake Hands With the Devil: The Failure of Humanity in Rwanda* (London: Arrow Books).

Darnolf, S. and Laakso, L. (eds) (2003), *Twenty Years of Independence in Zimbabwe: From Liberation to Authoritarianism* (Basingstoke: Palgrave Macmillan).

Davis, M. (2001), *Late Victorian Holocausts: El Nino Famines and the Making of the Third World* (London: Verso).

Diken, B. and Bagge Laustsen, C. (2005), *The Culture of Exception: Sociology Facing the Camp* (London: Routledge).

Duffield, M. (2002), 'Social Reconstruction and the Radicalization of Development: Aid as a Relation of Global Liberal Governance', *Development and Change* 33, 1049–71.

Escobar, A. (1995), *Encountering Development: The Making and Unmaking of the Third World* (Princeton: Princeton University Press).

Fanon, F. (1967), *Wretched of the Earth* (London: Penguin).

Foucault, M. (1980a), *Power/Knowledge: Selected Interviews and Other Writings: 1972–1977*, Gordon, C. trans. (New York: Pantheon).

—— (1980b), *The History of Sexuality* (New York: Vintage Books).

Gallagher, A. (1997), 'Ending the Marginalisation: Strategies for Incorporating Women into the United Nations Human Rights System', *Human Rights Quarterly* 19, 283–333.

Hague Times (2005), 'Cabinet Minister Lashes Out at African Leader', 40, 4 March, 1.

Hove, C. (1988), *Bones* (Harare: Baobab Books).

Kapoor, I. (2004), 'Hyper-self-reflexive Development? Spivak on Representing the Third World "Other"', *Third Word Quarterly* 25:4, 627–47.

Kertesz, I. (2004), *Fatelessness* (New York: Vintage).

Lamb, C. (2005), 'Mugabe Policy Branded "New Apartheid"', *The Sunday Times* 12 June, 22.

MacNab, G. (2005), 'Back to Hell', *The Guardian*: section G2, 9.

Mandaza, I. (1986), *The Political Economy of Transition in Zimbabwe: The Political Economy of Transition 1980–1986* (Dakar: Codesria).

Mbembe, A. (2003), 'Necropolitics', Meintjes, L. trans., *Public Culture* 15, 11–40.

Moyo, S. (1999), 'Land and Democracy in Zimbabwe', *Monography* series No. 7 (Harare: Sapes Trust).

Nederveen Pieterse, J. (2000), 'After Post–Development', *Third World Quarterly* 25: 1, 175–91.

Orford, A. (2003), *Reading Humanitarian Intervention: Human Rights and the Use of Force in International Law* (Cambridge: Cambridge University Press).

Patel, R. and McMichael, P. (2004), 'Third Worldism and the Lineages of Global Fascism: The Regrouping of the Global South in the Neoliberal Era', *Third World Quarterly* 25: 1, 231–54.

Pin–Fat, V. and Stern, M. (2005), 'The Scripting of Private Jessica Lynch: Biopolitics, Gender, and the "Feminization" of the U.S. Military', *Alternatives* 30, 25–53.

Raftopolous, B. and Campagnon, D. (2003), 'Indigenization, State Bourgeoisie and Neo–authoritarian Politics', in S. Darnolf and L. Laakso (eds), *Twenty years of Independence in Zimbabwe: From Liberation to Authoritarianism* (Basingstoke: Palgrave Macmillan), 15–33.

Roessler, P. (2005), 'Donor–Induced Democratization and the Privatization of State Violence in Kenya and Rwanda', *Comparative Politics* 37, 207–27.

Roy, A. (2002), *Fascism's Firm Footprint in India* (The Nation: 30 September, 18).

Sandbrook, R. and Romano, D. (2004), 'Globalisation, Extremism and Violence in Poor Countries', *Third World Quarterly* 25, 1007–30.

Spivak, G. (1988), 'Can the Subaltern Speak?', in C. Nelson and L. Grossberg (eds), *Marxism and the Interpretation of Culture* (Urbana: University of Illinois Press), 271–313.

Stannard, D.E. (1992), *American Holocaust: The Conquest of the New World* (New York: Oxford University Press).

Sylvester, C. (1991), *Zimbabwe: The Terrain of Contradictory Development* (Boulder: Westview).

—— (1999), 'Development Studies and Postcolonial Studies: Disparate Tales of the "Third World"', *Third World Quarterly* 20, 703–21.

—— (2000a), 'Development Poetics', *Alternatives* 25, 335–51.

—— (2000b), *Producing Women and Progress in Zimbabwe: Narratives of Identity and Work From the 1980s* (Portsmouth: Heinemann).

—— (2002), *Feminist International Relations: An Unfinished Journey* (Cambridge: Cambridge University Press).

—— (2003), 'Remembering and Forgetting Zimbabwe: Towards a Third Transition', in P. Gready (ed.), *Political Transition: Politics and Cultures* (London: Pluto Press), 29–52.

—— (2004), 'Fictional Development Sovereignties', in J. Edkins, V. Pin–Fat and M. Shapiro (eds), *Sovereign Lives: Power in Global Politics* (London: Routledge), 141–64.

The Guardian (2005), 'Zimbabwe Child Death Rate Highest in the World', 18 March, 10.

Vera, Y. (1994), *Without a Name* (Harare: Baobab Books).

Virilio, P. (2003), *Art and Fear*, Rose, J. trans., (London: Continuum).

Way, L. (2005), 'Authoritarian State Building and the Sources of Regime Competitiveness in the Fourth Wave: The cases of Belarus, Moldava, Russia, and Ukraine', *World Politics* 57, 231–59.

Chapter 3

Fine Words, Failed Policies:
Gender Mainstreaming in an Insecure
and Unequal World

Jane Parpart

Introduction

At the dawn of the twenty–first century, the international development community, spearheaded by the United Nations, concluded that development to date had not brought the promised reduction in poverty around the world. Member states agreed to support a set of Millennium Development Goals (MDGs), which promised to cut world poverty in half and to produce a more equitable, tolerant world by 2015. The third goal focused on promoting gender equality and the empowerment of women. Unlike the others, this goal was framed in the familiar development language of gender equality and empowerment. Despite the ambitious and lofty discourse, the carefully crafted policies and generous commitments of money and institutional support, implementation of the third MDG has been disappointing, both in the scope of its aims and the achievements of its goals (Johnson 2005; Kabeer 2005). This pattern of well–crafted gender policies producing disappointing results is not new. Gender mainstreaming policies, trumpeted as the technical fix for operationalizing gender equality and women's empowerment, have also achieved limited results (Moser and Moser 2005; Perrons 2005; Standing 2007).

As these failures have become increasingly apparent, some policy makers and development scholars have sought new ways to close the gap between policy and praxis. Their 'solutions' bring little new to the table, for the most part calling for more of the same – more resources, stronger institutions, more accountability and greater commitment. Even suggestions to include men fail to move beyond well worn strategies such as more gender sensitization workshops, more inclusive project administration, better laws and training in domestic violence (United Nations Population Fund for Activities (UNFPA) 2005). Clearly new thinking and new approaches are needed; ones that interrogate the consequences of an uncritical, triumphalist discourse on gender mainstreaming, gender equality and women's empowerment as well as the need to address the challenges thrown up by the increasingly masculinist, violent and unequal world emerging in the wake of global economic restructuring and the neoliberal (dis)order.

Gender equality and women's empowerment: Discourse and policy

While the language of empowerment had been popularized in the 1970s by critical educationalists such as Paulo Freire (1970) and small NGOs,[1] who adopted it as a tool for encouraging social transformation from the bottom–up/grassroots, mainstream development agencies generally regarded empowerment as a minor sideshow to the real issues of economic growth and modernization. However, as economic inequality and social dislocation intensified in the 1980s, the World Bank sought to mitigate the harsher effects of neoliberal policies (without disturbing their core values) by adopting the language of empowerment and participation (Hales 2007; Kerr and Tsikata 2000). Pressured by the Beijing Declaration and Platform for Action's call for globally empowering women,[2] empowerment moved from the margins to the centre, becoming a central pillar of gender policies and praxis. The United Nations Development Program (UNDP 2002, v; see also UNDP 2003) declared gender equality and women's empowerment 'central to human development', boldly arguing that 'gender inequality is an obstacle to progress, a roadblock on the path of human development. When development is not "en–gendered" it is "en–dangered"'. Government development agencies, such as the Canadian International Development Agency (CIDA 1999), adopted similar language and in 2001, a World Bank (2001, 35) policy report, *Engendering Development*, identified gender equality and women's empowerment as core development issues, 'whose failure both harms well–being and hinders development.'

The link between gender equality and women's empowerment inspired a shift from earlier concerns with gender equity – seen as 'the process of being fair to women and men' – to a focus on gender equality, defined by CIDA (1999, 7) as 'the equal valuing by society of both the similarities and differences between women and men, and the varying roles that they play.' Similarly, the World Bank (2001, 35) defined gender equality as 'equality under the law, equality of opportunity… and equality of voice.' While acknowledging the challenges to achieving gender equality, the report optimistically called for a three pronged strategy involving: reform of institutions to establish equal rights and opportunities for women and men, fostering more gender sensitive economic growth and taking active measures to redress persistent disparities in command over resources and political voice. Women's empowerment was seen as a critical element of this strategy (World Bank 2001, 231, 272).

---

1   As Batliwala (2007, 558) points out, empowerment has a long history that can be traced to the Protestant Reformation in Europe, Quakerism, democracy, early capitalism, Black Power and other social justice movements. It has also been adopted to serve more conservative agendas, including management gurus and neoliberal political agendas.

2   The 1995 Beijing meeting was the Fourth UN Global Women's Conference and its support for women's empowerment and gender mainstreaming entered into national planning documents around the world.

Scholars and practitioners of gender and development contributed to these discussions. Caroline Moser (1993) called for placing gender and women's empowerment at the centre of development planning. Drawing on lessons from empowerment practice in South Asia, in 1993, Srilatha Batliwala (2007, 560) rejected one–shot 'solutions', emphasizing process and the importance of challenging ideological and institutional practices supporting gender inequality. While acknowledging the problems of measuring empowerment, Naila Kabeer (1999, 437; see also Kabeer 1994) defined women's empowerment as 'the process by which those who have been denied the ability to make strategic life choices acquire such an ability.' Her focus on *agency*, seen as actively exercising choice in ways that challenge power relations; *resources*, which are necessary for exercising such choices and *achievements*, namely the degree to which the potential to choose is realized, has had considerable influence on development policy and praxis (Kabeer 2005,13–16). While adopting a more nuanced approach to power, Jo Rowlands (1997, 129–130) also equated empowerment with increased self–confidence, self–esteem and agency while Jane Parpart, Shirin Rai and Kathy Staudt (2002) called for more attention to political processes at all levels. Despite the caveats, the tone of this literature has been optimistic – women's empowerment was seen as a laudable and reachable goal.

Policy makers and practitioners in development agencies picked up the celebratory language of choice and agency, while largely ignoring caveats about measurement and broader ideological and institutional issues (Cornwall, Harrison and Whitehead 2007; Mukhopadhyay 2007).[3] CIDA defined empowerment as being 'about people – both women and men – taking control over their lives: setting their own agendas, gaining skills, building self–confidence, solving problems, and developing self–reliance' (1999, 8). Similarly, the World Bank (2001) defined empowerment as 'the process of enhancing individual's or group's capacity to make purposive choices and to transform those choices into desired actions and outcomes'. Empowerment discourse became shorthand for women/gender–friendly World Bank policies and projects. By 2005 over 1,800 World Bank projects mentioned empowerment in their documentation (Alsop, Bertelsen and Holland 2006, 1). The UNDP (2002) also claimed empowerment and gender equality as central pillars of their work, placing both at the centre of human development, with an emphasis on enlarging women's choices and addressing gender inequities in social, economic and political spheres. Resistances melted away as development agencies lauded the possibilities of gender equality and women's empowerment.

Development institutions (and supportive scholars) soon set about trying to operationalize these goals through gender mainstreaming, which became the approved mechanism for achieving gender equality and women's empowerment. This has been defined by the United Nations Economic and Social Council (ECOSOC) as:

---

3   Anne Marie Goetz (1994) points out that development bureaucracies tend to incorporate information that fits in with their own views.

> ...a strategy for making women's as well as men's concerns and experiences an integral dimension of the design, implementation, monitoring and evaluation of the policies and programmes in all political, economic and societal spheres so that women and men benefit equally and inequality is not perpetuated (1997, chapter IV).

Gender Mainstreaming soon became a central pillar of UN development efforts. The UNDP predicted that gender mainstreaming would contribute to profound organizational transformations 'by taking account of gender equality concerns in all policy, programme, administrative and financial activities' (UNDP 2000). In collaboration with the United Nation Development Fund for Women (UNIFEM), UNDP optimistically predicted that gender mainstreaming would 'transform the gender order throughout society, including organizations, programmes and projects...through deliberate and focused interventions at every level' (de Waal 2008, 210). As a UNDP (2002, 6) report triumphantly exclaimed, the 'why' had been supplanted by the 'how' of gender work.

Policy makers, practitioners and scholars soon constructed measurements for ensuring the success of gender mainstreaming, gender equality and women's empowerment. Responding to the requirements of results based management and intense governance oversight, development agencies ignored Kabeer's (1999) warnings; empowerment frameworks and gender mainstreaming guidelines proliferated (Alsop Bertelsen and Holland 2006; Narayan 2005). Specific measurements for relevance, effectiveness, efficiency, impact and sustainability were drawn up for project managers and development agencies (de Waal 2008; Malhotra, Schuler and Boender 2002). An impressive array of analytical tools, such as checklists, Gender Impact Assessments, awareness raising, training manuals, hearings, expert meetings, databases and measurements of participation in decision making reinforced arguments that empowerment could be both achieved and measured. Gender mainstreaming moved 'beyond politics', beyond resistance and became 'something that just needs to be done' (Verloo 2005, 351–52; Verloo 2001). 'The political project of gender and development had been reduced to a technical fix', guaranteed to work when applied with rigour and care (Cornwall, Harrison and Whitehead 2007, 7–8).

The MDGs adopted the same tone and strategies, particularly the technical language so characteristic of development discourse. The MDGs set out eight targets for action, including number three, dedicated to promoting gender equality and empowering women. More specifically, the third goal called for the elimination of gender disparities in primary and secondary education, on the assumption that this would improve women's literacy, employment opportunities and involvement in national parliaments. Despite slow progress, the language has remained optimistic (UN 2007; Kabeer 2003). A recent UNFPA document describes the MDGs as 'an unprecedented opportunity to realize the promise of equality and freedom from want and gender mainstreaming is seen as central to the process' (UNFPA 2005).

These lofty goals with their optimistic projections have continued to dominate development discourse and praxis. This optimism is no doubt reinforced by a neoliberal discourse that assumes women are relatively free agents, able to speak out and confront gender bias; that education and argument can effect change; that most societies believe in and support law and order; and that widespread support exists for gender equality and women's empowerment. The possibility that profound and intractable resistances to gender mainstreaming might derail these plans has received little attention from the development community. The problem has been seen as finding the right technical fix, the right formula for success, not interrogating complex and often deeply held resistances to gender transformation.

The gap between policies and praxis: Challenges of implementation

Some success stories can be found, and many proponents of gender mainstreaming and the MDGs continue to insist that 'rapid and large–scale progress is feasible', especially when strong government leadership and appropriate policies are combined with adequate financial and technical support from the international community (UN 2007). Gender has been mainstreamed into law reform in Botswana, almost half of the Rwanda parliament is female, women have joined men in the Burundi peace process and many national machineries for women have gained skills and voice. As Rao and Kelleher point out, 'these examples are not the norm' (2005, 57). Fundamental change remains uneven and largely elusive; successes are few and failures depressingly common (United Nations Research Institute for Social Development (UNRISD) 2005). Evaluations of gender mainstreaming for some mainstream development agencies and NGOs report patchy and often ineffective efforts to address gender mainstreaming (Moser and Moser 2005, 15). Moreover, the third MDG promise that education for women would bring quality employment and political participation has proven illusory (United Nations Economic Commission of Latin America and the Caribbean 2005, 3).

Gendered assumptions and practices continue to impede women's economic and political progress. In the Caribbean, for example, women outperform and outnumber male students in secondary and university education, yet they continue to have a higher unemployment rate and fewer well paying jobs than their male counterparts (Johnson 2005, 61). While involvement in waged labour has increased, women continue to cluster in the less skilled, poorly paid and most insecure jobs. Many have to migrate to find employment, usually poorly paid and sometimes illegal and dangerous. Increasing global competition and economic turbulence is undermining corporate commitment to gender balance (Rao and Kelleher 2005). Moreover, while political participation is increasing, the rise is painfully slow – only 0.5 per cent a year (UNRISD 2005, 147–49). High levels of participation in politics have often failed to improve women's lives. The impressive number of women parliamentarians in South Africa has not stopped South Africa from having one of the worst rape and gender based violence records in the world (Rao and Kelleher 2005, 58).

It is in regard to gender based violence, largely but not entirely perpetrated against women, that the possibilities for gender equality and women's empowerment seem most depressingly slow and even retrograde. In South Asia, 'one in every two women faces violence in her daily life, and social customs and attitudes that support violence against women are entrenched and institutionalized at all levels – home, family, community, society, and the state' (Mehta and Gopalakrishnan 2007, 41). Women around the world are more often killed or hurt by people they know. The WHO reported that almost half the women raped in Alexandria, Egypt, were soon killed by a relative determined to protect family/male honour. In Australia, Canada, Israel, South Africa and the United States, over half of women murder victims were killed by their partners, frequently in the context of an ongoing abusive relationship (WHO 2002, 93). Gender based violence is further fuelled by global economic restructuring, with the rise of female earners and the loss of many 'masculine' jobs leaving many men feeling displaced and devalued (Nurse 2004; Perrons 2005).

Gender based violence is particularly common in conflict and post–conflict societies. Attacks on civilians, including women, have escalated as civilian involvement in conflict has increased. The ratio of military to civilian casualties has moved from 8:1 (military to civilians) in 1900, to the opposite. Fighting is increasingly carried out by untrained forces, often young males with little concern for civilian lives, and an inclination towards rape and sexual savagery as a means to control frightened populations (Kaldor 2001, 8; Munkler 2005, 20). In these circumstances, rape, particularly group rape, provides an opportunity to humiliate enemy males by physically and symbolically 'marking' enemy women's bodies with semen, a site for performing loyal masculinity to comrades and a vehicle for educating or training reluctant soldiers in the practices of violence (Kaldor 2001, 44–53; Munkler 2005). These practices often continue in post–conflict societies. Liberia is experiencing an epidemic of violence, especially against young girls. Rape and domestic violence rates are escalating in South Africa, Rwanda, Peru and many other post–conflict societies, despite official support for gender equality and women's empowerment (Kelly 2000, 55; Pederson 2008).

War and conflict, within and between nations, intersect with poverty and gender discrimination with deadly effect, destroying health infrastructure and consequently increasing maternal and child mortality as well as spreading HIV/AIDS, particularly among women who are more physically vulnerable to the disease. War related violence along with widespread domestic violence has created an epidemic of abuse with gendered consequences. While some of this crisis can be attributed to poverty, violence against women cuts across class, religious and cultural contexts (WHO 2002). Clearly, widespread official commitment to gender mainstreaming and the MDGs has not disrupted long established gender hierarchies and masculinist practices. Gender equality and women's empowerment remain distant goals.

Looking for solutions in all the same places

The failures of gender mainstreaming (and the third MDG) have inspired some reflection on problems and possible solutions. Senior gender experts in the UNDP successfully lobbied for evaluations of gender mainstreaming within the organization and its programmes (Rosina Wiltshire, personal communication, 2008). The first report, published in 1998, highlighted a number of organizational constraints, most notably: the isolation of working level staff from management, a weak gender skill–base, weak accountability demands from headquarters, isolation from other focus areas, limited opportunities for sharing experience and organizational learning, a hierarchical organizational culture, and reluctance to recognize gender personnel as professional colleagues (Schalkwyk 1998, 4–5). Eight years later, another evaluation reiterated many of these concerns, describing UNDP gender mainstreaming policies as 'good starts and lost momentum, intermittent declarations and mixed signals' (UNDP 2006, vi). The report called for more proactive leadership by senior management; accountability and incentives for gender mainstreaming at all levels, monitored by senior management and the Executive Board; the revitalization of gender mainstreaming programming and the strengthening of its institutional framework at headquarters; developing capacity in gender analysis in country offices as well as among all UNDP staff; providing adequate financial resources; clarifying coordination with UNIFEM; and strengthening advocacy and partnerships (UNDP 2006, 45–51). Noeleen Heyzer, Director of UNIFEM, worried about many of the same issues, particularly the need to hold stakeholders, such as governments, UN agencies, the private sector, and civil society, accountable for implementing both gender mainstreaming and the MDGs (Heyzer 2005).

The UNDP evaluations raised both institutional and operational questions. At an institutional level, the emphasis on strengthening leadership of senior managers at both the international and country offices suggests some serious doubts about the degree of understanding, sympathy and commitment to gender mainstreaming of at least some of UNDP's top management. The reports also reveal concerns about the knowledge, communication skills and capacity of local UNDP gender experts, particularly the gender focal points. Both reports emphasize the need for greater accountability, driven from the top, including oversight by the Executive Board. While some new suggestions emerge, such as offering prizes for successful gender work and setting up a UNDP Corporate Gender Development Office at headquarters and country offices, for the most part the reports return to familiar development practices, calling for more commitment and oversight by administrators at all levels, more technical gender experts in practice areas/thematic foci, more financial support and more training/capacity building. To date solutions have been largely sought within established institutional structures and practices (UNDP 2006; Schalkwyk 1998).

The UNDP evaluations also return to established strategies for improving implementation of gender mainstreaming. They assume that strengthened and more committed management will enforce accountability and consequently ensure better performance of operational programming. Accountability surfaces repeatedly, presented as a magical solution to weak commitment and implementation. The Corporate Gender Development Office is expected to get the UNDP 'on the right track' by setting targets and monitoring policies and action plans (UNDP 2006, 47). Moser and Moser (2005) produce similar arguments, calling for consistent and systematic monitoring and evaluation of gender mainstreaming outcomes and impacts. World Bank gender experts argue or assume that the problem of gender mainstreaming implementation can be solved by using the 'right' gender empowerment framework (Alsop, Bertelsen and Holland 2006, 64–81). These frameworks and measurements have been used in the past, often with little success, but this has not undermined faith in their relevance. As Moser and Moser (2005, 18–19) argue, the solution is to try harder, to seek 'conceptual clarity, appropriate and consistent methodologies, and organisational support and institutional consistency.'

Deeper and more intractable resistances to gender equality and women's empowerment are rarely mentioned in development documents, and when they are, the answers generally focus on familiar 'solutions', largely considered the responsibility of women. The *UNFPA State of World Population 2005* acknowledges that men must join the struggle for gender equality as partners if real change is to be achieved. Its chapter on 'Partnering with Boys and Men' is a welcome balance to development discourse that generally ignores men as gendered beings. Drawing largely on literature from development meetings, the report acknowledges the many ways gendered assumptions and practices about masculinities tend to reinforce male authority over women. The report highlights the global rise in gender based violence and the complications raised by the masculine crises emerging from an increasingly unequal and violent world. Yet its recommendations return to the usual calls for empowering young people, transforming and engendering health systems and increasing resources (2005, 57–63, 85–92). The deeply held, subtle resistances to gender equality and women's empowerment (by many men and women) are largely ignored, as is the possibility that fresh insights and solutions might be gained from relevant feminist and masculinity studies scholarship.[4]

Scholars and activists concerned with gender and development propose many similar 'solutions'. They call for more specific, high level accountability, stronger leadership, more training and capacity building at all levels and greater

---

4   Ian Bannon and Maria Correia's collection, *The Other Half of Gender* (2006) is a welcome exception to this trend, along with Francis Cleaver's *Masculinities Matter* and the work of Andrea Cornwall (2000). However, all of these authors agree that men and masculinity has not been sufficiently integrated into development policy and practice. Moreover the development literature largely ignores the literature on masculinism (Connell 1995, 2005; Hooper 2001) as well as the feminist literature on masculinities, masculinism, gender, politics, war and violence (see Cockburn 2007; Enloe 1993; Halbertsam 1998; Parpart and Zalewski 2008; Wiegman 2001; Zalewski and Parpart 1998 and many others).

financial commitment to gender programmes (Moser and Moser 2005; Rao and Kelleher 2005; Tiessen 2007). Some concern with deeper resistances to gender transformation has been raised in the scholarly literature, particularly Rao and Kelleher's call for more attention to organizational culture, including male bias, which, whether conscious or unconscious, can affect organizational gender relations by fostering 'heroic individualism; the split between work and family; exclusionary power; and the "monoculture of instrumentality"' (2002, cited in Moser and Moser 2005, 16; see also Mukhopadhyay 2007, 138–39). Rao and Kelleher argue that deep structures of organizations, the collection of taken–for–granted values and ways of thinking and working often obscure entrenched beliefs and practices undermining gender transformation. These forces work through political access, accountability systems, cultural systems and cognitive structures (existing norms and understandings). Challenges to these structures are sought in familiar places: from women's activism, internal negotiations, leadership for cultural change, organizational process and programmatic interventions (Rao and Kelleher 2005, 64–66). Moser and Moser (2005, 17) agree, calling 'for work on transforming attitudes, and for training', including culturally sensitive gender training within institutions trying to carry out gender mainstreaming. Resistance to gender mainstreaming may be overcome by women organizing and pushing for change, by better laws, more accountability, gender sensitive training and more financial support (Moser and Moser 2005; Rao and Kelleher 2005). The possibility that the discourses, definitions and approaches to empowerment and gender equality, along with a failure to look beyond established development literature, may be contributing to the problems facing those trying to implement gender mainstreaming has largely been overlooked.

Rethinking and refocusing gender mainstreaming policy and praxis

New ways of thinking and acting are required to overcome the gap between gender mainstreaming policy and praxis. As discussed, development discourse on gender mainstreaming, women's empowerment and gender equality has focused on women's (and marginalized men's) ability to make choices, to speak out and to challenge established social, political and economic structures. This rather triumphalist discourse has presented empowerment and gender mainstreaming as a doable, technical problem that can be overcome with sufficient determination and commitment. Gender mainstreaming policies promise not only to empower women, but also to change the gender order of society. Potential resistances disappear in the optimism of this language (Cornwall 2008, 159). The possibility that gender equality and women's empowerment are often partial, that these have to take into account many obstacles, and that they can be expressed, but not always in the manner predicted by gender and empowerment discourse, has largely been ignored.

The triumphalist tone of the development literature on gender equality and empowerment is reinforced by a widely held neoliberal perspective which posits a world where rational arguments can win out and where gender inequality and women's empowerment can be ensured through constructive engagement with rational state actors, supportive institutions and law–abiding citizens (Harvey 2005). As Judith Squires points out, this world view has inspired two dominant approaches to gender mainstreaming: the strategy of inclusion, which aims to integrate women as equals into a world that excludes them; and the strategy of reversal/difference, which calls for greater acknowledgment and tolerance for difference based on non–hegemonic gender identities and cultures (usually female). Neither approach challenges the gendered nature of established power structures; rather they call for more inclusion and greater tolerance for those allowed into the inner circles of masculinist power without questioning the nature of that power and the transformative potential (or not) of such a move (Squires 2005; Verloo 2005, 345–46).

Efforts to destabilize gender hierarchies and empower women from within established structures have not lived up to their promises. Gender based violence is on the rise and neither laws nor institutions of governance have proven capable of bringing this violence under control. The new wars continue to fester and expand around the world, women and girls continue to suffer disproportionately and supposed 'solutions' like more education have failed to ensure success in economic and political arenas. These failures have inspired a third approach to gender mainstreaming, the strategy of displacement/transformation (Squires 2005). Drawing on postmodern thinking, this strategy 'aspires to move "beyond gender"'. It aims to destabilize the assumption that progress will be gained by simply including women and marginalized groups, instead problematizing 'not (only) the exclusion of women, or men as a norm, but the gendered world in itself' (Verloo 2005, 346). This approach challenges established assumptions about gender and power, acknowledging the struggles involved in such reordering, and the need to address powerful resistances to gender transformation (Verloo 2005, 352). The challenges to such a move are many, both at the level of understanding and praxis.

Transforming gender power relations requires a more profound understanding of how existing gender practices operate. As Diane Perrons points out, 'for gender mainstreaming to become genuinely transformative and retain feminist aspirations, an understanding of the processes leading to gender inequality is crucial' (2005, 405). While attention to women's voices, collaboration with gender sensitive organizations and building alliances with institutions, programmes and persons committed to gender equality and women's empowerment are important forces for change, transforming gender relations requires attention to how systemic blockages to gender equality and women's empowerment operate and maintain their grip on power. Failure to address this process, in all its variations, leaves proponents of gender equality and women's empowerment operating in the dark, with little appreciation of the often deeply held, but subtle and persistent resistances to their efforts (Verloo 2005). A deeper analysis of the masculinist operations of power reveals the limits of the 'body count' to gender transformation.

Simply allowing women (and marginalized men) into the inner circles of power does little to change the way the 'rules of the game' are played, the predominance of a 'common sense' equation between certain forms of masculinity and power. 'Outsiders' soon find themselves pressured to 'play by the rules' and given the flexibility of gendered practices, and the separation of sexed bodies from gendered practices, it is quite possible (and even probable) for women and marginalized men in positions of power to adopt hegemonic masculine traits (Hooper 2001; Hutchings 2008; Zalewski and Parpart 2008; Wiegman 2001). This is a common practice that continues to reinforce the common sense nature of masculinist power and feminine disempowerment around the world.

Attention to the workings of masculinist practices helps to explain why so many women support the status quo. These women have been dismissed as disempowered, ignorant of their own needs. Large numbers of women have chosen to side with male authority and it is necessary to understand why that choice is seen as more attractive and empowering than opposition to gender hierarchies. In Rwanda many Hutu women actually killed and/or actively supported the 1994 genocide (El–Bushra 2000, 74, 81). Women have also played a crucial role in legitimating war by applauding their troops and celebrating harm to enemy women (Enloe 1993). Some women have developed a warrior style femininity such as the Amazonian guard around Charles Taylor (one of the warlords in the Liberian struggles), who wore tight fitting camouflage uniforms with matching handbags, high heels and pistol holsters. They reeked of perfume and bristled with side–arms and assault rifles (Moran 1995, 84). How do we understand this kind of empowerment? Is El–Bushra right when she argues that women's involvement in nationalist wars should not be seen 'as an aberration but rather as a component of "agency", or ways in which individuals carve out an acceptable life for themselves within the constraints imposed by their various and possibly conflictual identities'? (2000, 81). Can we dismiss this behaviour in a world where gender based violence continues to flourish? An all or nothing approach to women's empowerment and gender equality does not help.

Moreover, the empowerment/disempowerment binary, with its emphasis on choice as agency, does not allow an understanding or evaluation, that could be partial, incomplete, tentative and sometimes barely voiced steps towards empowerment and gender transformation (Parpart 2009). In many situations, particularly within conflict and post–conflict zones, and societies with widespread criminal activities, gender violence and deeply masculinist practices, the choice to publicly challenge male power is often extremely dangerous and even foolhardy. A World Health Organization (WHO) study on violence and health concludes:

> …most abused women are not passive victims…Some women resist, others flee, while others attempt to keep the peace by giving in to their husbands' demands. What may seem to an outside observer to be a lack of positive response by the women may in fact be a calculated assessment of what is needed to survive in the marriage and to protect herself and her children (2002, 95).

Many individuals and communities have quietly, even secretly, sought to protect victims of violence (El–Bushra 2000, 69–70). Others have risked their lives, such as a woman running a soup kitchen in Somalia in the early 1990s who was driven into exile (UNRISD 2005, 225). How do we evaluate these small steps, these acts of courage in a dangerous world? I think they need to be seen as empowering, and as crucial building blocks for future change, not as failures to choose, to speak and to transform the world for gender.

Nor can a binary model of empowerment/disempowerment explain silence and secrecy as a survival strategy in the face of overt violence. How do we understand refusal to admit to rape? We understand it by acknowledging the real fear of honour killing and the courage required to choose silence. We need to stop thinking that voice/choice is an easy option; in situations of terror and rape, silence can be a considered and intelligent option. In Zimbabwe, Everjoice Win concludes: 'As any woman in a violent situation will tell you, there are no prizes for speaking out. If anything, you are ostracized by your own family and community. You are branded a bad woman, or worse, you are violated all over again for daring to open your mouth' (2004, 76). Often, 'there is only personal survival under abnormality, especially when there is a subverted state without an intervening free civil society' (Chan 2005, 372). The costs of speaking out have to be acknowledged, and alternative options considered as potentially empowering, with potential to unsettle and possibly undermine gendered hierarchies.

Resistance to masculinist power can also take the form of silent acts and everyday performances. Just as wearing a veil has been a symbolic performance of opposition to colonial rule or to the right–wing anti–Muslim politics emerging in many parts of the world (Butler 2004; Sullivan 1998, 228), so too are acts of resistance to patriarchal oppression around the world. In Afghanistan, for example, wearing western clothes and platform shoes, makeup and jewellery, painting toenails and other prohibited practices are small, silent protests/performances in an oppressive situation (Armstrong 2002, 3, 112; Hans 2004, 244). In French immigrant housing projects many young Muslim women have challenged the authority of their fathers and elders by wearing revealing clothing, dressing in Western fashions and using makeup, sometimes outrageously. They want individual freedom and the right to equality and respect with young men. 'Makeup has become war paint, a sign of resistance. It is their way of fighting' (Amara 2006, 75).

Given the resilience of masculinist power, in all its many variations, and the discouragingly tentative steps taken to improve gender equality and strengthen women's empowerment, it is easy to understand why some gender specialists have called for abandoning the language of transformation. Hilary Standing, for example, contends that sectoral bureaucracies, which have often been posited as sites for gender transformation by the gender mainstreaming literature, are actually dedicated to maintaining and reinforcing the status quo. Certainly most of the few success stories in gender mainstreaming praxis have focussed on capacity building within established structures, particularly the gender machineries in many nations of the Global South. Standing sees sectoral bureaucracies as appropriate sites for a gender mainstreaming dedicated to increasing inclusivity and difference within established structures, arguing that 'the appropriate space and place for driving transformation is in the political arena' – 'the apparatus of gender mainstreaming can at most make a modest contribution to political transformation' (2007, 105, 110). She would like to see gender mainstreaming rescued from its impossible mission with the hope that instead, real progress can be made in the lives of women and men (Standing 2007, 110; Subrahmanian 2007).

This argument is persuasive on some levels. It is true that 'despite decades of struggle, large parts of "the mainstream" in all our societies, including their androcentrism and male bias, remain stubbornly intact' (Woodford–Berger 2007, 131). It is also true that the technical bias of gender mainstreaming has created an obsession with matrixes, frameworks and measurements for processes that are inherently extremely difficult to measure (Woodford–Berger 2007, 131). Yet the argument that gender transformation should be left to politics ignores the daily struggles around gender, the everyday contestations over gendered assumptions and practices that are taking place in every corner of the world. Struggles to redefine and reshape gendered practices also bleed into institutions and structures, yet they are often difficult to understand or control. To argue that gender transformation should be left to political processes ignores their internal, fragile, complex and multileveled nature. As Judith Butler points out, transforming gender requires staying on the edge of what we know, questioning our own certainties and through that, creating openness to risk that allows 'another way of knowing and of living in the world' …that expands 'our capacity to imagine the human' (2004, 228). This is no small task, and it is understandable that people committed to measurable change regard such statements with suspicion. Yet gendered struggles are taking place all around us, and are critical for understanding the trajectory of much of the global gender based violence.

Developmental praxis that pays attention to feminist and masculinity studies' writings on masculinist power provides an entry point for understanding both the way power is gendered and the limits and possibilities for gender transformation. Moving beyond established development literature to incorporate insights from the burgeoning masculinities and feminist literature dealing with masculinities, sexualities, gender and power (see Connell 2005; Cornwall 2000; Cornwall, Harrison and Whitehead 2007; Cornwall, Correa and Jolly 2008; Parpart and Zalewski 2008) holds open the possibility that gender transformation can be understood and encouraged. This literature both helps to explain the resilience of masculinist power and the need to understand the many ways that resistance to that power can emerge, often through subtle strategies and small triumphs that deserve support and respect. It is this literature that reminds us that spaces need to be found where non hegemonic actors can struggle to transform/perform gendered practices so that they begin to reframe the 'normal'. It is this literature that reminds us that there are many actors, of all sexual orientations, who are dedicated to gender equality and empowerment for all. We need to encourage these actors, to remain open to risking untested waters, and above all, to adopt a gradual, process–oriented approach while never losing sight of the ultimate goal (Verloo 2005, 347, 350; Kesby 2005).

Conclusion

Gender transformation has become another development buzzword, bandied about as if it were easily achieved with the right mix of gendered policies, plans, measurements and accountability. This language has been particularly commonplace since the adoption of the discourse of empowerment and gender equality, with its reliance on transformational imagery and symbols. As discussed, mainstream development agencies have promised to transform the gender order throughout society, including organizations, programmes and projects. This ambitious, even triumphalist language has been presented as a reasonable, reachable goal that simply required the right mix of technical solutions or drivers, the will to put them to work and the necessary accountability to ensure implementation. The possibility that deeply held resistances might subtly (and not so subtly) undermine attempts to alter gendered power relations and hierarchies has rarely been raised as a serious reason for abandoning such grand and ambitious goals.

Yet masculinist power has long proven difficult to destabilize, let alone dislodge. Feminist struggles over the centuries have demonstrated the difficulty of disturbing the commonsense link between hegemonic masculinity and power in both the public and private realms. Efforts to incorporate symbolic 'others' – such as women and marginalized men – into the inner circles of power have done little to loosen the grip of cognitive shortcuts equating certain styles of masculinity with power – in all its variations (Hutchings 2008). The introduction of women and some non–traditional men into circles of power have also done little to detach femininity from disempowerment. Emasculation continues to be a synonym for loss of power. The struggle to maintain masculine privilege is clearly ongoing, particularly in the boardrooms and bureaucracies, but also on the battlefields, in the streets and in the bedrooms. The current epidemic of gender based violence around the world is a sorrowful testimony to this truth. The child soldiers using their guns to threaten and humiliate civilians, the frightening rise in rapes in war and in post–conflict societies, the defence of honour killings and widespread domestic violence all testify to the intensity of the current gender wars – worsened no doubt by global economic restructuring and a winner take all mentality in an increasingly unequal, crisis ridden world (WHO 2002; UNRISD 2005; Munkler 2005).

In such a world, Standing's (2007) warning about the transformative limits of gender mainstreaming policies within sectoral bureaucracies and most institutions has some appeal. Given the impediments to gender transformation, it can be seen why many would be ready to jettison the language of transformation. It could be argued that the less ambitious, but more doable goals of inclusivity and diversity may be all the gender transformation that can be reasonably expected. Certainly given the long history of opposition to more ambitious gendered reordering, there is nothing wrong with focusing on strengthening these more limited approaches to gender mainstreaming. Even they will encounter plenty of resistance, which will need to be dealt with. Even modest goals will require a clear understanding of the resilience of masculinist power, its many allies and its disciplinary power over those who might disturb the status quo. Modest goals will still require a more flexible understanding of empowerment and gender equality, wherein small, tentative steps can be acknowledged as critical building blocks for change. Given the historical resistance to gendered equality, progress will be slow, but at least gender mainstreaming will not be promising the impossible.

This is an attractive solution for many who have found comfortable (or at least paying) positions within the development enterprise and its cognate institutions. Yet the incorporation of a few women and marginalized men into established power structures seems a hollow victory when so many continue to suffer the brunt of masculinist power. Moreover while the current epidemic of gender based violence could be seen as evidence of hardening gender hierarchies, it also suggests intensifying struggles over gendered meanings and relations. Challenges to masculinist privilege, and their many allies, as well as to established gendered practices/'traditions' are being launched in many places and contexts. They are often tentative, sometimes unspoken, embodied subversive practices. Some challenge directly, others work through established channels, aiming at slow subversion from within. Men and boys are involved, seeking new ways to think about and perform gender in a changing world. Allies have to be sought in unexpected places. Safe places/spaces have to be created where new ways of being gendered can be performed and practiced. Possibilities will vary with contexts, but the goal has to remain the same – to understand and overcome resistance to gender transformation, to seek ways to foster a world where masculinity can be more vulnerable and femininity more assertive and authoritative, where fixed practices dividing notions of the masculine and feminine will decline and openness to new ways of thinking and ordering the world will become possible both to think and do. This seems an impossible goal. Indeed if it is just empty rhetoric, it is worth abandoning. However, if gender mainstreaming can become a venue for opening up new ways of thinking and performing gender, particularly in this time of global economic crisis and reactionary politics, then the promise of a new gender order just may become a possibility worth dreaming and fighting for.

References

Alsop, R., Bertelsen, M.F. and Holland, J. (2006), *Empowerment in Practice: From Analysis to Implementation* (Washington, D.C.: World Bank).

Amara, F. (2006), *Breaking the Silence: French Women's Voices from the Ghetto* (Berkeley: University of California Press).

Armstrong, S. (2002), *The Hidden Power of the Women of Afghanistan* (New York: Four Walls, Eight Windows).

Bannon, I. and Correia, M.C. (eds) (2006), *The Other Half of Gender: Men's Issues in Development* (Washington, D.C.: World Bank).

Batliwala, S. (2007), 'Taking the Power Out of Empowerment – An Experiential Account', *Development in Practice* 17:4–5, 557–565.

Butler, J. (2004), *Undoing Gender* (London: Routledge).

Canadian International Development Agency (CIDA) (1999), *CIDA's Policy on Gender Equality* (Ottawa: CIDA).

Chan, S. (2005), 'The Memory of Violence', *Third World Quarterly* 26:2, 369–382.

Cleaver, F. (ed.) (2003), *Masculinities Matter! Men, Gender and Development* (London: Zed Books).

Cockburn, C. (2007), *From Where We Stand: War, Women's Activism and Feminist Analysis* (London: Zed Books).

Connell, R.W. (1995), *Masculinities* (Berkeley, CA.: University of California Press).

—— (2005), 'Change Among the Gatekeepers: Men, Masculinities, and Gender Equality in the Global Arena', *Signs* 30:3, 1801–1825.

Cornwall, A. (2000), 'Missing Men? Reflections on Men, Masculinities and Gender in GAD', *IDS Bulletin* 31:2, 18–27.

—— (2008), 'Myths to Live By? Solidarity and Female Autonomy Reconsidered', in A. Cornwall, E. Harrison and A. Whitehead (eds), *Gender Myths and Feminist Fables* (Oxford: Blackwell), 145–163.

Cornwall, A., Correa, S. and Jolly, S. (eds) (2008), *Development with a Body: Sexuality, Human Rights and Development* (London: Zed Books).

Cornwall, A., Harrison, E. and Whitehead, A. (2007), 'Gender Myths and Feminist Fables: The Struggle for Interpretive Power in Gender and Development', *Development and Change* 38:1, 1–20.

de Waal, M. (2008), 'Evaluating Gender Mainstreaming in Development Projects', *Development in Practice* 16:2, 209–214.

El–Bushra, J. (2000), 'Transforming Conflict: Some Thoughts on a Gendered Understanding of Conflict Processes', in S. Jacobs and R. Jacobson (eds), *States of Conflict: Gender, Violence and Resistance* (London: Zed Books), 66–86.

Enloe, C. (1993), *The Morning After: Sexual Politics at the End of the Cold War* (Los Angeles: University of California Press).

Freire, P. (1970), *Pedagogy of the Oppressed*, trans. by M.B. Ramos (NYC: Continuum).

Goetz, A.M. (1994), 'From Feminist Knowledge to Data for Development: The Bureaucratic Management of Information on Women and Development', *IDS Bulletin* 25:2, 27–36.

Halbertsam, J. (1998), *Female Masculinity* (Durham: Duke University Press).

Hales, J. (2007), 'Rhetoric and Reality: World Bank and CIDA Gender Policies', *Convergence* 40:1, 147–169.

Hans, A. (2004), 'Escaping Conflict: Afghan Women in Transit', in Giles, W and Hyndman, J. (eds), *Sites of Violence* (Berkeley, CA.: University of California Press), 232–48.

Harvey, D. (2005), *A Brief History of Neoliberalism* (Oxford: Oxford University Press).

Heyzer, N. (2005), 'Making the Links: Women's Rights and Empowerment are Key to Achieving the Millennium Development Goals,' *Gender and Development* 13:1, 9–12.

Hooper, C. (2001), *Manly States: Masculinities, International Relations and Gender Politics* (New York: University of Columbia Press).

Hutchings, K. (2008), 'Cognitive Short Cuts', in J. Parpart and M. Zalewski (eds) *Rethinking the Man Question: Sex, Gender and Violence in International Relations* (London: Zed Books), 23–46.

Johnson, R. (2005), 'Not a Sufficient Condition: The Limited Relevance of the Gender MDG to Women's Progress', *Gender and Development* 13:1, 56–66.

Kabeer, N. (1994), *Reversed Realities: Gender Hierarchies in Development Thought* (London: Verso).

—— (1999), 'Resources, Agency, and Achievements: Reflections on the Measurements of Women's Empowerment', *Development and Change* 30:3, 435–64.

—— (2003), *Gender Mainstreaming in Poverty Eradication and the Millennium Development Goals* (London: Commonwealth Secretariat).

—— (2005), 'Gender Equality and Women's Empowerment: A Critical Analysis of the Third Millennium Development Goal', *Gender and Development* 13:1, 13–24.

Kaldor, M. (2001), *New and Old Wars: Organized Violence in a Global Era* (Stanford: Stanford University Press).

Kelly, L. (2000), 'Wars Against the Women: Sexual Violence, Sexual Politics and the Militarised State', in S. Jacobs and R. Jacobson (eds), *States of Conflict: Gender, Violence and Resistance* (London: Zed Press), 45–65.

Kerr, J. and Tsikata, D. (eds) (2000), *Demanding Dignity: Women Confronting Economic Reforms in Africa* (Ottawa: North–South Institute).

Kesby, M. (2005) 'Retheorizing Empowerment–Through–Participation as a Performance in Space: Beyond Tyranny', *Signs: Journal of Women in Culture and Society* 30:4, 2037–2065.

Malhotra, A., Schuler, S.R. and Boender, C. (2002), 'Measuring Women's Empowerment as a Variable in International Development', Working Paper (Washington, D.C.: World Bank).

Mehta, M. and Gopalakrishnan, C. (2007), '"We Can": Transforming Power in Relationships in South Asia', *Gender and Development* 15:1, 41–49.

Moran, M. (1995), 'Warriors or Soldiers? Masculinity and Ritual Transvestism in the Liberian Civil War', in Sutton, C.R. (ed.), *Feminism, Nationalism and Militarism* (New York: American Anthropological Association), 73–88.

Moser, C. (1993), *Gender Planning and Development: Theory, Practice and Training* (London: Routledge).

Moser, C. and Moser, A. (2005), 'Gender Mainstreaming Since Beijing: A Review of Success and Limitations in International Institutions', *Gender and Development* 13:2, 11–22.

Mukhopadhyay, M. (2007), 'Mainstreaming Gender or "Streaming" Gender Away: Feminists Marooned in the Development Business', in Cornwall, A., Harrison, E. and Whitehead, A. (eds), *Feminisms in Development* (London: Zed Books), 135–49.

Munkler, H. (2005), *The New Wars* (Cambridge: Polity Press).

Narayan, D. (2005), *Measuring Empowerment: Cross–Disciplinary Perspectives* (Washington: World Bank).

Nurse, K. (2004), 'Masculinities in Transition: Gender and the Global Problematique', in R. Reddock (ed.), *Interrogating Caribbean Masculinities* (Kingston: UWI Press), 3–37.

Parpart, J. (2009), 'Choosing Silence: Rethinking Voice, Agency and Women's Empowerment, in R. Ryan–Flood and R. Gill (eds), *Secrecy and Silence in the Research Process: Feminist Reflections* (London: Routledge).

Parpart, J., Rai, S. and Staudt, K. (eds) (2002), *Rethinking Empowerment: Gender and Development in a Global/Local World* (London: Routledge).

Parpart, J. and Zalewski, M. (eds) (2008), *Rethinking the Man Question: Sex, Gender and Violence in International Relations* (London: Zed Books).

Pedersen, J. (2008), 'In the Rain and in the Sun: Women in Peace–building in Liberia', mimeo.

Perrons, D. (2005), 'Gender Mainstreaming and Gender Equality in the New (Market) Economy: An Analysis of Contradictions', *Social Politics* 12:3, 389–411.

Rao, A. and Kellcher, D. (2002), 'Unravelling Institutionalised Gender Inequality', Occasional Paper Number 8 (Washington, D.C.: Association of Women in Development).

—— (2005), 'Is there Life after Gender Mainstreaming?', *Gender and Development* 13: 2, 57–69.

Rowlands, J. (1997), *Questioning Empowerment* (Oxford: Oxfam Publications).

Schalkwyk, J. (1998), *Building Capacity for Gender Mainstreaming: UNDP's Experience* (New York: UNDP).

Squires, J. (2005), 'Is Mainstreaming Transformative? Theorizing Mainstreaming in the Context of Diversity and Deliberation', *Social Politics* 12:3, 366–88.

Standing, H. (2007), 'Gender, Myth and Fable: The Perils of Mainstreaming in Sector Bureaucracies', in A. Cornwall, E. Harrison and A. Whitehead (eds), *Feminisms in Development: Contradictions, Contestations and Challenges* (London: Zed Books), 101–11.

Subrahmanian, R. (2007), 'Making Sense of Gender in Shifting Institutional Contexts', in A. Cornwall, E. Harrison and A. Whitehead (eds), *Feminisms in Development: Contradictions, Contestations and Challenges* (London: Zed Books), 112–121.

Sullivan, Z.T. (1998), 'Eluding the Feminist, Overthrowing the Modern', in L. Abu–Lughod (ed.), *Remaking Women* (Princeton: Princeton University Press), 215–242.

Tiessen, R. (2007), *Everywhere/Nowhere* (Hartford: Kumarian Press).

United Nations (UN) (2007), *The Millennium Development Goals Report*, Inter–Agency and Expert Group on MDG Indicators (New York, United Nations).

United Nations Development Programme (UNDP) (2000), *Learning and Information Pack. Strategy Development*, Gender in Development Programme (updated 19 April 2006) <www.undp.org/women/docs/GM_INFOPACK/Mainstreaming1.doc>.

—— (2002), *Gender Equality: Practice Note*, November (New York: UNDP).

—— (2003), *Transforming the Mainstream: Gender in UNDP* (New York: UNDP).

—— (2006), *Evaluation of Gender Mainstreaming in the UNDP* (New York: UNDP).

—— 'Women's Empowerment', <http:www.undp.org/women/> accessed 18 March 2009.

United Nations Economic Commission of Latin America and the Caribbean (ECLAC) (2005), 'Gender and the Millennium Development Goals', special issue of *Gender Dialogue* (Port of Spain, Trinidad and Tobago: ECLAC), December.

United Nations Economic and Social Council (ECOSOC) (1997), 'Mainstreaming the Gender Perspective into all Policies and Programmes in the United Nations System' (New York: United Nations).

United Nations Population Fund (UNFPA) (2005), *UNFPA State of World Population 2005: The Promise of Equality* (New York: UNFPA).

United Nations Research Institute for Social Development (UNRISD) (2005), *Gender Equality: Striving for Justice in an Unequal World* (Geneva: UNRISD).

Verloo, M. (2001), 'Another Velvet Revolution? Gender Mainstreaming and the Politics of Implementation', IWM Working Paper No. 5/2001(Vienna: IWM).

—— (2005), 'Displacement and Empowerment: Reflections on the Concept and Practice of the Council of Europe Approach to Gender Mainstreaming and Gender Equality', *Social Politics* 12:3, 344–65.

Wallace, T. (1998), 'Institutionalising Gender in UK NGOs', *Development in Practice* 8:2: 159–171.

Wiegman, R. (2001), 'Object Lessons: Men, Masculinity, and the Sign Women', *Signs* 26:2, 355–388.

Win, E. (2004), 'Open Letter to Nkosazana Dlamini–Zuma and Other Women in the South African Cabinet', *Feminist Africa* 3 (October/November), 74–76.

Woodford–Berger, P. (2007), 'Gender Mainstreaming: What is It (About) and Should We Continue Doing It?', in A. Cornwall, E. Harrison and A. Whitehead (eds), *Feminisms in Development: Contradictions, Contestations and Challenges* (London, Zed Books), 122–134.

World Bank (2001), *Engendering Development Through Gender Equality in Rights, Resources and Voice. A World Bank Policy Research Report* (Washington, D.C.: World Bank).

World Health Organization (WHO) (2002), *World Report on Violence and Health* (Geneva, WHO).

Zalewski, M. and Parpart. J. (eds) (1998), *The 'Man' Question in International Relations* (Boulder, CO.: Westview).

—— (2008), 'Introduction: Rethinking the Man Question', in J. Parpart and M. Zalewski (eds), *Rethinking the Man Question: Sex, Gender and Violence in International Relations* (London: Zed Books), 1–20.

Chapter 4

The Macroeconomics of Human Insecurity: Why Gender Matters

A. Haroon Akram–Lodhi

Human security and the Millennium Development Goals

The global food and economic crisis of 2008 has strongly reinforced the evidence that across the developing world there is a marked lack of human security.[1] Prior to the food crisis it was estimated that at least 854 million people suffered from the insecurity of chronic hunger and malnourishment (Weis 2008). In 2008, according to the World Bank, the food crisis pushed a further 100 million people into poverty and eradicated seven years of poverty reduction across the developing world (Akram–Lodhi and Kay 2009). Moreover, for tens – and possibly hundreds – of millions more people, the global food crisis undermined their livelihoods and made life dramatically more insecure. This dramatic deterioration in the immediate circumstances facing the world's insecure was then compounded by the global economic crisis: collapsing exports meant collapsing incomes for those working in export–oriented activities and rendered unemployed; remittances, which play a key role in sustaining livelihoods, were cut as employment dropped; and bilateral aid flows were reduced as governments in the developed world focused upon using their revenues for domestically–targeted fiscal stimuli. For the world's insecure, the situation has become even more dire than was previously the case.

The principal means by which global human insecurity is to be addressed in the contemporary world is the Millennium Development Goals (MDGs). These are a consequence of the Millennium Declaration, signed by 189 countries at the September 2000 Millennium Summit of the United Nations (UN), which unequivocally stated that in an insecure world there were essential values and inalienable rights that were shared by humanity: the right to be freed from hunger

---

1　A preliminary version of this chapter was presented to the Annual Meetings of the Canadian Association for the Study of International Development in Vancouver in June 2008. In developing this chapter, the work of Diane Elson, Nancy Folbre and Lucia C. Hanmer has been extremely influential. So too has been the opportunity, over a prolonged period, to work with Irene van Staveren. Thanks also to Jacqueline Leckie for giving me the opportunity to contribute to this volume and for her careful editorial oversight. The writing of this chapter has not been a gender–neutral task, and I thank Catherine, Cameron and Róisín for putting up with early morning absences. The usual disclaimers apply.

and fear; the right to equality, solidarity and tolerance; the right to expect that nature would be respected; and the right to expect that the international community had a shared responsibility for development. The Millennium Declaration has formalized a long standing shift in the understanding of what is meant by 'development' towards a so–called 'rights–based' approach to development designed to enhance 'human security': the social, political, economic, environmental and cultural conditions that guarantee an individual and collective right to physical safety, basic wellbeing, a sustainable livelihood and the opportunity to strengthen core capabilities.

As a rights–based approach to human insecurity there can be little doubt that the MDGs have transformed the practice of development in the early years of the twenty first century. Within the UN system analytical and technical reportage as well as development policies and programmes quickly and explicitly came to reflect the focal concerns of the MDGs. Simultaneously, bilateral donors began to structure their independent development cooperation flows around the consistency of such assistance with the MDGs. Finally and crucially, the International Monetary Fund and World Bank overtly incorporated the MDGs into the policy framework and monitoring arrangements used for the release of resources under the aegis of Poverty Reduction Strategy Papers (PRSPs). As a consequence, the aim of global, national, and subnational interventions designed to challenge human insecurity by enhancing social and economic development, at least in the official rhetoric employed by global political appointees, international and national civil servants, and the array of consultants currently employed in the 'business of development', is now about achieving the MDGs.

The purpose of this chapter is to use feminist development economics to critically evaluate the capacity of the MDGs to confront human insecurity.[2] It builds the discussion around the macroeconomics that underpins MDG–consistent policy and programme interventions, to argue that this analytical framework is, from a gender perspective, fundamentally compromised because of its failure to take account of the allocation of time. This renders the macroeconomics of the MDGs as being at best incomplete and at worst incoherent. As a result, it comes as no surprise that it is probable that the MDGs will not be achieved; the analytical framework that is used to drive the policies and programmes designed to achieve the MDGs and enhance human security offer only a partial transcript of existing social and economic processes.

The chapter is structured as follows. Following this introduction, the next section introduces the MDGs and critically highlights, in particular, how they are often thought to represent a new mode of thinking about development policy and practice. Section three discusses the macroeconomic foundations upon which the MDGs are constructed. Section four provides a gender based critique of those

---

2   To my knowledge, the phrase 'feminist development economics' was first used by myself and Irene van Staveren at the Institute of Social Studies in The Hague, the Netherlands in 2002. It remains an uncommon phrase, even within feminist economics.

Table 4.1   The Millennium Development Goals and Targets

Goal	Target
1. Eradicate extreme poverty and hunger	1. Halve, between 1990 and 2015, the proportion of people whose income is less than one dollar a day
	2. Halve, between 1990 and 2015, the proportion of people who suffer from hunger
2. Achieve universal primary education	3. Ensure that, by 2015, children everywhere, boys and girls alike, will be able to complete a full course of primary schooling
3. Promote gender equality and empower women	4. Eliminate gender disparity in primary and secondary education, preferably by 2005, and in all levels of education no later than 2015
4. Reduce child mortality	5. Reduce by two thirds, between 1990 and 2015, the under–five mortality rate
5. Improve maternal health	6. Reduce by three quarters, between 1990 and 2015, the maternal mortality ratio
6. Combat HIV/AIDS, malaria and other diseases	7. Have halted by 2015 and begun to reverse the spread of HIV/AIDS
	8. Have halted by 2015 and begun to reverse the incidence of malaria and other major diseases
7. Ensure environmental sustainability	9. Integrate the principle of sustainable development into country polices and programmes and reverse the loss of environmental resources
	10. Halve, by 2015, the proportion of people without sustainable access to safe drinking water and basic sanitation
	11. By 2020, to have achieved significant improvement in the lives of at least 100 million slum dwellers
8. Develop a global partnership for development	12. Develop further an open, rule–based, predictable, non–discriminatory trading and financial system
	13. Address the special needs of the least developed countries
	14. Address the special needs of landlocked developing countries and small island developing states
	15. Deal comprehensively with the debt problems of developing countries through national and international measures in order to make debt sustainable in the long term
	16. In cooperation with developing countries, develop and implement strategies for decent and productive work for youth
	17. In cooperation with pharmaceutical companies, provide access to affordable essential drugs in developing countries
	18. In cooperation with the private sector, make available the benefits of new technologies, especially information and communications

Source: United Nations 2009.

foundations. Section five discusses aspects of the macroeconomics of gender and care that must be captured within the macroeconomic foundations of the MDGs if they are to offer a fuller account of the processes upon which human security is or is not enhanced.

The MDGs: What's new for development and human security?

What's new about the MDGs?

The MDGs, as the framework by which enhanced human security might be achieved, are listed in Table 4.1, in terms of the 8 specific goals of the MDGs and the 18 targets associated with attaining those goals. In addition, 48 specific indicators were identified so as to be able to monitor and evaluate progress towards meeting both the goals and the targets within the stipulated time frame, if one is attached, of each target.

The use of a set of clearly stated intentions as a means of galvanizing political will and public support are as old as the 'development industry', largely because they act as a simple, easily understood, heuristic device. Although in this regard the MDGs tread a familiar path they are different in seven ways. This emerges from Table 4.1 and distinguishes the MDGs from previous sets of stated intentions.

The first difference is that the MDGs clearly offer a broader understanding of 'development' than economic growth, being rooted in a perspective that requires improving wider human capacities and capabilities. In this sense, the MDGs are focused upon enhancing human security rather than merely fostering economic development. The second difference, which follows, is the ambition of the MDGs, which set them apart from previous efforts to target development outcomes. As is clear from Table 4.1, the MDGs cover the range of human security and economic development indicators first identified by the United Nations Development Programme's *Human Development Reports* in the early 1990s as constituting a broader and more meaningful conception of 'development' than that associated with income–based measures. Moreover, the MDGs simultaneously provide targets for these indicators. Achieving the MDGs would, in a globally unprecedented way, begin the process by which it would be possible to enhance human security and 'make poverty history' in the broadest sense in the countries of Africa, Asia, Latin America and the tropical Pacific.

The third difference is that the targets are not merely descriptive statements of aspiration. They are specific, in a measurable and quantitative sense, in ten out of eighteen cases. Of significance is that the MDGs suggest that efforts to enhance human security can be measured rather than being merely described. The fourth difference is that each quantified target is placed within a particular and specific time horizon, which again raises the MDGs above being more than mere aspiration by placing an additional quantifiable emphasis on both the ambition and specificity of the targets contained within the MDGs. The fifth difference is that MDGs can provide a basis upon which to judge policies and programmes and hold governments, donors and international institutions accountable for their interventions. As a mechanism of accountability, the sixth difference of the MDGs is that they provide a basis upon which non state actors from within civil society can critically intervene in global policy making debates from a rights–based and human security standpoint.

One final difference distinguishes the MDGs from previous sets of publicly stated intentions: they are underpinned by an unprecedented degree of global political agreement, by the national political consensuses that sustain them, and the extent of civil mobilization that seeks to achieve them. This is despite the reality, that for some officials in global institutions and national governments, attachment to the MDGs is merely rhetorical. Nonetheless for many, whether within civil society, government or the international development institutions, the MDGs serve to align a broad and diverse set of concerns into a reasonably coherent and consistent vision of the ends of development in practice. In this sense, the MDGs are the most successful and important set of development goals that have yet been articulated.

The MDGs, structure and agency

In establishing a set of intended results that global institutions and national governments should seek to achieve, the MDGs fall squarely into the trend towards evidence based interventions and outcomes that has been articulated by the theorists of 'new public sector management' (Pollitt 2003). For these theorists, development is represented by the targets and indicators of the MDGs, the attainment of which will constitute, the 'end' of development. The processes by which these ends are attained do not represent a set of moral and ethical decisions regarding the meaning of global social justice. Indeed, theorists of the new public sector management explicitly eschew philosophical standpoints in favour of a 'third way', that are supposedly pragmatic choices in which (significantly but not stated) the ends determine and justify the means.

However by eschewing the moral and ethical decisions that must be made to sustain the possibility of development, theorists of the new public sector management do not question the set of social relations that serve to constrain the set of pragmatic choices that are ultimately capable of being made and which subsequently structure the development outcomes and degree of human security that are capable of being achieved. The 'technocratic instrumentalism' that underpins the new public sector management and the MDGs contains within it the germ of an explanation as to why achieving the MDGs was always going to be problematic.

The MDGs offer easy answers to complex, systemic questions rooted in an overriding global, national and local geopolitical context dominated by neoliberal globalization. The MDGs do not challenge the prevailing set of global capitalist social relations that foster insecure, unequal, market–embedded, neoliberal outcomes. The MDGs are technocratically instrumentalist in aspiration so are not predicated upon human insecurity as the outcome of a set of socially constructed poverty creating processes. This set of structural constraints is not recognized within the development paradigm of the MDGs. For all their florid rhetoric, the MDGs are not intellectually entrenched within a humane, democratic, alternative and socially embedded development paradigm that highlights the agency–led systemic changes necessary to achieve human security. Enhancing human security to the extent necessary to achieve the MDGs requires a degree of agency capable of challenging the structure within which the MDGs are located. This contradiction between agency and structure (Long and Long 1992) is at the heart of the conundrum that is the MDGs.

The macroeconomics of the MDGs

Orthodox approaches

The contradiction between agency and structure that is most vividly demonstrated by the technocratic instrumentalism of the MDGs is most easily witnessed in the macroeconomic analytical framework upon which the MDGs are predicated. Given the ambition of the MDGs, it might be expected that they were developed after careful consideration of the macroeconomic dynamics necessary for their fulfilment. This suggests that the MDGs were developed within an alternative macroeconomic paradigm but this was not evident. Indeed when seeking to investigate the macroeconomics of the MDGs there is remarkably little that emerges as an explicit macroeconomic analytical framework. Rather, when researching the macroeconomics of the MDGs what consistently emerges is another target: the resources that must be mobilized in order to generate the possibility of meeting the MDGs.[3] The macroeconomics of the MDGs is usually portrayed as a function of the financial cost of meeting the MDGs.[4] This requires a series of implicit and

---

3   Googling macroeconomics and MDGs results in 29,000 hits; the highest results are dominated by documents dealing with the costs of meeting the MDGs.

4   I do not discuss possible criticisms of the various estimates of the cost of meeting the MDGs, other than to note that some assumptions underlying estimates may not be robust and that the data provided for estimates may be of suboptimal quality – which suggests that MDG estimates may be methodologically dubious. Nonetheless, a number of alternative estimates of the cost of meeting the MDGs have been generated. The Zedillo Report, prepared for the Monterrey Conference, estimated in 2001 that achieving the MDGs would require an additional US$50 billion a year in aid by donors to 2015 (United Nations 2001). The World Bank's initial estimates in 2002 of the cost of achieving MDG 1 ranged between US$54 billion and US$62 billion a year in additional aid by donors to 2015 (Devarajan, Miller and Swanson 2002). The other seven MDGs added estimated costs of between US$35 and US$76 billion a year to donors to 2015, meaning that comprehensively achieving the MDGs would cost between US$89 and US$138 billion a year in additional

explicit assumptions concerning appropriate and inappropriate macroeconomic strategy to meet the MDGs but is not addressed.

There is a remarkably widely held assumption that there is agreement over the macroeconomic analytical framework of the MDGs. This assumed consensus has allowed the World Bank, as the globally preeminent development cooperation institution, to take the lead in crafting 'second–generation' PRSPs that are 'MDG–consistent'. MDG based PRSPs require development partners to establish MDG–consistent priorities on the basis of political consultation between state and civil society. Once priorities have been politically determined, the partners then identify the funding gap between available and necessary domestic and foreign resources so that the priority becomes achievable. Having established a set of domestic budgetary allocations and necessary foreign resources the PRSP is then designed based upon meeting a set of core macroeconomic policy objectives that are not directly referred to within the MDGs but which, according to the Bank, are a necessary policy precondition if the MDGs are to be met.

Not surprisingly, these core macroeconomic policy objectives replicate those prior to the MDGs: macroeconomic stability based upon budgetary balance, an 'enabling' environment for the private sector based upon internal deregulation and external trade liberalization, a 'realistic' exchange rate, and export led growth. In most instances, discussion of the macroeconomics of the MDGs, whether by international institutions or national governments, focuses upon the most cost efficient way of achieving these ends within the prevailing macroeconomic orthodoxy espoused by international financial institutions. The prevailing macroeconomic orthodoxy is not usually challenged despite a staggering over 25 years of failure in many developing countries and particularly in sub–Saharan Africa. This failure was starkly illustrated in 2008 when the world was hit with simultaneous food, fuel and financial crises.

Heterodox approaches

There is some institutional dissent to this orthodoxy within most notably, the UN's World Institute for Development Economic Research and the United Nations Development Programme's International Poverty Center (IPC). The IPC has produced a ream of research that challenges the macroeconomic orthodoxy of the World Bank and that of many client governments. Key issues that have been raised by the IPC include: the poverty elasticity of income under alternative income distribution scenarios, which suggest that income redistribution may be a necessary

---

donor–financed development cooperation to 2015. Finally, the UN's Millennium Project, led by Jeffrey Sachs, prepared a costing of the resources necessary to comprehensively attain all of the MDGs (United Nations Millennium Project 2005). The Project estimated that there was a need to gradually increase net flows of official development assistance from their 2002 levels from an extra US$70 billion in 2006 to US$130 billion in 2015 if the MDGs were to be met.

condition of facilitating the growth necessary to achieve the MDGs; assumptions concerning input–output flows, capital–output ratios and national savings rates, all of which have implications for the macroeconomic dynamics of growth that underpin the possibility of achieving the MDGs; and, perhaps most significantly, the extent to which countries are capable of absorbing the additional resources implied by MDG–predicated increases in official development assistance.

However, even the more heterodox analysis developed by the IPC, frames much of its discussion within quantitative variables, estimated costs, and resource flows. Less discussion is given to more fundamental questions regarding what constitutes the nuts and bolts of macroeconomic processes. Is the approach to macroeconomics appropriately reflective of the social and economic processes that currently sustain human insecurity?

The need to undertake a deeper, more fundamental 'root and branch' reassessment of the conceptualization of macroeconomics that underpins the MDGs has important implications for the attainability of the MDGs. In *The Millennium Development Goals Report 2008* the UN Secretary General unambiguously states that 'we are not on track to fulfil our commitments' (United Nations 2008, 3). I argue that going off track was preordained because of the analytical framework that is used to array discussion of the macroeconomics of the MDGs. More specifically, conventional macroeconomics, in both orthodox and heterodox forms, fails to adequately account for the role of gender in macroeconomic processes. Considering macroeconomics from a gender perspective both challenges the underlying macroeconomic analytical framework of the MDGs and suggests why achieving the MDGs is currently off track. It was always problematic that the MDGs would be achieved because they were constructed on the basis of a macroeconomic analytical framework that failed to take into account the gendered allocation of time in human households. This phenomenon has pivotal implications for human security and insecurity.

Gender relations and macroeconomics

What is macroeconomics?

A standard dictionary defines macroeconomics as 'a branch of economics that focuses on the general features and processes that make up a national economy and the ways in which different segments of the economy are connected' (Microsoft Ltd. 2001). Macroeconomics emphasizes aggregate output levels, price levels and employment, focusing on either short run fluctuations around a trend or the factors that contribute to the long term expansion of economic activity. Macroeconomic theory is concerned with understanding the relationship between a set of variables that determine national output and income, including consumption, investment, savings, government expenditure and trade, while macroeconomic policy seeks to alter the relationship between these variables so as to alter the overall level of economic activity. MDG–consistent macroeconomic policy, such as that proposed within MDG–consistent PRSPs, seeks to increase the rate of growth of aggregate output and income and lay the foundations by which the MDGs might be met.

Gender relations

For most macroeconomists the focus of attention on aggregate variables appears to preclude an analysis that integrates gender relations. Gender relations are a set of social norms, values, conventions and rules that informally or formally regulate practical daily relationships between men and women (Akram–Lodhi 1996). However, one aspect of gender relations transcends the complex gender based cultural differences that can be found across societies – the systemic and structural asymmetries of social power between men and women that benefit men. The universality of these systemic and structural asymmetries lies behind the placement of goal 3 within the MDGs. These systemic and structural asymmetries are constructed on the basis of dominant gender ideologies that emphasize those aspects of life that differ between men and women. The power of gender ideology lies in its capacity to conflate the biological with the social and render as 'natural' the allocation of tasks by gender.

The most notable material impact of gender ideologies is in the division of labour within the household, where women usually have a distinct role in performing the caring, maintenance and service activities that comprise 'household production'. At the most minimal, these activities often consist of the biologically necessary tasks of food preparation, child and familial care, sanitation and family reproduction.

It is difficult to precisely trace the impact of macroeconomic processes on gendered individuals. Households mediate the relationship between macroeconomic variables and outcomes and understanding the ways in which this mediation takes place is essential if the identification of the gendered individual effects of macroeconomics is to be made (Akram–Lodhi 2002). Moreover, in households three material elements affect the pattern of gendered social relations and the mediation between macroeconomic variables and outcomes: production, consumption, and reproduction. Three types of reproduction simultaneously occur: biological reproduction, labour force reproduction and social reproduction (Edholm, Harris and Young 1977). Social reproduction can be unpacked into its obligatory and relational components (Himmelweit 1995).

Gender, economics and macroeconomics

The focal role of the household in mediating economy wide trends with individual impacts has resulted in the analysis of the economic role of the household being dominated by a branch of neoclassical microeconomics termed the 'new household economics' (Becker 1981). In contrast, the macroeconomic analysis of the household and the gender relations that operate within it remains, despite a great deal of work (Çağatay, Elson and Grown 1995; Grown, Elson and Çağatay 2000), in its infancy. The analytical variables that are considered relevant to macroeconomics are, as aggregates, deemed by most macroeconomists to not be relevant in understanding the social identities that reflect and affect gender relations in households. As a consequence the tools of macroeconomic theory and policy are seen as being gender neutral. However, this perception of gender neutrality is incorrect, for two interrelated reasons.

The first reason is that the perception of gender neutrality largely reflects an orthodox neoclassical conceptualization of the domain of macroeconomic analysis that assumes that the distribution of aggregate output is given, and is analytically exogenous. This assumption is not shared by heterodox macroeconomists working with the IPC on the MDGs, and is also fundamentally challenged by feminist economists (Çağatay and Erturk 2004) because it is at best, misleading and at worst, wrong. This error is because the distribution of aggregate output is the outcome of a series of explicit and implicit social choices (Evers 2003). Gender relations are an extremely important determinant of the structure of these choices and of the distribution of aggregate output, particularly with regard to implicit choices.

This has three implications. The first is that factors effecting the distribution of aggregate output must be investigated. The second is that gender relations are likely to be a key factor in structuring the distribution of aggregate output. The third is that this has implications for those policies and programmes designed to alter economic outcomes that will advance the MDGs and enhance human security. Gender, as a power relationship, affects the division of labour in the performance of household maintenance and service activities and consequently the division of labour between paid work in the commodity producing economy and the caring labour engaged in household production. As a result, the labour market is segmented on the basis of gender.

This gender based distortion can be transmitted into other economic processes that can be segmented on the basis of gender. For example, constraints on female labour supply as a result of the gender division of labour have implications for the output gap between potential and actual production, which has implications for the ability to meet the MDGs. Therefore, factor market segmentation affects production, productivity and incomes, and the distribution of aggregate output, macroeconomic growth processes and the resulting capacity to attain the MDGs.

As a consequence, the distribution of time, income and wealth, all often gender differentiated within and between households, can affect consumption and investment choices, productivity, and the distribution of aggregate output, macroeconomic growth processes and consequently the capacity to meet the MDGs. Gender inequalities can generate 'hidden' structural inefficiencies that affect aggregate investment, aggregate production, distribution and economic growth, leading to the suboptimal outcomes that the MDGs seek to address (Hanmer, Pyatt and White 1999).

For example, it is well established that gender inequality in early childhood education for females reduces long term economic growth (King and Hill 1995). This is one reason why goal 2 has been placed within the MDGs. The response of a government to such gender based inefficiencies can affect its budgetary position, in that, in response to suboptimal growth, it must spend more relative to its tax revenues. Moreover, the efficiency and equity of public spending can be subject to gender based distortions. These two reasons are cited to justify the economic case for public intervention with notably market failure and redistribution; both the outcome of the structure of gender inequalities (Akram–Lodhi 2002). Thus, gender relations can act as a structural constraint on the economy as a whole (Folbre 1994).

The second reason that the perception of macroeconomic gender neutrality is incorrect is related to the first. The behaviour of economic agents reflects their social identity as gendered individuals (Çağatay and Erturk 2004; Akerlof and Kranton 2000). This microeconomic phenomenon has macroeconomic implications, suggesting that patterns of consumption (Dwyer and Bruce 1989), investment (Arndt and Tarp 2000; Warner and Campbell 2000) and savings (Seguino and Floro 2002) at an aggregate level may be gender differentiated. This has clear implications for the ability to meet the MDGs. Again it appears that gender relations can act as a structure of constraint on the economy. This suggests that macroeconomic variables should not necessarily be treated as homogenous. This perspective is inconsistent with orthodox neoclassical macroeconomics.

Following from these points, it is necessary to introduce three key propositions that differ from those in orthodox macroeconomics but which are essential to an engendered macroeconomic analysis (Grown, Elson and Çağatay 2000). These aim to integrate gender structures into the macroeconomic analysis that underpins the policies and programmes designed to meet the MDGs. First, economic institutions – international organizations, states, markets and households – bear and transmit gender bias. Second, the economy must be defined to include the unpaid caring labour that goes into household production and whose supply is generally inelastic with respect to non caring labour. Third, gender relations affect the division of labour, the distribution of productive inputs, the distribution of employment, income, output and wealth. In so doing, gender relations structurally affect aggregate production, savings, investment, net exports and macroeconomic processes. All three propositions have implications for the MDGs.

Engendering the macroeconomics of the MDGs: Implications for human security

Achieving the MDGs through increased gender inequality

The promotion of gender equality and empowering women's agency is both an important goal in its own right and critical to the achievement of the human security that underpins the MDGs. However, gender equality is neither a necessary or sufficient condition for the fulfilment of the MDGs; the fulfilment of the MDGs is consistent with increased gender inequality. For example, it is feasible to construct a scenario in which MDG 1 is achieved, but at the cost of increases in the allocation of female time towards household production and care. It can be suggested that this is not consistent with improvements in gender equality. Similarly, it is possible to construct a scenario in which MDG 4 is achieved, but again, at a cost of increases in the allocation of female time towards household production and care. This logic can be applied to the range of the targets used to indicate progress towards achieving the MDGs.

While MDG 3 is explicitly about gender relations, engendered macroeconomic dynamics permeate the goals, targets and indicators of the other MDGs. Consequently, progress towards achieving the MDGs could be profoundly gendered unless MDG 3 is more broadly defined and is mainstreamed across all goals and targets. Not doing so has profound implications for human security. The following section offers some suggestions to tentatively regard ways in which economic policies need to be reconsidered to take account of the structurally engendered character of macroeconomic dynamics. I argue that it is only by integrating gender into macroeconomics that the attainment of the MDGs in a manner consistent with aggregate improvements in human security could become even a remote possibility.

Time and care

Time is central to a structurally engendered understanding of macroeconomic dynamics, and feminist development economics, as suggested above, argues that the economy has to be defined to include the unpaid caring labour that goes into household production and which sustains commodity production. It is important to clarify what is meant by 'care'. Susan Himmelweit (1995) has persuasively argued that tasks such as childcare are not work because the task cannot be separated from the person that performs the task. This means, that while a wide range of household production can be commodified, caring labour, whether it is for children, older family members, the differently–abled, or others, cannot be totally commodified. Caring labour is different from other forms of social reproduction because quality is a function of the social relations that connect those that give and receive care. Himmelweit argues that treating care as work devalues what is performed.

It could be suggested that from a gender perspective, to accommodate the macroeconomic dynamics of care time is a 'missing' MDG, cutting across all the goals in ways that have clear implications for human security. Women supply their labour to household maintenance activities at no cost, often for relational and self fulfilling reasons of care but also often for socially necessary and obligatory reproductive work. Such labour affects the allocation of resources by imposing a structural constraint upon the agency of women in other activities beyond the household. Ingrid Palmer (1995) has termed this the 'reproduction labour tax'. The structural constraint upon women's agency imposed by care and household maintenance activities places fundamental limits upon the capacity of gendered economic agents to strive to achieve the MDGs in a manner that enhances human equality and security.

The care regime

There is a need to transform the dynamics of the 'care regime' to ease the 'time poverty' that women bear because of their performance of socially necessary, if at times relational, tasks. A care regime can be defined as the basis on which care responsibilities are allocated, with particular reference to the specific balance between the household, the market and the state as the providers of care (Bettio and Plantenga 2004). In recent comparative research on Europe 'the relative reliance on informal care and formal care, and the different modalities of formal care provisioning, like leave arrangements, financial provisions and social services' (Bettio and Plantenga 2004, 108) were identified as important markers of the pattern of care provision. Links from the care regime to labour markets, poverty and macroeconomic dynamics have also been identified in this research.

A key implication from the concept of the care regime is the need to boost investment in the social and physical infrastructure that reduces structural constraints on women's time and which enhances women's access to social assets: the relational rules, norms, and values of civic responsibility and social community. Both would alter the dynamics of the prevailing care regime.

In developing countries poor women in particular spend significant parts of their day collecting water and fuel as well as transporting people and goods. This is done as women try to combine their caring labour, household maintenance activities, and income generating work, tasks that take place in infrastructural environments that place heavy time burdens on women, and particularly poor women. Increased investment in physical and social infrastructure that is designed to overcome women's time poverty will have the potential to enhance the capacity to meet women's human security needs by freeing up the time to undertake tasks such as education, participation in governance, as well as paid employment (Akram–Lodhi and Hanmer 2008). This is consistent with the aims of MDG 3, but cuts across the other MDG goals, once the need to more broadly conceptualize the economy is recognized.

Questioning efficiency

A set of assumptions within conventional economic thinking about efficiency must be questioned, because these assumptions are predicated upon failing to recognize the specific structural burdens placed upon women as a result of care. As discussed, one rationale for state intervention in the provision of services is the failure of markets to provide 'public goods'. The 'cult of efficiency' (Stein 2002) implicitly propagated by neoclassical economics assumes that there is a free supply of unpaid caring labour, which acts, as a public good subsidizing the commodity–producing economy. Women's unpaid care substitutes for the provision of publicly provided healthcare and education within poor families. Women's unpaid care produces goods and services that both markets and states fail to provide or which are provided in ways that price women out of the market despite need. Caring labour is a social asset central to the macroeconomic dynamics of the care regime, but conventional measures of efficiency take this for granted. Once care is recognized not as a public good but as a relational service and that more obligatory household maintenance services can be substituted by public or private provision there is a need to consider ways of developing the social infrastructure that facilitates meeting some degree of household maintenance services and as a result reduces time constraints.

Consider, for example, water privatization. Water privatization, as often proposed by the World Bank under PRSPs, may bring long term supply improvements but the immediate cost prices many poor users out of the market which increases ill health. The task of caring for this ill health usually falls to women even when most are unable to participate in the market because of their time poverty. A direct consequence of privatization, through its impact on wealth differentiated access to services, is an increase in women's time poverty as households and communities place greater reliance upon more fully using the social asset that is women's caring labour. Many similar examples can be provided, suggesting that the fulfilment of MDG 3 requires an awareness of time as a key component of a gender aware macroeconomics. Time is a completely missing consideration from the existing macroeconomic analysis that underpins the MDGs.

Conventional macroeconomics, as noted, have set assumptions about distributional parameters. As stressed, time affects the division of labour. Similarly, policies within PRSPs promoting the establishment of user fees for services are clearly predicated upon a gender–blind view of the distribution of income and expenditure. As a result, payment systems for public services are not designed upon the distribution of income and expenditure within households, which is often inequitable, as resources are not pooled. These distributional parameters have the potential to affect macroeconomic dynamics. There is a need to reconsider the terms and conditions under which men and women access and use consumption and investment commodities and social and physical assets. Market and non market based payment structures and systems, including both 'private' decision making and publicly mandated taxation, are constructed on the basis of ability to pay, which is predicated upon how households allocate time, wealth and money both within and between themselves. It is suggested that efforts designed to meet the MDGs requires consideration of these macroeconomic distributional parameters if human security is to be enhanced in a gender equitable fashion.

In terms of the distribution of work in the commodity economy, there is clear gender inequality with gaps in pay, security and protection. Women are concentrated in poorer paid jobs, with greater degrees of casualization and lesser degrees of formality, and with lower elements of social protection that may sometimes be absent. Labour market inequality is predicated upon the assignation of women to care within the home and the community, generating the previously noted structural time constraint that formal employment cannot accommodate but which casual and informal employment can partially accommodate, even as household income requirements places the onus on women to seek out casual and insecure work to sustain gendered household expenditure patterns.

The improved investments in 'human capital' suggested by MDG 4 therefore appear inadequate. Improved training and education for females, important as that is, may not obviate labour market discrimination or the time poverty that results in underutilized human resources, lesser incomes, and poverty. The economy needs to be unpacked, to recognize the ways in which the provision of care and social assets generates macroeconomic processes that foster discriminatory outcomes that are inconsistent with MDG 3. This also suggests the need for greater social investment in the public provision of childcare, to reduce time poverty, as well as enhanced social transfers to better meet the costs of raising children. Both have implications for state budgetary positions, especially under the terms of PRSPs, but the target of fulfilling MDG 3 suggests the need to creatively and explicitly recognize the role of caring labour and social asset investment in macroeconomic processes and dynamics (Akram–Lodhi and Hanmer 2008).

The open economy

The discussion so far has been that of a 'closed' economy; that is, one without international flows. Opening this up, the liberalization of trade, investment and finance has globally increased the participation of women in paid employment. However, it has not reduced gender inequality in labour markets; by affecting the types of jobs that are available, it may have exacerbated labour market inequality. The implications of economic liberalization for gender equality or otherwise in the labour market must be considered when trade, investment and finance policies are developed. Liberalization must be placed within the binding structural constraint that is the provision of care. It cannot be assumed that the liberalization of trade, investment and finance has no effect on time poverty; rather, the dynamics of the open economy must be investigated and evaluated from a gender perspective.

Global, national and local markets are very important in the transmission of goods and services. Such markets cannot be assumed to be gender neutral; overt and covert discrimination against women often occurs, in the markets for both services and goods. This has implications for macroeconomic dynamics, generating gender based distortions that engender human insecurity and which have the potential to reduce the capacity to meet the goals of the MDGs. Moreover, participation in markets is predicated upon the provision of care, which must be provided prior to market based activity. As stressed, the provision of care is the binding constraint that structures market oriented decision making.

Economic governance

In that markets can be subject to gender based distortions, this suggests that there is a need for fundamental change in the institutions that govern economic processes. In other words, there is a need for economic reform, albeit economic reform that differs from that suggested by PRSPs. In particular, there is a fundamental need to reform economies to better achieve *de facto* rights that are currently *de jure*. This includes legal reform, embracing effective implementation, and programmes promoting legal literacy regarding property and inheritance rights.

The importance of this for enhancing human security cannot be overstressed. Bina Agarwal (1994), for example, has extremely successfully argued for the need of effective and independent land rights for women to improve welfare, equality and empowerment, while simultaneously promoting more productive use of resources. The achievement of MDG 1 requires, in part, effective and enforced land rights for rural women. In so doing, agency is enhanced even as structures are reformed.

Meanwhile, given the macroeconomic dynamics of market based provision of consumption and investment commodities, it cannot be assumed that markets do not require substantive regulation if social inefficiencies and discriminatory outcomes are to be avoided. The establishment of land markets that may accompany the provision of land rights for women can lead to a reconcentration of land in the hands of richer owners, including foreign owned agribusiness. In such circumstances, women's ownership may only be temporarily effective and enforced, after which both women and men working in agriculture begin to become landless labourers or tenant farmers working under conditions of contract farming to agribusiness. In such circumstances, *de facto* rights, once established, may be quickly lost, compromising the ability to attain the human security objectives that underpin the MDGs.

This suggests a need to reconsider systems of economic governance. In particular, there is a need to consider systems of economic governance that sustain the care of human capabilities and nurture human security. Governance systems should be constructed that foster the provision of gender equitable social assets, that reinforce the capacity of household to provide care in gender equitable ways and which ensure that social and physical investments are made that reduce time poverty (Akram–Lodhi and Hanmer 2008). The task is to construct systems of economic governance that are consistent with enhanced, gender equitable human security. For example, the effective privatization of social provisioning under the aegis of structural adjustment and PRSPs has effectively eliminated ways of developing 'collective, egalitarian and solidaristic' (Elson 2004, 11) systems of social provisioning that have a greater potential to promote gender equality, the empowerment of women, and meet MDG 3 than do market based mechanisms of social provisioning. There is a clear need to connect goal 3 with goal 8, as economic governance structures nationally and internationally need to be considered for their impact on the gender relations that structure macroeconomic dynamics.

This means, at the very least, the facilitation of an effective and resourced women's machinery in government, the strong presence of women in legislatures, accountability mechanisms within government and between government and civil society and sustained efforts to estimate the direct and shadow costs of gender inequalities, as well as directing the resource flows necessary to obviate such inefficiencies. In so doing, women's agency is enhanced.

Internationally, it suggests the need to deepen efforts at gender mainstreaming into both international institutions, bilateral donor agencies, as well as with partners. There is the need to create a gender aware global partnership for human security and economic development, a creation that would be very different to the current notion of partnerships for development that would institutionalize an engendered understanding of agency into the interstices of governance in order to offset the transmission of gender bias in economic processes.

Conclusion

The MDGs represent a global compact designed to enhance rights–based human security. However, the MDGs are in danger of not being met. In many ways this is not surprising. Macroeconomic policies that flow from MDG–consistent PRSPs do not recognize the limitations inherent in the orthodox macroeconomic analytical framework that is used to craft MDG–consistent economic policies and programmes. In particular, gender relations act as a structural constraint on macroeconomic processes and this has implications for the capacity of the MDGs to actually enhance women's agency, both individually and collectively and improve human security.

A gender analysis of the macroeconomics of the MDGs reveals that time is a missing structural constraint on agency, and that, as such, time is the 'missing' MDG. Perhaps time cannot be added to the MDGs, but certainly targets and indicators should be reconsidered in light of their impact upon the gendered allocation of time. Moreover, the integration of time – and care – into the MDG framework would lead into a reconsideration of the prevailing care regime as well as questioning orthodox understandings of efficiency, which may be predicated upon the introduction of economic reforms promulgated in the name of MDG–consistent PRSPs that are not gender neutral. This is turn suggests that economic governance, of which the MDGs are now clearly a part, needs to be fundamentally rethought in ways that both enhance women's agency and in so doing challenge the prevailing structures of power and privilege that place women in the most insecure strata within society.

In short, the MDGs should challenge the prevailing set of global capitalist social relations that foster insecure, unequal, market–embedded, neoliberal outcomes, and in so doing transcend a prevailing development paradigm that creates human insecurity. The objective of such a challenge would be to achieve gender equitable human security. That such a challenge is not currently on the agenda suggests that addressing human insecurity is also fundamentally not on the agenda.

References

Agarwal, B. (1994), *A Field Of One's Own: Gender and Land Rights in South Asia* (Cambridge: Cambridge University Press).

Akerlof, G.E. and Kranton, R.E. (2000), 'Economics and Identity', *Quarterly Journal of Economics* 115:3, 715–753.

Akram–Lodhi, A.H. (1996), '"You Are Not Excused From Cooking": Peasants and the Gender Division of Labor in Pakistan', *Feminist Economics* 2:2, 87–106.

—— (2002), '"All Decisions Are Top–Down": Engendering Public Expenditure in Vietnam', *Feminist Economics* 8:3, 1–20.

Akram–Lodhi, A.H. and Hanmer, L.C. (2008), 'Ghosts in the Machine: A Post Keynesian Analysis of Gender Relations, Households and Macroeconomics', in F. Bettio and A. Verashchagina (eds), *Frontiers in the Economics of Gender* (New York: Routledge), 77–98.

Akram–Lodhi, A.H. and Kay, C. (2009), 'The Agrarian Question: Peasants and Rural Change', in A.H. Akram–Lodhi and C. Kay (eds), *Peasants and Globalization: Political Economy, Rural Transformation and the Agrarian Question* (New York: Routledge), 3–34.

Arndt, C. and Tarp, F. (2000), 'Agricultural Technology, Risk and Gender: A CGE Analysis of Mozambique', *World Development* 28:7, 1307–1326.

Becker, G. (1981), *A Treatise on the Family* (Cambridge, MA: Harvard University Press).

Bettio, F. and Plantenga, J. (2004), 'Comparing Care Regimes in Europe', *Feminist Economics* 10:1, 85–113.

Çağatay, N., Elson, D. and Grown, C. (1995), 'Introduction', *World Development* 23:11, 1827–1836.

Çağatay, N. and Erturk, K. (2004), 'Gender and Globalization: A Macroeconomic Perspective', International Labour Organization World Commission on the Social Dimensions of Globalization Working Paper no. 19.

Devarajan, S., Miller, M. and Swanson, E.V. (2002), 'Goals for Development: History, Prospects and Costs', World Bank Policy Research Working Paper no. 2819.

Dwyer, D. and Bruce, J. (eds) (1989), *A Home Divided: Women and Income in the Third World* (Palo Alto, CA: Stanford University Press).

Edholm, F., Harris, O. and Young, K. (1977), 'Conceptualizing Women', *Critique of Anthropology* 3:9 and 10, 101–130.

Elson, D. (2004), 'The Millennium Development Goals: A Feminist Development Economics Perspective', Institute of Social Studies *Dies Natalis* Address, October.

Evers, B. (2003), 'Broadening the Foundations of Macro–economic Models Through a Gender Approach: New Developments', in M. Gutierrez (ed.), *Macro–economics: Making Gender Matter* (London: Zed Press), 3–21.

Folbre, N. (1994), *Who Pays for the Kids? Gender and the Structures of Constraint* (London: Routledge).

Grown, C., Elson, D. and Çağatay, N. (2000), 'Introduction', *World Development* 28:7, 1145–1156.

Hanmer, L.C., Pyatt, G. and White, H. (1999), 'What do the World Bank's Poverty Assessments Teach us About Poverty in Sub–Saharan Africa?', *Development And Change* 30:4, 795–823.

Himmelweit, S. (1995), 'The Discovery of "Unpaid Work": The Social Consequences of the Expansion of "Work"', *Feminist Economics* 1:2, 1–19.

King, E. and Hill, A. (1995), 'Women's Education and Economic Well–Being', *Feminist Economics* 1:2, 1–26.

Long, N. and Long, A. (eds) (1992), *Battlefields of Knowledge: The Interlocking of Theory and Practice in Development Research* (London: Routledge).

Microsoft Ltd. (2001), *Microsoft Encarta* (Seattle: Microsoft Ltd.)

Palmer, I. (1995), 'Public Finance from a Gender Perspective', *World Development* 23:11, 1981–1986.

Pollitt, C. (2003), *The Essential Public Sector Manager* (Milton Keynes, UK: Open University Press).

Seguino, S. and Floro, M. (2002), 'Does Gender Have Any Effect on Aggregate Saving? An Empirical Analysis', *International Review of Applied Economics* 17:2, 148–166.

Stein, J.G. (2002), *The Cult of Efficiency* (Toronto: House of Anansi Press).

United Nations (2001), *Report of the High Level Panel on Financing for Development* (New York: United Nations).

United Nations (2008), *The Millennium Development Goals Report 2008* (New York: United Nations).

United Nations (2009), 'UN Millennium Project: goals, targets and indicators', available at <http://www.unmillenniumproject.org/goals/gti.html>, accessed 11 June 2009.

United Nations Millennium Project (2005), *Investing in Development: A Practical Plan to Achieve the Millennium Development Goals* (New York: United Nations Development Programme).

Warner, J. and Campbell, D.A. (2000), 'Supply Response in an Agrarian Economy with Non–symmetric Gender Relations', *World Development* 28:7, 1327–1340.

Weis, T. (2008), 'The (Not–so) Sudden Crisis of the Global Food Economy', *Canadian Dimension* 42:4, 13–16.

Chapter 5

Gender and Social Justice Beyond the Millennium Development Goals: Challenging Human Insecurity

Helen Hintjens

This chapter outlines challenges for rights–based action by global social and gender justice movements in the current climate. Non Governmental Organizations (NGOs), civil society groups, grassroots organizations and loose transnational (or translocal) networks of actors build sets of social and gender justice claims that are much broader and more structurally interconnected than the limited quantitative targets of the Millennium Development Goals (MDGs). My main argument is that the 'complex internationalism' of global gender justice movements emphasizes basic rights, and that this challenges the bureaucratic logic, or 'frozen architecture' of more formal, institutional approaches to development (Della Porta and Tarrow 2005). This latter approach is typified by the adoption of the fixed, quantitative targets of the MDGs.

If the MDGs were ever achieved in the future, the best way to ensure that they remained sustainable would be by linking them with broader social and gender justice aims. Unlike the specific results sought by the MDGs, social movements tend to tie their various demands together into complex, interwoven bundles of rights claims. For example, gender justice would be seen as completely tied up with equal access for girls and women to education, but also to prioritizing women's rights to have adequate food, clothing and shelter, as well as clean water, minority rights protection and health entitlements, among others. Elements of the distinctiveness of gender justice movements/NGO/civil society in relation to security and insecurity will be explored in this chapter using two main examples.

Each case shows, in a different way, how demands and rights claims from below can be integrated and combined with legal and policy prescriptions from above. The first case concerns the implementation processes embedded in CEDAW (Convention on the Elimination of all Forms of Discrimination against Women) and how its gender justice demands have been put into practice. This case shows how important it is to mobilize civil society actors so that a legally based set of 'corrective mechanisms' can work effectively. The second case is a social movement of women demanding gender equality 'from below', that of SEWA, the Self Employed Women's Association of India. Together with other similar movements, during the 1990s, SEWA helped form translocal networks that pressed for rights claims to be formalized into the International Labour Organisation (ILO) Convention on Home Work (finalized in 1996 and coming into force in 2000) (ILO 1996). SEWA was the prime mover behind this Convention, which has in turn become a tool for advocacy for some of the world's most vulnerable women workers to claim their basic rights (Gallin 2007). This chapter uses these examples to show how chinks in the armour of global neoliberal capitalism can be used to open up challenges to the neoliberal dominance of market values. The globalized market economy cannot be replaced in the near future but a more socially based economic system based on different values, is an alternative. This chapter outlines how a global politics of security and insecurity has been challenged both from above, through law, especially international human rights law, and from below by social movements and NGOs, to include issues of wider social justice in the global agenda.

Why social movements?

Social movements are important because they can both expose and respond to the paradoxes and inherent contradictions of the liberal paradigm of security and political economy. Systemic legitimacy failures, especially the structural incapacity to meet the most basic rights of the poorest populations, open space for such social movements and NGOs. This is not to romanticize the possibilities for action, since: 'glorification of the splendid underdogs is nothing other than glorification of the splendid system that makes them so' (Adorno 1974, 28). Even so, over the past two decades at least, global women's movements and other social justice movements have organized across borders leading to major rights claims being recognized, including by the UN and member states (Sen 2005). In this chapter, two examples illustrate how political spaces can be used to promote social and gender justice alongside strategic use of national and international legal and policy instruments. The emergence of CEDAW (The Convention on the Elimination of all Forms of Discrimination against Women) as a process shows the importance for implementation processes to be embedded in civil society. This example highlights the facilitating role of UNIFEM in bringing together the inductive levels of claims among gender justice NGOs and deductive formal legal processes, to overcome this artificial distinction.

Such complex interconnections between social justice movements and wider rights–realizing institutions like the UN, states and transnational corporations are generally ignored within, for example, the targeted approaches underpinning the MDGs. As authors in this volume emphasize (see chapters by Sylvester, Akram–Lodhi), it is not expected that targets can adequately deal with processes as complex as those involved in social transformation. The global social and gender justice movements expose the reality that even full attainment of the MDGs would not pull the world's population out of structural poverty (Prontzos 2004). Those who comprise the 'wasted humanity' of the global system, and fall through the cracks of market failures, are most in need of advocates (Bauman 2005).

In stating that human rights are transformational and 'performative i.e. they require action on the part of those who hold them', Bas de Gaay Fortman (2006, 41, 37) provides an avenue to the examples I consider, The second example, SEWA is simultaneously a registered trade union, social movement, local organization, part of a global network as well as an NGO. SEWA promotes women's organizational ability on the basis of social insurance schemes that remove some of the very lowest status women workers from debt. Through an innovative mix of national and translocal strategies of applying pressure in certain areas (legal, professional and political) SEWA has forged networks and connections that stretch to Europe, Mexico, Thailand and elsewhere. While the ILO played a central role in the SEWA case, UNIFEM has been the main facilitating agency for CEDAW. Each of the two cases in this chapter involves gender issues as central in a broader rights–based approach. There is also a constant emphasis on linking up policies and legal processes at different levels with organized, socially grounded claims, demands and pressures from below, expressed for example through citizens' claims or NGO–led campaigns. Sometimes the environment may not be conducive to campaigns, demands or claims to essential rights, or may 'actually be hostile to any effort for the protection of basic human dignity' (de Gaay Fortman 2006, 38).

Some (Roberts 2008; Richmond 1994; Alexander 1996; Bond 2001) argue that today's world, because of its gross inequalities and tight restrictions on movement, closely resembles pre–democratic South Africa, with its rampant, legally enforced and arbitrary inequalities. In this 'global apartheid': 'people with greater power control safer land, and governments and political institutions determine where poor and vulnerable people live by denying access to better land through a range of means and justifications' (Roberts 2008, 1). In this context, progressive social justice movements and NGOs are like a global anti–apartheid movement. Simply by advocating equal rights, gender and other social justice movements start to expose the deep democratic deficits and qualitative shortcomings in the dominant system. State authorities have a tendency to exaggerate the level of threat to their own and by implication their citizens' security. Social movement organizers can easily find themselves accused of a form of 'terrorism' or some other crime of thought or association. When campaigns start to identify the root cause of people's poverty as being inside the routine structural violence of the global economic system, this alarms those in power (Prontzos 2004). Some even claim that global neoliberalism takes the form of a 'war on the poor', and especially a 'war on women' (Sen 2005; Roberts 2008). Screened from accountability, neoliberal economic policies continue to be imposed even during a crisis that they arguably created.

Peaceful social movements for gender and social justice are often faced with deeply unpopular policies. They can expose the defects of 'free' market economic and social policies, the criminality of the 'war on terror', and the draconian surveillance of citizens and restrictions against human movement across borders. Politics designed to shore up untenable national ideals; to bully and bamboozle the emerging global solidarity movements need to be exposed. Otherwise, the politics that goes with neoliberal hegemony tends to find new victims at home and abroad to blame for our problems.

'Joined up' rights–based approaches are supposed to widen room for manoeuvre by people themselves, using a mix of skill in timing, arguments based on economic self–interest and moral persuasion (de Gaay Fortman 2006; Gready and Ensor 2005). Compared with the static targets of the MDGs, the more holistic goals of creating 'alternatives' to existing forms of globalization provoke enormous engagement of various publics. The real challenge is to enable other, sentiment–driven and non–market–reducible values to penetrate the debate at key moments (Goodwin, Jasper and Polletta 2000; McDonald 2006). The 'loose activist networks adopting self–organizing communication technologies, and advocating multiple issues, multiple goals and inclusive identities' pose a real challenge for fixed outcome targets (Della Porta and Tarrow 2005, 17).

A lack of fixed structures and permanent organizations signal, from this perspective, the effectiveness and creativity of global gender and social justice movements compared with many more conventional forms of national organizations (Albert 2002). Fluidity in form matches the fluidity of global capital, and the 'social energy' released can accumulate over time and be used for many different goals and campaigns (Hirschman 1983). Despite some serious resource and capacity constraints, social movements act at different levels to move the debates beyond the static quantitative goals typified by MDG targets.

Even so, by being widely known and discussed, and holding governments accountable internationally, MDGs have usefully encouraged broader demands to be made. Promoting a genuine politics of human security in the face of the insecurity engendered and exacerbated by neoliberal deregulation and marketization is seen as a matter of urgency (George 2004). In this chapter, one of the key points is how broad social and gender justice strategies, working on a rights–based foundation, need social movements, NGOs and UN agencies to work hand in hand. The central organizing principle is laid out by Bas de Gaay Fortman (2008), when he explains that for social justice, rights–based approaches must combine 'deductive' and 'inductive' elements in order to start to be effective.

Mapping the global: Lethal outcomes

Warfare is not the most significant cause of preventable deaths in the world today (Pogge 2008; Prontzos 2004; Roberts 2008). While whole countries are left to rot as so–called failed states, ecosystems decay, and millions face displacement from their livelihoods (Bauman 2005; Ziegler 2008). The global economic system continues to be geared around high cost and 'hard' security surveillance and military spending. The global security business sector has sprawled into areas previously confined to the state, such as detention, prison and policing. New technologies of control and surveillance have created business opportunities for the sector (Bauman 2004; Nederveen Pieterse 2004). Amid a race for strategic resources by huge corporations and postindustrial countries, the focus since at least the late 1990s has been on global military security first, and human development second (Chomsky 2003). The failure of the 'system' to create possibilities for the real improvement of the lives of the majority of the world's population has become quite apparent, even to a child (Prontzos 2004).

Struggles over development – and debates over reaching the MDGs – are also conflicts about where responsibility should lie for the deprivation and economic misery of the poor, of women and of the most vulnerable people on the planet. The struggles of illegally housed, landless and undocumented people, of those trafficked and smuggled, of stateless or indigenous minorities not given recognition as full citizens, are everywhere apparent. Even for many of the poorest people, to claim their rights, such as food, housing, water and education, is a life threatening challenge. Irene Grootboom, whose name became famous from a legal battle around low cost housing in South Africa, died in August 2008 in her shack, still awaiting implementation of the judge's final decision in the Grootboom case in 2000. She was just 39 (Joubert 2008). Asking for decent housing, land, food, health and schooling, falls within the scope of the MDGs, yet even the most basic rights claims (land, housing, water, education, health) may seem to be extremely challenging to politicians, lawyers and business people. This may be because such rights violations against the poor are structurally embedded (the very need to invent the MDGs in the first place suggests this is the case) (Roberts 2008; Pogge 2008; George 2004). Consumption is still confined mainly to those who can afford it, and many have to fall by the wayside, dying young and living in misery (Bauman 2005; Prontzos 2004).

With the current economic crisis, whatever the impact on high income consumerist value systems and lifestyles, although global consumption may be reduced, ecosystemic imbalances and resource exploitation are likely to continue to worsen. Meagre sources of sustenance are likely to diminish further for the poor. With economic decline, the dominant neoliberal order is entering a phase of chronic legitimacy crisis, which no amount of global consensus building on basic development goals like MDGs can resolve. An economic system that is completely unable to ensure 'full stomachs' for a large part of the population has a serious legitimacy deficit (Ziegler 2008; Golay 2008). A result of social problems is the tendency to blame them on victims, including migrants, refugees, poor people, and especially poor women (Bauman 2005; Ryan 1971).

In this context of state failure, global social movements – including women's movements and civil society NGOs – may need to help with alternative modes of rights realization and mass provisioning, and this relationship can be highly problematic, leaving social movements with little autonomy in relation to the state or NGOs (Bendana 2006). Civil society cannot make up for deficiencies in the market and the state, both of which are very apparent. State structures will need to be recuperated and reconstructed before even the most basic entitlements to food, shelter and a sustainable livelihood can be better ensured for women and the poor in general. Although the state remains crucial to this, the examples presented in this chapter provide some hope of other ways of promoting rights for the poorest and particularly for women.

Paradoxes in the status quo

There are some clear paradoxes in the current state of affairs. Increasingly more governments fall under the purview of international UN legal institutions and these governments' accounts of gender and justice progress are confronted with 'shadow reporting' by NGOs and other civil society organizations. For example, CEDAW means that signatory governments should become more accountable for fulfilling their wider obligations towards all citizens, and ensuring equal outcomes for men and women (Hintjens 2008). Governments should be more actively accountable to their citizens than before, to poor women, minority groups and others with low status and poor life chances.

The paradox is that those same governments that are required to report regularly on progress in terms of meeting MDGs, such as ensuring access to free education for girls, for example, are also subjected to international structural adjustment regimes which require them to meet financial and trade deregulation conditions that in turn reduce these governments' longer term capacity to meet both MDG goals and basic rights claims from the poor and vulnerable. Instead of responding to criticism of their record by political opponents, governments square the circle by fighting 'dirty wars' of violence and propaganda against political opponents, especially the organizers of the poor, who may be falsely charged with 'terror' or other criminal associations, disappeared, incarcerated or killed.

This paradox results from the contradictions between economic and political liberalism. The same states obliged to respect principles of equality and rights protection, which are striving to meet MDG goals, are also required to take economic and financial deregulation measures that make it less and less likely that they can ensure that the poor have access to the most basic economic and social rights. The rights to land for subsistence agricultural food production, access to clean and low cost urban housing, provision of broad and adequate health care and access to affordable or free education, all appear out of reach so long as a high proportion of revenues, GNP and taxes are gobbled up by the neoliberal machine. Spilling externalities onto the surrounding and distant population, this economic machine, driven by politically embedded global corporations mashes up the global stratosphere and the subsoil in its wake. It dumps toxic by–products especially onto minorities, women, children and the socially vulnerable. David Roberts (2008, 12) calls this 'non–military violence against civilians' and includes the use of food as a weapon to reinforce, for example, what both South African transnational activists and the Brazilian citizenship movements have termed 'global apartheid' (Bond 2001; Dagnino 2005; Kent 2005, 152; Stendile 2002).

This implies a renewal of older notions of democratic participation, whereby elections and competing parties no longer define politics and political power.

Prontzos (2004, 319) notes: 'Ultimately, the only way in which structural violence will be significantly reduced is if the political economy of each nation, and of the world as a whole, is effectively democratized.' If this is to happen, then it will have to be a collaborative task, which combines the energies of global social movements, women's organizations, trade unions, citizens' campaigns and the like, with the legal, institutional and economic capacity of international organizations and perhaps even some transnational companies. Campaigns that express popular and widespread disenchantment with the conventional business order can achieve their goals (such as 'Jubilee 2000', 'blood diamonds', the campaign to ban land mines)[1] but are usually brief and have to respond to the prevailing logic of the market in order to be successful (Gready 2004).

The global social justice movement, with its many NGO and grassroots components, campaigns and alliances, offers a different form of engagement from the dominant liberal model, where citizens, essentially atomized, combine along class, party or identity lines. There are few 'central command' structures among social movements today; information is much too diffuse to be controlled or filtered systematically. The prevailing culture of fear and apathy has been identified by Noam Chomsky (2003). This can be contrasted with the model proposed by Alain Touraine (2005) where the consumer, as individualized as s/he is, responds as an organized social actor, someone who does not confine their sense of autonomy to voting every few years, or to consuming various products.

CEDAW: From deductive to inductive

In an unpromising wider global context, it is worth considering how international rights discourses can positively influence social change. CEDAW emerged after many years of discussion, lobbying, campaigning and negotiation among well meaning governments, an international array of women's and feminist NGOs and gender experts. CEDAW obliges ratifying governments to promote, protect and fulfil the equal rights of men and women in their own jurisdictions. Complex oversight mechanisms are attached to the Convention, which amount to a form of global governance around gender justice (Sen 2005).

From around the mid 1990s, when the UN started to reintegrate human rights into its internal operations, there has been a positive commitment made to mainstream human rights–based approaches across all UN agencies and policies. Prioritizing gender equality and empowerment became a way of ensuring that

---

1   Jubilee 2000 was an international coalition movement in over 40 countries that called for cancellation of third world debt by the year 2000. Blood diamonds are also known as conflict diamonds, diamonds that are used by rebel groups to fuel conflict and civil wars. See http://www.globalwitness.org/pages/en/conflict_diamonds.html. See <http://www.icbl.org/intro.php> on the international campaign to ban land mines.

UN agencies were committed to a human rights–based approach. Gender equality goals come into all programming, as do the priorities of securing human rights, and should be given practical expression in terms of goals and outcomes of UN policy processes (UNIFEM 2007).

The United Nations Development Fund for Women (UNIFEM) has recently been identified by the UN Secretary General as the key agency, tasked with coordinating both gender justice and human rights–based approaches as shared goals across the main UN agencies. Gender justice and rights are to be more and more coordinated and mainstreamed. The *UNIFEM Strategic Plan for 2008–2011* (UNIFEM–Plan 2007) noted however, that if CEDAW was to continue to 'bite back' against resistance to gender equality and human rights agendas, then additional resources would have to be found to match the organization's growing responsibilities.

The CEDAW Committee sporadically receives government reports, sometimes accompanied by 'shadow reports' from monitoring NGOs or NGO coalitions in the country concerned. Shadow reports can play a disciplining role; helping to unpack the claims of governments and expose some of the neglect that underlies declared achievements. UNIFEM mainly relies on persuasion, on reassuring dialogue with governments, and behind–the–scenes meetings with officials. Through trained negotiators and gender experts, the organization tries to persuade bureaucrats and ministers to see the advantages of greater transparency. UNIFEM filters the more strident voices but endorses their expression within NGO fora and networks. Gender related NGOs and movements therefore have an input, however indirect, into the counterweight of the shadow reporting process, an integral part of CEDAW implementation. UNIFEM acts as broker and mediator, both supporting inter–organizational collaboration in–country, and negotiating access to key policy makers for organized opinion 'from below' (Hintjens 2008).

Playing both ends of the advocacy game makes UNIFEM a powerful actor, not because it can control the outcomes, but because it sets processes in motion, which can sometimes develop their own momentum, pushing for positive change. Linking deductive, legally based actors, like lawyers and officials, with more inductive grassroots based groups, NGOs and movements, is the key contribution that UNIFEM has made in countries where its work has been prolonged and sustained, like the Philippines case considered below (Hintjens 2008). UNIFEM is supportive of even minor improvements in performance by government, while simultaneously supporting and facilitating shadow reporting processes and being constructively critical of those policies. CEDAW's own mechanisms of reporting and comment make this double role possible and a vital part of the accountability process.

A recent UNIFEM–CEDAW report exposed some of the contradictions that can arise between principles and institutions of international legal CEDAW machinery, and the priorities and working habits of UNIFEM (UNIFEM 2007). Combining gender equality and a human rights–based approach within a single framework is perhaps the major contribution of UNIFEM and the remit it has been given internally within the UN system. UNIFEM's impact can only be measured as a catalyst but quantifying such impacts is very difficult. Ironically UNIFEM must generate change that promotes gender equality at government level and inside the UN, and demonstrate this impact. In the context of mainstreaming human rights–based approaches across the UN system (UNIFEM 2007, 5), UNIFEM has a good track record, as relatively flexible and responsive to those governments and coalitions of actors willing to innovate in gender responsive social technologies.

In contrast, the MDGs are much more easily measurable and achievable than gender justice and a human rights–based approach, even within the UN system. Yet measurability is not proof of inherent significance, as processes often prove more significant than 'targets' which can be measured as outcomes at specific moments. Some of the most important forms of social change, where pressure brings about a change in values, attitudes and perceptions of interests, are not easily quantified. How UNIFEM's impact could be assessed remains a puzzle, but this does not undermine the important potential work of the organization in promoting and realizing greater gender equality.

The task of unearthing the reality of women's rights in different countries is facilitated by UNIFEM supporting a 'shadow reporting' process from NGOs, especially women's NGOs, often representing social movements and grassroots organizations of the poor. By commenting on the official CEDAW report of the national government presenting to the CEDAW Committee (UNIFEM 2007, 10–12), the NGOs and civil society organizations are able to provide a deeper contextual analysis of gender equality problems. This is vital, as one report notes: '(a) universal set of gender equality requirements could actually be an obstacle rather than an asset for gender equality work, if it was too abstract or rigid' (UNIFEM 2007, 13). What are needed are more responsive guidelines that acknowledge (just as CEDAW mechanisms do) that women's social organizations, already established in particular societies, play a vital role in holding governments accountable for promoting human security, gender equality and transparent political practices.

CEDAW's national level impacts and outcomes in terms of gender equality and social justice are significant because of their quality, not their measurable impact. 'The fundamental innovation of the *substantive model of equality* is to use the conditions of women's actual lives, rather than the wording used in laws, as the true measure of whether equality has been achieved' (UNIFEM 2007: 52, emphasis added). In line with this, UNIFEM engages in interventions that seek to relate official government reports to CEDAW with particularly the substantive impacts on poor women's lives. This provides crucial 'evidence' for that policy to be based on, rather than relying only on official documents.

CEDAW's substantive model of equality makes it an interesting and useful vehicle for women's justice movements and NGOs concerned with gender justice, worldwide. One of the more original features of CEDAW is that equality is detached from its minimalist liberal frame and reinserted into a socialist understanding of reality. Equality thus implies much more, under CEDAW, than the state desisting from discrimination. It means more than the absence of gender discrimination; indicative that policies and actions should be undertaken that will overcome the structural disadvantages suffered by women compared to men, with other factors being equal.

Other forms of structural inequalities in society can also be viewed through this lens, such as class, cultural and religious identity, age and sexuality. The poor, landless, slum dwellers and indigenous people can all suffer from compound discrimination, especially if they are also women. The notion of equality should not be coopted by the liberal concept of a market economy, in which, economically rational and gender neutral actors operate each with their own separate maximizing strategy of indifference and non–cooperation. In terms of human security, this model leads to lose–lose outcomes rather than the win–win outcomes generally sought by NGOs, women's movements and social movements for whom social and gender justice are core values. In relation to property, work and how it is defined, and reproductive rights, the implications of the substantive equality model of rights can potentially be far reaching, especially when adopted by state institutions (Williams 2006).

Under conditions of endemic economic insecurity, employment opportunities appear and soon vanish. Workers are obliged to be constantly mobile in the hope of finding some kind of livelihood security, and the substantive model of equality can appear utopian. Yet from within the mechanisms and provisions of CEDAW, UNIFEM tries to ensure that some of the substantive equality demands that have motivated gender justice social movements and NGOs are fed back into the policy process. The human rights–based approach to programming that has become part of the UNICEF and other UN agencies' core agendas and modes of operation, is of potentially great significance for women's organizations, especially in the 'global South'.

In comparison to other UN agencies, UNIFEM is considered 'ahead of the game' in relation to understanding equality as substantive, as well as formal. UNICEF also has been making practical headway in terms of realizing gender equality, by working at different levels simultaneously, including with community based networks and NGO alliances. Like UNIFEM, UNICEF also works: (i) at the macro, national or regional levels to help reform laws and policies; (ii) at the meso level to support institutions, undertake advocacy and enhance evaluation capacities; and (iii) at the micro level in communities, to help support organizations that have engaged with shifts in attitudes towards citizenship rights, gender rights and overall value systems conducive to more inclusive social change in future (UNIFEM–Plan 2007, 25).

Some positive experiences have emerged from countries such as the Philippines, and this example is briefly considered in the wider context of UNIFEM's work within CEDAWSEAP programme ('Facilitating CEDAW Implementation Towards the Realization of Human Rights in South East Asia').[2] This programme operates

---

2   The experiences of women's NGOs in the Philippines are illustrative of the possibilities for NGOs to hold government accountable through CEDAW mechanisms, which UNIFEM has been instrumental in developing. More information on this is available

in seven countries of East and Southeast Asia (Cambodia, Indonesia, Laos, Philippines, Thailand, Timor–Leste and Vietnam), and supports women's NGOs by training them about CEDAW's provisions and mechanisms. The main idea is to enhance the local organizations' ability to gather and independently analyse data available on gender equality outcomes, from a rights–based perspective. National and local NGOs use these data to make their own collective recommendations in individual country shadow reports. The CEDAWSEAP programme also trains NGO representatives in how to present shadow reports and how to engage in dialogue with CEDAW experts during CEDAW Committee sessions in Geneva (Rodriguez in Hintjens 2008).

In most Southeast Asian countries, many women's organizations and social movements did not understand the significance of CEDAW's provisions and implementation mechanisms prior to UNIFEM's intervention. They did not know how the shadow report could be compiled, why it was vital to do this, and why it mattered that evidence should be effectively presented. In many Southeast Asian countries, shadow reports were either not presented, or written by a few unrepresentative NGOs. According to Luz Rodriguez of UNIFEM, the work of UNIFEM in the Philippines promoted an environment more conducive to CEDAW implementation. A small number of Philippino women's NGOs were encouraged to file the first shadow report in 2006. When a second shadow report for the Philippines was filed, 95 NGOs and women's organizations were involved. Taking safety in numbers, the second shadow report was more assertive about a number of gender equality issues, including reproductive rights.

The interesting lesson from this case is that a broader notion of 'civil society' and security, as proposed in this study, is being worked out through the CEDAW reporting process. Through increased involvement in advocacy at all levels, UNIFEM can develop its substantive rather than formal equality approach more consistently in a country like the Philippines.

Homeworkers: From inductive to deductive rights

Across the world, millions of women earn a pittance. In India some of the lowest paid women sew garments, grow and sell vegetables, head load construction materials, pick up scrap, and roll cigarettes or incense. Most are paid by the piece, and self employed and homeworking women and their families are often heavily in debt. In the early 1970s, the Textile Labour Association Women's Wing (created in 1954) gave rise to SEWA, the Self Employed Women's Association. Led by Ella Bhatt, SEWA had roots in the cooperative movement in Ahmedabad (Rose 1992).

---

in UNIFEM's report, *Going CEDAW in the Philippines*, which provides detailed information on various experiences with the shadow reporting process in the Philippines. Available at: <http://cedaw-seasia.org/philippines_resources.html#goingcedaw > Section 2, Chapters 2 and 4 are particularly relevant to the argument here.

The textile workers' radical history inspired SEWA ideals, giving the association a form of historical legitimacy in the anti–colonial national movement. SEWA activities now bring together groups of women homeworkers in rural areas and urban slums in several regions of India. SEWA encourages groups of self employed women to become more self reliant. It has features of a NGO in its funding structures, while continuing to work like a social movement and registered as a trade union, with the SEWA umbrella connecting networks of women's groups. Services are provided by the central SEWA organization and in 2002–2006, total membership was estimated at between half and three–quarters of a million.

Court cases against government and employers have been one tactic used by SEWA, along with negotiations and bargaining, microcredit and savings schemes and environmental and health actions (Rose 1992). Naming and shaming is carried out through media campaigns, such as fighting corruption by exposing poor employment practices. Community video and the internet are also used to encourage learning among SEWA members about how to organize. After serious riots and killings of Muslims in Gujarat in 2002, SEWA members took the lead in rehabilitation and reconciliation efforts, drawing on funds from government and donor agencies like Oxfam (Jhabvala and Kanbur 2002). Security, in the widest sense, was the priority for SEWA member groups, who continued with this work despite efforts by the Gujarat government to stop the organization working with Muslims. SEWA has been central to the global network that has campaigned for rights for homeworkers, in coordination with homeworkers' movements from the United States, the Netherlands, the Philippines, South Africa and elsewhere. As mentioned earlier, this global network was instrumental in the formulation of the 1996 ILO Convention 177 on Home Work (SEWA website; Gallin 2007; Jhabvala and Kanbur 2002).

A feature of global social and gender justice movements, and for people entering such movements or campaigns, is a sense of hope that they can act constructively in a collective way. What Adorno (1974) called the politics of love, or solidarity, involves seeing the 'similarity in the dissimilar' and has informed many women's movements worldwide. SEWA brought together many women workers with disparate, but almost equally insecure, forms of self employment and piecework, often carried out at home. Member organizations sought a new notion of authenticity that departed from the collective bargaining of trade unions when they were unable to work within mainstream trade unions. Abstract, grand schemes were rejected and instead the practices of SEWA centre on the 'politics of the possible', working with groups of women in a range of very disparate, but uniformly poorly paid, professions (Rose 1992). The gender related MDG 3 is part of SEWA's repertoire, but even all the MDGs together might prove inadequate to meet the organization's members' needs, because of their special vulnerabilities as home–based, often self–employed workers. Instead, SEWA women members' rights claims centre on a basket of goods and services, private and public, which all aim to end their indebtedness. Significantly, debt is not mentioned in the MDGs.

SEWA arose from a refusal to see marginal, poorly paid and previously poorly organized, women as obstacles to progress. Instead, as low status workers, slum dwellers, and poor people who cross caste, race, and religious divides in terms of identity, SEWA groups of members have produced some answers to their extreme poverty and low status, without waiting for the MDGs to be achieved. The women who comprise the movement are assumed to be resourceful, capable of organizing themselves and of identifying how they can best promote their own interests. They organize peacefully; using legal weapons but also nonviolent civil disobedience, involving thousands in marches, films about their experiences, and legal advocacy and lobbying work. The members of SEWA propose how they can repay debts, and support themselves and their families. SEWA offers its members the chance to exercise their popular power, to renew their social relationships with women around them, and to construct a 'politics of hope' for others who may despair (Hintjens 2009). The government of India has been one of the main interlocutors of SEWA, mainly but not only through the process of legal claims in court around SEWA members' conditions of work, and the duties of those who supply and purchase their goods. The aim is to make both public and private patrons behave more responsibly, by using the law to expose their neglect and even intimidation. This social movement thus challenges market led economic choices with actions that can affect the government in all domains of governance and public policy, from health care to water and gene pools, via criminal justice, the position of women, children and the press (Gallin 2007).

For the state and for corporations, social movements like SEWA do pose a challenge. State repression and violence can often be defended against through nonviolent forms of organizing, but this depends vitally on the support of key professionals: lawyers, doctors, agronomists, journalists and politicians as well as business people. Global support and solidarity networks may perform a similar role in keeping open the route of peaceful social action rather than armed rebellion. The security claims of states can be hard to reconcile with security claims of the poorest and most marginalized people. Often those who lack the most basic needs want material security first, though not at the expense of other forms of freedom. They may even be obliged to use illegal means to obtain a minimal life, let alone a decent one (Zikode 2006, 185–9).

Global insecurity, translocal justice

It seems the nation state has less and less autonomous control over the movements of global trade and capital. What little autonomous policy making there was in the 'South', following colonial withdrawal or expulsion, has been stripped from postcolonial states by processes of forced deregulation and structural adjustment. Social movements that have grown in many parts of the globe, and processes of accountability that start to be embedded in international institutions like UNIFEM, focus on the state, of necessity. Social movements can bring many people from the middle class strata together with some of the most excluded people (such as landless, low caste women, indigenous people, the indebted and disabled). These movements are increasingly translocally interconnected, as the SEWA and Philippines cases illustrate. New media and internet, film and other forms of networked communication can help social movements, for whom: '…the generation of transnational support may be crucial for their survival' (Olesen 2005, 213). Internet and new media can help to create the transnational 'local' forms of identities that are mobilized by gender justice movements and cut across differences of caste, class, religion and political ideology (Castells 2008; Hintjens 2006; Nederveen Pieterse 2004).

Many global social justice movements – such as those that meet in the annual World Social Forum each year – claim to represent the 'global South', and those excluded from the benefits (though not costs) of globalization. These claims have little resonance unless there is some hope of 'being heard' at decision–making levels. Among urban slum dwellers, rural landless, small farmers, poor women, long term jobless and indigenous people, organizing is a visible vector of social demands in relation to higher level institutions. Inequalities and forms of exclusion can only be addressed by claiming spaces on the basis of justice. In Brazil, among the citizenship movements that emerged during the late 1990s, it was hoped that the state would take on the citizenship demands as its own (Dagnino 2005). This social meaning of class and citizenship was to propose a more inclusive notion of citizenship as the basis for social, political and economic life. These ambitions have been realized only in part under the government of Lula. Even in the heartlands of the United States, United Kingdom, France and Australia, social renewal and community regeneration are the only way forward for some of the poorest communities (Wainwright 2003), who are faced with devastated postindustrial landscapes, neglect, crime and structural unemployment. Democratising political and social life, whether in the 'global South' or 'global North', requires clearer provisions over how citizens' control services and utilities, electricity costs, water supplies and schooling and affordable basic commodities (Williams 2006).

Economic change swallows lives and spits them out, to high mortality, poor health and poverty leaving them to be 'supported' (and frequently left to starve) by systems that are unable to ensure basic subsistence (Pogge 2008; Prontzos 2004). They look to the state, and can sometimes get a small pension or allowance, but as in Brazil, for example, the right to food remains far from realized, as does the right to land. In the case of Brazil the rapid increase in the minimum wage paid in the formal sector, over the past decade or so, has had the greatest impact on reducing poverty, rather than the social measures targeted particularly at the elderly, disabled and children. People will find it almost impossible to work themselves out of the dire poverty and marginality in which they find themselves unless they can shake off the parasitical strata that lived off the difference between their incomes and expenditures; in other words off their debts (Kent 2005, 151–55).[3]

---

3   Thanks to Brazilian PhD student, Larissa Barbosa da Costa, for providing this information, May 2009.

Promoting gender security and social justice

In the struggles to defend social and economic justice for workers, men or women, organization remains a key weapon. People may operate independently, unable to manage the resources that are required to build collective solutions to commonly faced problems. This is how privatization works; it fragments social movements, disorients NGOs by generously funding their activities and may divert gender justice movements from their collective and feminist goals into 'coping' mode, as services are cut. The deceptions of sponsorship, corporate social responsibility and environmental respect by oil conglomerates, continue to deprive social movements of some of their authenticity, turning them against themselves, with one part of many movements being attracted to more and more violent solutions. This is often the result of severe legal and politico–military persecution, of the more 'moderate' leaders of social movements of the dispossessed and downtrodden.

In many parts of the world, the rise of the informal sector in the 1980s accompanied the undermining of formal state structures under the impact of austerity packages, whether homegrown or IMF (International Monetary Fund) and World Bank imposed. As developmental and welfare states were cut back, people resorted – through necessity rather than choice – to informal economic activities and self–help social relations, and this included the middle classes, who started to face an insecure future. New movements emerged from an era of state cutbacks and acceleration of privatization policies. Such movements work in ways, nationally and globally that are only partly understood by social scientists.

Most contemporary social movements view neoliberalism and economic restructuring of the global economy as key threats to human security and well being across the planet (Olesen 2005). In various guises, deregulation, privatization and corporate control of the economy and of politics are blamed for war, chaos, unemployment, poverty and political crisis. Social movements have tended to respond to upheaval, disorder and changing social structures, transnationally, nationally and locally. Revolutionary movements are also social movements, which today operate across borders and differences, gathering up people's capacity for autonomous agency and giving this capacity direction. In seeking to change things for the better, social movements: 'relate not only mechanically' to external constraints, economic and security challenges, but 'also shape and create political opportunities through their actions' (Olesen 2005, 36).

As Arundhati Roy (2004, 53) reminds us, 'under the spreading canopy of the War against Terrorism, the men in suits are hard at work.' Social and women's movements need particularly strong organizational capacity during this period. Loose alliances, sometimes with the overarching support of NGOs, can provide needed organizational funding (such as for the World Social Forum, for meetings and websites). Social movements are almost always alongside NGOs: 'think of any of the grand issues of our time, of peace, environment, gender, development, or identity, and the depiction of some kind of social movement seems to follow automatically' (Walker 2005,140). This list includes land rights, employment and labour rights, equal access for boys and girls, decent housing, clean water, food and even free movement across borders.

Conclusion

Exercising social and political power has generally unpredictable outcomes, not reducible to competing or converging interests or identities. Instead of a block confronting the security state, new social movements are akin to a long wave, breaking and reforming at different points along a shore, at various angles, and over various surfaces. Each has their own sense of time, relational values and new technologies that produce new, complex and multilevel relations and forms of action. They are part of a wave in that they respond to and seek to replace globally generated processes of change. When people become more open to the experience of others elsewhere in the world, in comparable circumstances to their own, they may become willing and able to act collectively. Self interest is redefined to include engagement and cooperation with others across social movements, in order to secure much wider goals. Human security, thus conceived, goes well beyond usual understandings of liberal theory, rooted in the isolated individual self.

As Bauman (2005, 50) puts it: '…on a full planet, the messages of emancipation need to be legible to sailors sailing all of the planet's oceans and seas, to stand a chance of having a radical effect.' Since 'no life of dignity or gratifying human life are conceivable without an admixture of *both* freedom and security', and since: '…a fully satisfying balance between the two values is seldom achieved' (Bauman 2005, 35), the job of social movements is never likely to be done. Specific social movements may rise and fall but the need for social movements will remain latent, to be realized with the emergence of new informal associations when the time is ripe. In historical terms, the evidence of rights struggles suggests that no targets or charters achieved can ever bypass this necessity.

As narrow forms of state based security take centre–stage in global realities, people use whatever weapons they have left at their disposal – collective actions, legal or not, their own bodies, the networks they communicate with, social and organizational skills and creativity, and education and the media – in order to defend themselves against threats to their broadly defined human security and their dignity as citizens. Sometimes the wolf comes in sheep's clothing, as with a recent proposal to provide 'Legal Empowerment for the Poor'.[4] This recommended that the best way to resolve the poverty of 4 billion people was to ensure that they have legal title to property. Yet these same people have been pushed into marginality by just such a system; one based on recognition of legal title to property. The 'Legal Empowerment' proposals did include a nod in the direction of collective property rights, but it was just a nod. This kind of measure is very risky, and can deepen

---

4   See <http://www.undp.org/legalempowerment/>.

rather than resolve the economic crisis for the poorest and most vulnerable. It may make the poor more bankable, marketable and visible, but it may expose them to additional controls, surveillance and modes of discipline. Determined states can respond by tightening security unilaterally and by making it difficult for democratic alternatives to emerge within the formal or informal public arena. Legal title is little protection against arbitrary exercises of political and corporate power. Demands for peace, global justice, environmental protection, cultural identity, indigenous rights, land rights, free movement, gender equality and distributional justice will continue whatever is achieved by the MDG process. Precisely because processes of social transformation are inherently discordant, alive and ongoing, pressures from below will continue to shape changes in international, regional and national law. Global gender and social justice movements will remain closely connected. Globally, social movements are unlikely to disappear so long as human insecurity remains.

References

Adorno, T. (1974), *Minima Moralia: Reflections from Damaged Life* (London: New Left Books).

Albert, M. (2002), *The Trajectory of Change: Activist Strategies for Social Transformation* (Cambridge, MA: South End Press).

Alexander, T. (1996), *Unravelling Global Apartheid: An Overview of World Politics* (Cambridge: Polity Press).

Bauman, Z. (2004), *Wasted Lives: Modernity and its Outcasts* (Cambridge: Polity Press).

—— (2005), *Liquid Life* (Cambridge: Polity Press).

Bendana, A. (2006), *NGOs and Social Movements: A North/South Divide?* UNRISD Civil Society and Movements Programme, Paper No. 22, June.

Bond, P. (2001), *Against Global Apartheid: South Africa meets the World Bank, IMF and International Finance* (Landsdowne: University of Cape Town Press).

Castells, M. (2008), 'The Network Society: from Knowledge to Policy', in M. Castells and G. Cardoso (eds), *The Network Society: From Knowledge to Policy* (Washington: Centre for Transatlantic Relations, John Hopkins University), 3–22.

Chomsky, N. (2003), *Hegemony or Survival: America's Quest for Global Dominance* (New York: Metropolitan Books).

Dagnino, E. (2005), '"We all have rights, but…" Contesting concepts of citizenship in Brazil', in N. Kabeer (ed.), *Inclusive Citizenship: Meanings and Expressions* (London, New York: Zed Press), 149–63.

de Gaay Fortman, B. (2006), 'Poverty as a Failure of Entitlement: Do Rights–Based Approaches Make Sense?' in L. Williams (ed.), *International Poverty Law: An Emerging Discourse* (London, New York: Zed Books), 34–48.

Della Porta, D. and Tarrow, S.G. (2005), 'Transnational Processes and Social Activism: an Introduction', in D. Della Porta and S.G. Tarrow (eds), *Transnational Protest and Global Activism: People, Passions and Power* (Lanham MD: Rowman and Littlefield), 1–21.

Gallin, D. (2007), *The ILO Home Work Convention – Ten Years Later,* paper presented to *Women Work and Poverty: SEWA/UNIFEM Policy Conference on Home Based Workers of South Asia,* 18–20 January, New Delhi, <http://www.wiego.org/program_areas/org_rep/Gallin_homework_speech.pdf>, accessed 2 May 2009.

George, S. (2004), *Another World is Possible If...* (London, New York: Verso Books).

Golay, C. (2008), *The Global Food Crisis and the Right to Food,* CETIM (Europe–Third World Centre), Critical Report No. 3, December, <http://cetim.ch/en/publications_cahiers.php>, accessed 2 May 2009.

Goodwin, J., Jasper, J. and Polletta, F. (2000), 'The Return of the Repressed: The Fall And Rise of Emotions in Social Movement Theory', *Mobilization: An International Quarterly* 5:1, 65–83.

Gready, P. (ed.) (2004), *Fighting for Human Rights* (London, New York: Routledge).

Gready, P. and Ensor, J. (eds) (2005), *Reinventing Development? Translating Rights–Based Approaches from Theory into Practice* (London, New York: Zed Books).

Hintjens, H. (2006) 'Appreciating the Movement of the Movements', *Development in Practice* 16: 6, 628–43.

—— (2008), 'UNIFEM, CEDAW and the Human Rights–Based Approach', *Development and Change* 39: 6,1181–92.

——(2009), 'Social Movements', in *Globalisation and Security: An Encyclopaedia* (Preager Press).

Hirschman, A.O. (1983), 'The Principle of the Conservation and Mutation of Social Energy', *Grassroots Development* (Journal of Inter–American Foundation), 7:2, 5–13.

ILO (1996), C177 Home Work Convention, 1996, available at <http://www.ilo.org/ilolex/cgi-lex/convde.pl?C177>.

Jhabvala, R. and Kanbur, R. (2002), *Globalization and Economic Reform as Seen From the Ground* (SEWA), available at <www.wiego.org/.../global_markets/Jhabvala%20Kanbur%20Globalization%20as%20see%20from%20the%20ground.pdf>.

Joubert, P. (2008), 'Grootboom Dies Homeless and Penniless', *Mail and Guardian online* 8 August 2008, <http://www.mg.co.za/article/2008-08-08-grootboom-dies-homeless-and-penniless>, accessed 31 May 2009.

Kent, G. (2005), *Freedom from Want: the Human Right to Adequate Food* (Washington: Georgetown University Press).

McDonald, K. (2006), *Global Movements: Action and Culture* (Malden, Oxford: Blackwell).

Nederveen Pieterse, J. (2004), *Globalization or Empire?* (New York, London: Routledge).

Olesen, T. (2005), *International Zapatismo: The Construction of Solidarity in the Age of Globalization* (London, New York: Zed Books).

Pogge, T. (2008), *World Poverty and Human Rights: Cosmopolitan Responsibilities and Reforms*, 2nd Edition (Cambridge, Malden: Polity).

Prontzos, P. (2004), 'Collateral Damage: The Human Cost of Structural Violence', in A. Jones (ed.), *Genocide, War Crimes and the West: History and Complicity* (London, New York: Zed Books), 299–324.

Richmond, A. (1994), *Global Apartheid: Refugees, Racism and the New World Order* (Oxford, Toronto, New York: Oxford University Press).

Roberts, D. (2008), *Human Insecurity: Global Structures of Violence* (London, New York: Zed Books).

Rose, K. (1992), *Where Women are Leaders: The SEWA Movement in India* (New Delhi, London: Vistaar, Zed Press).

Roy, A. (2004), 'Confronting Empire', in J. Sen, A. Anand, A. Escobar and P. Waterman (eds), *World Social Forum: Challenging Empires* (New Delhi: Viveka Foundation).

Ryan, W. (1971), *Blaming the Victim* (New York: Pantheon Books).

Sen, G. (2005), *Neo–Libs, Neo–Cons and Gender Justice: Lessons from Global Negotiations*, UNRISD Occasional Paper, No. 9, September.

SEWA website, available at <http://www.sewa.org/>.

Stendile, J.P. (2002), 'Landless Battalions: the Sem Terra Movement of Brazil', *New Left Review* (Movements – 7), New Series, 15: May–June, 77–85.

Touraine, A. (2005), 'The Subject Is Coming Back', *International Journal of Politics, Culture and Society* 18, 199–209.

UNIFEM (2007), *CEDAW and the Human Rights–based Approach to Programming* (New York: UNIFEM), available at <http://www.unifem.org/resources/item_detail.php?ProductID=94>.

UNIFEM–Plan (2007), *UNIFEM Strategic Plan for 2008–2011* (New York: UNIFEM), available at: <http://www.unifem.org/attachments/products/UNIFEM_SP_2008–2011_eng.pdf>.

Wainwright, H. (2003), *Reclaim the State: Experiments in Popular Democracy* (London, New York: Verso).

Walker, R.B.J. (2005), 'Social Movements/World Politics', in L. Amoore (ed.), *The Global Resistance Reader* (Oxford, New York: Routledge), 136–49.

Williams, L. (ed.) (2006), *International Poverty Law: An Emerging Discourse* (London, New York: Zed Books).

Ziegler, J. (2008) *Promotion and Protection of All Human Rights, Civil, Political, Economic, Social and Cultural Rights, including the Right to Development. Report of the Special Rapporteur on the Right to Food,* United Nations General Assembly, General Report No. A/HRC/7/5, 10 January, available at: <http://www.righttofood.org/new/PDF/CHR2008.pdf>.

Zikode, S. (2006), 'The Third Force', *Journal of Asian and African Studies* 41:1–2, 185–9.

PART III
Localizing Development
In An Insecure World

Chapter 6
Costly Development?
Gendered Insecurity in a Militarized Pacific

Ronni Alexander

I am one of the victims of army abuse. A military policeman named Robin Monai raped me. He buggered me and raped me wearing a coffee mug handle on his penis… This caused me internal damage. This man is still here on Buka and nothing has been done to correct this injustice. This is a man who used to cut the ears off and then kill our men. He is still here. Nothing has been done; there is no justice. There are many women's organizations, but they are of no help. They have funding but I do not know what they do with this money. They do not fight for our women's rights and they do not help us, the victims. Today we must try to forgive and forget (Miriori 2004, 65).

As in many former colonies, the euphoria that followed independence in the island countries of the Pacific has faded, or perhaps morphed, into a militarized postcolonial mish–mash characterized by rhetoric of development and human rights, in stark contrast to the realities of everyday life. Despite their reputation as 'paradise,' colonization and militarization have made the Pacific Island Countries and Territories (PICTs) a part of the complex culture of violence that envelops our world. States and militias, hidden behind the cloak of national security or liberation struggle, legitimize much of that violence; most of the remainder is a by–product of the militarization of everyday life. Women and women's bodies are used to legitimize violence and militarization, even as states, development agencies and local leaders proclaim the need for special measures such as the Millennium Development Goals (MDGs) to address the needs of women and children.

This chapter interrogates the intersection of militarization, gender(ed) violence and resistance within gendered and militarized spaces in the Pacific Islands. It explores how current cultural governance which emphasizes 'gender' (in this case generally meaning women) both creates spaces for resistance to violence and recreates the militarized culture of violence in the region.

Gender(ed) violence is both pervasive and elusive; I recognize its existence in some forms and spaces, but not in others. I suggest that to eliminate gendered violence, we must also address the intricate web of violence created by militarism and militarization, much of which is promoted through neoliberal strategies for development that glorify consumption while also destroying traditional livelihoods. Resistance results in both internal and external militarization, increasingly legitimized by invoking the 'threat of terrorism'.

To address these questions, this chapter first looks at the concepts of cultural governance, militarism/militarization and gender(ed) violence in the context of the Pacific Islands region. It then introduces three brief case studies to offer diverse illustrations of how these concepts intersect. The first illustration offers a regional perspective for addressing women's issues and violence, including the implementation of the United Nations Security Council Resolution 1325. The second addresses an armed conflict – the Bougainville crisis – focusing on the role played by women in peace making. While this conflict occurred before the adoption of Resolution 1325, it is typical of the kind of conflict that that resolution hopes to address. The third case study examines a problem beyond the realm of Resolution 1325 – the situation of the removal of US troops to Guam from US bases on Okinawa. It suggests that to be transformative, resistance must address not only gender and gender(ed) violence, but also militarism/militarization and demilitarization.

Colonization and militarization in the Pacific Islands region

The Pacific Ocean covers approximately one–third of the globe and many of its island countries encompass more water than land. With the exception of Tonga, the Pacific Islands dotting the ocean surface were all colonized, and most achieved independence in the 1970s. While island products and mineral resources were coveted by outside powers, from the perspective of the colonizers, the value of the Pacific Islands lay not so much in the exploitation of the land resources so much as in the access they provided to ocean spaces and resources. The strategic importance of marine and deep–sea spaces to the extra–regional powers remains significant today, even after decolonization.

The colonization and militarization of Pacific spaces has not been limited to physical spaces, but has created militarized cultures, identities and bodies. Military coercion has become embodied through the intergenerational effects of nuclear and toxic contamination on Pacific peoples, their forced migration or relocation due to the contamination of their living spaces, and the Amerasian[1] and other children of mixed background living near military bases. It is visible

---

1 According to the instructions for filling out US Citizenship and Immigration Service Form I–360 (Petition for Amerasian, Widow(er), or Special Immigrant), an Amerasian is 'Any person who…was born in Korea, Vietnam, Laos, Kampuchea, or Thailand after 31 December 1950, and before 22 October 1982, and was fathered by a US citizen' (US Public Law 97359;1982) <http://www.uscis.gov/files/form/i-360instr.pdf >, accessed 4 January 2008. The Amerasian Foundation defines an Amerasian as, 'any person who was fathered by a citizen of the United States (an American servicemen, American expatriate, or US Government Employee (Regular or Contract)) and whose mother is, or was, an Asian National Asian' <http://amerasianfoundation.org/?page_id=15>, accessed 10 January 2008.

as well in the Pacific Islanders serving overseas in Peace Keeping Forces, those working for private security companies in Iraq, and the families those soldiers are supporting both through wages and sometimes through death.[2] It is also visible in the ways women's bodies and gender roles have been shaped by Western values and development strategies.

The militarized Pacific is also visible in the increase in intra–regional and internal conflicts since the end of the Cold War. Militarization has exacerbated the difficulty of post–independence negotiations, resulting in, for example, several coups in Fiji, armed conflicts in the Solomon Islands, Papua New Guinea, Timor Leste and West Papua. While Tonga was never colonized, it has been the site of political violence in recent years in response to demands for democratization, and blood has been shed in the struggle for decolonization in New Caledonia, although that country has yet to achieve independence. As Asian countries such as the Philippines and Japan attempt to reassert their sovereignty and oust US bases, the relative importance of military facilities on US Pacific territories grows. An example that will be considered here is the current US plan to relocate roughly 8,000 marines and their families from Okinawa (Marine Corps Air Station Futenma) to Guam.

Cultural governance and the management of identity

Colonized spaces are controlled not only through military coercion and economic regulation but also through the creation and management of identity. Colonization creates new and often artificial borders, while after independence, postcolonial states take over the attempt to align territorial and cultural boundaries. The creation and maintenance of gendered identities plays an important role in this cultural governance, which often seeks legitimacy in militarism and capitalist modernity. Resistance comes from many places, some of which may reinforce the objectives of the state while simultaneously working to eliminate or stop violence, and create peace.

Cultural governance creates and destroys both personal and collective identities. Colonization created 'the Pacific,' an entity composed of islands in a far sea but the Pacific is also a sea of islands, a holistic totality of oceans and islands (Hau'ofa 1993, 7). In the binary world view of the West, the Pacific Islands

---

2   In 2005 an estimated 1,000 Fijians were working as private security contractors in Iraq and another 2,000 former Fijian soldiers were working for the British army. See for example Inter Press Service News Agency, 'Fijian Deaths in Iraq Revive Mercenaries' Issue,' <http://ipsnews.net/print.asp?idnews=33580>, accessed 27 December 2007. By December 2006, 13 Fijians had been killed. The number of military personnel from American Samoa killed in Iraq on a per capita basis is almost 13.5 times the US national average. News: US Department of the Interior, <http://www.doi.gov/news/06_News_Releases/060706.htm>, accessed 16 November 2006.

were neither Orient nor Occident; even today they are neither East nor West, but 'other.' The mission of 'civilizing' the 'savage' Islander was a powerful tool in the colonization process (for example, Callahan 2006; Hau'ofa 1993). Unlike the Caribbean, where indigenous Island cultures were exterminated, indigenous Pacific Islanders have remained, although the experience of colonization brought many changes to the nature of that 'indigeneity'. In those islands that remain under foreign rule, indigenous people are marginalized, their rights and sometimes their very existence denied by majority populations and colonial governments. Examples include the Native Hawaiians in Hawaii, the Chamorus in Guam and Kanaks in New Caledonia.

Beginning with the independence of Samoa in 1962, most of the Pacific Islands have now moved to independent or self–governing status. Despite this, the extra–regional powers have continued to view the Pacific Islands as strategic spaces and to use them for military purposes. The US Navy from 1899 to 1950, for example, governed Guam, and World War II brought intense fighting and the establishment of military bases and facilities to many Pacific Islands. An extreme example of the militarization of the post–World War II Pacific was its use by the US (in Micronesia), Britain (in Australia) and France (in French Polynesia) to test nuclear weapons. The end of US testing in 1963 did not end militarization, but did allow for the negotiation of new political status for the Micronesian countries. In contrast, French nuclear colonialism and testing continued until 1995, and French Polynesia, New Caledonia and Wallis and Futuna remain as French territories even today.

Military bases are one place where the priorities of cultural governance, militarization and militarized spaces are visible. Bases bring military activities and create military economies, but military and militarized cultures remain, even after the bases are gone. Violence, particularly gender violence, is one example. Often resistance to this violence seeks to be transformational, aiming at alternative cultural production, but much of it actually serves to promote hegemonic militarism and militarization.

Militarization as a tool for cultural governance

When societies and institutions commit themselves and their resources to the waging of war they are engaging in militarism (Reardon 1985). Militarism is most visible in militarization, a mechanism which privileges military concerns, giving 'value' to aspects of ordinary life normally not directly related to the military, such as fashion design, and making people accepting of military values and solutions without their necessarily being aware of what is happening. Often militarization and development go hand in hand, as in the privileging of military and police forces for reasons of security or to quell internal resistance to development projects.

Militarization is a powerful tool of cultural governance and uses gender to further its goals. The archetype of women as mothers, wives and caregivers commits women to bearing and raising sons to send off to war to fight for their nation. When care giving institutions are militarized, the people who work there (largely women) are serving military aims, even if they do not consciously support these. Similarly, when development agencies target women as 'vulnerable' and in need of 'protection,' they are legitimizing the use of violence for that purpose. Moreover, through the engendering of some women as 'good' and others 'bad,' cultural governance and militarization work together to legitimize some forms of gender violence but not necessarily others. For example, the construction of masculinity in the military is a major factor in prostitution and the gendered violence, which surrounds military bases, but the military often disregards or fails to give importance to that violence. In the words of Cynthia Enloe,

> Feminists from India, Zimbabwe, and Japan to Britain, the United States, Serbia, Chile, South Korea, Palestine, Israel, and Algeria all have found that when they have followed the bread crumbs of privileged masculinity, they have been led time and again not just to the doorstep of the military, but to the threshold of all those social institutions that promote militarization (Enloe 2000, 33).

Laura Kaplan (1994, 124) explains the relationship between privileged masculinity and militarization as 'patriarchal militarism,' which encourages men to create images of women as 'devalued others' and then use those images as a 'model for training and inspiring masculine warriors to devalue and distance themselves from enemies.'[3] Patriarchal militarism uses dual images of male and female, often moulding traditional gender roles to fit into the larger system of modern warfare.

Conflict and gender violence

In the Pacific as elsewhere, militarization and militarized mentalities do not necessarily take the form of direct violence. Often they constitute a form of structural violence, which is inherently gendered and but under certain circumstances results in direct violence. This often takes the form of gender violence, usually directed against women by men. Gender violence is 'a systematic, institutionalized and/or programmatic violence (sexual, physical, psychological) that operates through the constructs of gender and often at the intersection of sexuality, race and national identity' (Nayak and Suchland 2006, 469).

In the Pacific, conflict and gender violence are partially a legacy of colonial rule, which institutionalized male privilege through systems for control over social

---

3   Kaplan (1994, 124) lists two additional features of patriarchal militarism: (1) Since war is seen by many to be a creative masculine act, the commitment of social resources to war is a male project and (2) the public is convinced that militarism is necessary for safety because those who are different must be dominated for the good of both themselves and the dominators.

and economic resources such as land and social position, as well as recreating and reinforcing gendered roles. In addition to patriarchal militarism, colonization and cultural governance also created ethnic tensions as different ethnic and tribal groups were brought together, often in ways that suited the colonizers rather than the colonized and later the needs of local elites. In the postcolonial Pacific, these trends continue under the rhetoric of development. The privileging of gender, race and class has generally ensured certain men a secure spot on top and relegated indigenous women to the bottom.

Pacific women identify the following as the major causes of conflict in the region:

> ...increasingly unequal access to land, paid employment and economic resources, particularly when inequality is based on ethnicity; centralization of resources and services; lack of involvement in decision–making and authority; a weakening of traditional methods of dispute resolution; and the growth of a 'Rambo' culture of violence and guns among young unemployed men (Thomas 2005a, 157).

These causes occur against a background of changing demographics including migration and urbanization and a growing gap between a small wealthy minority that has profited from 'development' and an increasing number of impoverished people. Thomas identifies a lack of information about political processes as exacerbating the situation and draws links between the influence of media violence, domestic violence, a growing culture of violence and national conflict (Thomas 2005b, 3–4).

Particularly in recent years, the international development and security communities have attempted to address some of these issues of gender violence. Evidence of this is the adoption of Resolution 1325 by the UN Security Council in 2000. This resolution encourages member states to 'ensure increased representation of women at all decision making levels in national, regional and international institutions and mechanisms for the prevention, management, and resolution of conflict,' and calls on all involved actors, 'when negotiating and implementing peace agreements, to adopt a gender perspective' (UNSC 2000). The adoption of UNSC Resolution 1325 led to an increase in cooperation among governments, international governmental organizations (IGOs) and Non Governmental Organizations (NGOs) at transnational as well as local levels. This should have had enormous implications for organizations working with women in conflict situations. Although we hear more about the ways conflicts are affecting women, there is still a long way to go before those situations are rectified in the Pacific Islands region as elsewhere.

One reason for the seeming inability of transnational networks to end gender violence may be that the liberal gender perspective and the associated focus on women adopted by most agencies working in international development and human security seek to find solutions in increasing the number of women involved rather than changing structures, which adversely affect women. The terms gender and women are often conflated. Liberal feminism recognizes that women are absent from public view, but places responsibility for this on individuals rather than on gendered institutions. As a result, the reason for lack of access becomes one of individual prejudice. Connell (1990, 513) points out; liberal feminism '...has not been able to grasp the character of gender as an institutional and motivational system, nor to develop a coherent analysis of the state apparatus or its links to a social context.' Increasing the number of women can be effective for increasing access, but in failing to address gendered systems such as patriarchy which institutionalize gender hierarchies, it proves to be ineffective at addressing power imbalances, gendered and otherwise. States, through laws and administrative practices, create and reproduce gender relations. The state, using coercive and other methods, sets the limits for the use of personal violence but also '...protects property (and thus unequal economic resources), criminalizes stigmatized sexuality, embodies masculinized hierarchy, and organizes collective violence in policing, prisons, and war' (Connell 1990, 520).

Changing the ways that states produce and reproduce violence requires more than increasing the numbers of women involved. Concomitant changes must be made in the ways states negotiate gender and violence. This involves addressing gender hierarchies and patriarchy itself, looking at the ways in which women's 'free choices' are coerced by social norms and standards of behaviour. This does not imply that measures such as affirmative action or gender mainstreaming are meaningless; they are very important and can be effective. Simultaneously, an increase in the numbers of women does not necessarily change patriarchal structures or address the problem of marginalization of some women, because only the women who have successfully negotiated the existing system can become a part of it. Such measures can also reinforce the reproduction of patriarchal and traditional gender and power roles and the accompanied violence. Militaries engage in the production and reproduction of feminized others (for example, 'savage' and irrational men, uneducated women) on personal, social, and national levels. This othering creates hierarchies of authorized sexuality and behaviour that may both encourage soldiers to be 'men' and be critical of sexual violence. One result is that regardless of gender education and mainstreaming, much of the sexual violence in the military goes unreported and unpunished. The challenge is to find ways to challenge this process of othering so that women do not merely go from being othered to othering, but help to increase acknowledgement of diversity.

Case Studies: Working for peace and opposing violence in the Pacific

As discussed, militarization is a feature within the Pacific Islands. The presence of US military bases in Japan, Guam and Hawaii, linked with alliance partners in Australia and New Zealand encompass the region in a military circle. The primary focus of that circle of military installations has been outward toward Asia rather than inward toward the Pacific but in recent years the region has been the site of several armed conflicts (such as Papua New Guinea, Bougainville, Solomon Islands, Timor–Leste, West Papua) and political violence (including for example Fiji and Tonga). Women have been seriously affected by the militarization of the region, not only where direct conflicts have occurred but also in places where militarization is most visible, such as foreign military bases.

Measures such as Resolution 1325 have provided an impetus for work at the regional and national levels to deal with gendered violence, but so far the results have been limited. Here I examine the structures for dealing with gendered violence in the PICTs and then consider two contrasting examples of militarization, both of which include gendered violence: the Bougainville crisis and the relocation of US marines from Okinawa to Guam.

At first glance, there may be little to connect the three cases offered here. According to the norms purveyed by cultural governance, Japan (but not necessarily Okinawa) is outside the 'Pacific Islands Region' (but part of the Pacific). The political status of Guam is that of an unincorporated territory of the United States, locating it like Japan, outside the purview of regional organizations in the Pacific Islands Region.[4] The Bougainville crisis was a prolonged internal conflict which ended before UNSC Resolution 1325 was enacted; US military bases in Japan are not generally regarded as being within the intended realm of that resolution in the first place. This dissonance allows us to recognize how cultural governance imposes boundaries and how resistance can work to change them. It is hoped that these examples will help to promote discussion of the relationship between gendered violence and militarization and illustrate the ways in which these are influenced by cultural governance.

Addressing gendered violence at the regional level

In the Pacific region, the organization responsible for coordinating gender mainstreaming and equality at the regional level in the Pacific is the Pacific Women's Bureau (PWB).[5] Established in 1982, the PWB is the sole regional organization

---

4   Japan is an observer in the Pacific Islands Forum and other regional organizations and some regional bodies include non–independent entities such as Guam, American Samoa, New Caledonia and French Polynesia.

5   PWB is part of the Secretariat of the Pacific Community (SPC). Japan is not a member. Membership includes 22 Pacific Island countries and territories: American Samoa, Cook Islands, Federated States of Micronesia, Fiji Islands, French Polynesia, Guam, Kiribati, Marshall Islands, Nauru, New Caledonia, Niue, Northern Mariana Islands, Palau, Papua New Guinea, Pitcairn Islands, Samoa, Solomon Islands, Tokelau, Tonga, Tuvalu, Vanuatu, Wallis and Futuna. In addition, the 26 members of the Pacific Community include the four remaining founding countries: Australia, France, New Zealand, and the US. The United Kingdom withdrew at the beginning of 1996 from SPC, rejoined in 1998 and withdrew again in January 2005. <http://www.spc.int/corp/index.php?option=com_content&task=view&id=17&Itemid=46>, accessed 10 January 2008.

recognized by governmental and non governmental women's organizations as advocating gender awareness, gender mainstreaming and women's needs in the region. PWB belongs to the Social Resources Division of the Secretariat of the Pacific Community (SPC; former South Pacific Commission) and has as its goal to foster 'empowered Pacific Island women and young people and strong cultural identities'. It endeavours to improve the status of Pacific women through the monitoring of the implementation of the Pacific Platform for Action on the Advancement of Women and Gender Equality (PPA)[6] and the MDGs. The PPA has been used in conjunction with the Beijing Platform for Action to promote national and regional initiatives for empowering women in political, legal, social and cultural spheres. The Convention on the Elimination of all Forms of Discrimination Against Women (CEDAW) and the MDGs have provided a standard by which the progress of these endeavours is measured. This creates a political space for the promotion of women while simultaneously subjects all women to the gender mainstreaming lens invoked by the international development and human security community.

Although PICTs have established institutions for women at the national level and thirteen countries have ratified CEDAW, resources for these institutions are scarce. Few Pacific Islands countries mainstream gender, and compliance with CEDAW is minimal in some countries. The levels of women's participation in political and public decision making is generally low, and reduced budgets due to regional and local conflicts, structural reforms and financial crises have served to further marginalize women and women's issues. Women are under–represented in business, particularly in senior management positions, including the media and only a few countries have specific measures to foster women's economic participation. Despite many PICTs having achieved universal primary education, as a group, women, particularly rural women, are less well educated than men. Moreover, an Asian Development Bank survey shows that poverty is increasing overall in the region, particularly in women–headed households. The exploitation of women migrant workers and the impact of trade liberalization policies are further areas of concern. With regard to gender violence, violence against women and domestic violence are prevalent, as are teenage pregnancies, school dropouts and broken families. These trends are linked to alcohol and substance abuse, which remains common (Pacific Women's Bureau 2005, 2–3).

The PWB works in close collaboration with UN agencies in the region such as the United Nations Development Fund for Women (UNIFEM), other international organizations and in particular with the member organizations of the Council

---

6   The PPA was the result of wide regional and sub–regional consultations and was approved at the 6th Regional Conference of Pacific Women and the Ministerial Conference on Women and Sustainable Development, both held in Noumea in 1994. It was revised in 2004. This plan formed the basis for the Pacific region's contribution at the 1995 World Conference for Women in Beijing and the current PPA incorporates the Beijing +5 outcomes and commitments under CEDAW (Pacific Women's Bureau 2004).

of Regional Organizations in the Pacific (CROP).[7] It also works with national Women, Peace and Security (WPS) Coordinating Committees,[8] which tend to include government and women's NGOs, as well as other NGOs in the region concerned with security issues.

With regard to peace and security, a regional workshop was convened in 2006 on Gender, Conflict, Peace and Security under the auspices of the Pacific Islands Forum Secretariat with the support of AusAID (The Australian Government's Overseas Aid Programme), UNDP (United Nations Development Programme), UNIFEM, International Women's Development Agency and FemLink Pacific, and a follow–up meeting was held in April of 2007. The results of these consultations have been presented to the Pacific Islands Forum Secretariat in the context of human security.

The regional structure for handling security issues is based on the 2000 Pacific Islands Forum, Biketawa Declaration,[9] which mandates response to security issues at the regional level and reiterates the rule of law, individual freedoms, equal rights regardless of gender, race, colour, creed or political belief, and the right to participation in political processes. In 2005 the Pacific Plan adopted a broad definition of security that listed human security as one of four priority goals for the region and included gender equality as a cross–cutting strategic objective. The implementation of UNSC Resolution 1325 in all countries, including those that have not experienced recent violent conflict was considered useful as it provides a framework to ensure 'due consideration to gender dimensions of peace and stability, particularly with regard to the pervasive nature of violence against women, boys and girls in these countries' (see Pacific Islands Forum Secretariat 2006, 1).

---

7   These include the Pacific Islands Forum Secretariat, Forum Fisheries Agency, Pacific Islands Development Programme, Secretariat of the Pacific Community, South Pacific Applied Geoscience Commission, South Pacific Regional Environmental Programme, South Pacific Tourism Organization, South Pacific Board for Educational Assessment, University of the South Pacific, Fiji School of Medicine, START (Global Change System for Analysis, Research and Training) – Oceania Secretariat, PACSED (Pacific Centre for Environment and Sustainable Development).

8   These committees are affiliated with the UN WPS Coordinating Committee, established in 2005 to further implement UNSC Resolution 1325.

9   The Biketawa Declaration was signed in Biketawa, Kiribati in 2000. It is a security framework building on a number of other frameworks dating back to the Honiara Declaration of 1994. It has several key features that make it unique to the region. 'These include its commitment to upholding democratic processes and good governance, its recognition of indigenous rights and cultural values and the process for addressing crises in the region.' The Biketawa Declaration has been invoked twice since its promulgation in 2000, with the Regional Assistance Mission to Solomon Islands (RAMSI) and the Pacific Regional Assistance for Nauru (PRAN). Three successful election observer missions in the region – Bougainville, Solomon Islands and Fiji – have also been undertaken under this framework. < http://www.forumsec.org/_resources/article/files/Biketawa%20Declaration. pdf>, accessed 11 January 2008.

Civil society organizations in the Pacific are numerous and some are very active. A regional umbrella organization, Pacific Island Association of NGOs (PIANGO) has coordinating committees in most PICTs. Church affiliated groups are also prevalent. With regard to women's organizations, most PICTs have a National Council of Women or the equivalent, as well as a variety of primarily development–oriented organizations. Among the better known women's organizations working in the area of peace, security and violence against women are the Fiji Women's Crisis Centre, Fiji Women's Rights Movement, Bougainville Women for Peace and Freedom, and Leitana Nehan Women's Development Agency (Bougainville). Neither Guam nor Okinawa is involved in these organizations. Regional networking most often, although not exclusively, occurs within either the southern or northern Pacific region, and then along the lines of the colonizing power. Hence, Guam tends to be more involved in US–related, northern Pacific groups, while Bougainville and Papua New Guinea are in the southern Pacific.

In the Pacific, both women and men have worked to oppose violence and create peace. Women, often at great risk to themselves, have engaged in vigils and peace marches, lobbied political leaders, talked with soldiers and armed fighters, networked to provide information, shelter, food and other assistance and worked to restore their communities once the direct violence has ceased. Despite this, work for peace by women, like much of the other work performed by women, becomes virtually invisible as little consideration is given in peace and post conflict policy–making to '…the role that Pacific Island women have played, and continue to play, in establishing communication channels between warring parties, in restoring and maintaining peace, in rebuilding communities and in working to overcome the physical and psychological trauma of conflict' (Thomas 2005a, 155).

Women are also excluded or unacknowledged at the policy–making level on issues of security. For example, fewer women are actually engaged in fighting and are thus thought to have less legitimacy than men; it is assumed that what men want is also what women want; negotiation teams generally come from diplomatic and military circles where there are few women; women are often excluded from public life by custom or tradition; women's actions are not considered political nor is outright political action considered appropriate for women; logistical and security issues exclude women; and participation is limited by the inability of women to access resources or because of their caring commitments (Onubogu and Etchart 2005, 39). These factors serve to encourage women who want to be involved in resistance to do so in women's groups, but also make them subject to the limitations of gendered cultural governance which not only defines the ways in which women and men are expected to behave, but also whether, and in what ways the intersection of women, militarism and militarization and demilitarization will be addressed. Ironically, both the involvement of women in the work for peace and their invisibility occur for Pacific women because of the ways cultural governance constructs women; gender roles as peace makers and gendered power relations have given women a space from which to resist and a methodology for doing so within a patriarchal social discourse. Women have played important roles, yet their work often goes unacknowledged because it occurs within the parameters of and is made invisible by patriarchal militarism.

The Bougainville crisis

> One thing the army did was to make men strip and commit anal sex with each other at gunpoint. People were afraid of the gun and would do these things to avoid being shot (Miriori 2004, 64).

> Violence is glamorous masculinity in Melanesia (Macintyre 2000, 35).

Bougainville Island, together with neighbouring Buka Island and several small atolls, forms one of the nineteen provinces of Papua New Guinea. When Papua New Guinea attained independence in 1975, Bougainville likewise declared independence, but it lasted only one day. While Bougainville is geographically and ethnically closer to the Solomon Islands than to Papua New Guinea, the presence of the Panguna mine in central Bougainville ensured that independence would come at a high price, if at all. The mine, at the time of its opening in 1972, was the largest open–pit mine in the world and during the 1970s and 1980s, it was Papua New Guinea's main source of foreign exchange, serving as the backbone of the Papua New Guinea economy.

In 1989, a former mine employee Francis Ona, on behalf of all Bougainvilleans affected by the copper mine on their ancestral lands, formed the 'New Panguna Landowners Association' and demanded the company pay up 10 billion kina (AU$14.7 billion (1989 value)) in compensation for the impact of the mine (Garasu 2002). When his demands were not met, a campaign was launched to sabotage Bougainville Copper Limited and ultimately the national government. In June 1989, the Papua New Guinea government declared a state of emergency in Bougainville and the Papua New Guinea Defence Forces (PNGDF) were sent to quell the violence. A blockade, enforced with patrol boats donated by Australia, halted almost all air and sea transport, including emergency medical and food supplies. Ona declared independence for Bougainville on 17 May 1990, and a free–for–all of violence began. Local resistance forces armed and supplied by the PNGDF sprang up in communities, adding a new party to the conflict. Thousands fled into the bush in an effort to avoid the violence. The Bougainville crisis lasted for ten years. It was the longest and bloodiest clash in the Pacific since the end of World War II, and by its conclusion, more than 15,000 people had lost their lives, most of them civilians (Volker and Garasu 2004, 568).[10]

The war had an impact on all women and men on Bougainville, both in terms of their everyday lives and in terms of their communities. Bougainvilleans

---

10   Issue 12 of *Accord*, edited by Carl and Garasu (2002) provides much of the background information on the Bougainville conflict.

traditionally live by gardening, hunting and fishing and society is built around land, of which the women are the traditional custodians. In particular, it is the woman's line that determines inheritance and use of land. Women are therefore powerful, although they seldom raise their voices directly in the public arena but instead speak through male relatives. Due to their strong connection with the land, women are often referred to as 'Mothers of the land,' a term that has been used frequently in describing the role played by women during and after the conflict.

The development of the mine disrupted the social fabric not only through the presence of ethnically and culturally different workers but also through destruction of the land itself and forced relocation. Moreover, the Papua New Guinea constitution only provides for compensation for the surface of the land, giving complete ownership of everything else to the Papua New Guinea government. Compensation for use by the mine was made only once (if at all); there was no renegotiation.

> 'I can't pass the land on now because most of it has been covered up by the mine,' Patricia Dave said in 1988 as she stood among her grandchildren. 'The traditional system will never work again. The company has only paid the parents for this. What Ona is fighting for is that everybody, right down to the last born, should get compensation because our traditions have been broken and we will not be able to pass anything down to them.' It was this loss – the loss of land not to just one generation but to all the generations to come and all those that had been, that the miners did not seem to comprehend (O'Callaghan 2002, 8).

Women in government controlled areas had limited access to food, medicine and other necessities and could not go daily to their gardens due to restrictions and fear of violence. The breakdown of services affected women's reproductive health due to shortages of human and material resources including medicine. Interruption of the supply of sanitary protection made it difficult for women to leave their homes during menstruation.

Militarization and the presence of weapons brought rampant sexual violence to Bougainville. In the absence of traditional or modern cultural restraints, murder, rape and robbery in the name of the 'war' became everyday occurrences. Rather than being in the hands of chiefs, power was in the hands of young men because they had guns. Women were raped and tortured, often in front of their husbands and children (Hakena 2005, 162). Women in care centres were subject to sexual abuse by PNGDF and Bougainville Resistance Force soldiers, and were frequently required to pay for necessities with sexual acts. These problems were compounded for women in the Bougainville Revolutionary Army (BRA) controlled areas, as they not only suffered from sexual violence and harassment from the government and Resistance Forces, but from the BRA as well (Garasu 2002).

The breakdown of traditional social rules and conventions made childrearing difficult; many mothers complained that their children were growing up without any socialization and were running wild.

> Men, women and children as young as nine mix fruit juices with yeast and sugar, ferment it, and a few days later, drown their sorrows…Children who have seen close relatives die make their own home–brew because they have learnt from their mothers. Absenteeism from school is high and exam results are poor. Prior to the crisis the people were well–educated and went to university. Now, 80% of children don't go to school…Children who were eight or nine when the crisis started are in their late teens now. They have joined the fighting and they don't even know why they are fighting (Hakena cited in McCutchan 1997, 1).

Women in the BRA controlled areas had to endure attacks by the PNGDF and the Resistance, while the blockade prevented access to basic necessities and medical care. Those who fled into the bush had to plant new gardens and build shelters to live in, forcing people to put their skills and creativity to work. For example, they figured out how to make 'blockade soap' from cocoa pods, run their cars and trucks on coconut oil and store the hydroelectric power they generated from mountain streams in used car batteries. Women supporters of the BRA became 'mamas' for the men when they came to the villages, and in exchange for feeding and caring for them, the men brought smuggled supplies or smuggled sick children out to the Solomon Islands for treatment (Havini 2004, 70).

In terms of community and women's organizing, before the conflict, there were two women's organizations on Bougainville. During the 1960s, the Churches' Women's Organization held programmes for self–reliance in the villages, and the Northern Solomons Provincial Council of Women was active in the 1970s and 1980s. The latter was trying to form a network of women's organizations when the conflict began, putting an end to their efforts (Garasu 2002).

The 'divide and conquer' strategy of the PNGDF and Resistance Forces made networking difficult, and peace groups had to begin work within their own communities in isolation from one another. Women formed church and other groups to provide aid and assistance to one another and their children. Sometimes women used their traditional role as 'peacemakers' to go into the bush and bring their sons back from fighting; high status women served as intermediaries to help negotiate peace, sometimes going into the jungle to negotiate with the BRA. Using prayer meetings, reconciliation marches, peace marches, petitions and international support through contacts in Australia and New Zealand, women were able to influence the peace negotiations. For example, peace marches led by women in 1993 and 1994 instigated peace negotiations and in 1995 women from both sides sent delegations to the Beijing Women's Conference. The Bougainville Women for Peace and Freedom (BWPF)[11] was a group of BRA and Bougainville

---

11   The BWPF is an organization that developed a human rights programme in the formerly blockaded areas of Bougainville. Their meetings for women also attracted large crowds of men and chiefs. During the war, BWPF members recorded human rights abuses, often risking their lives to send information to Sydney. These lists have been recognized by both the Bougainville Interim Government and the BWPF as their own documents although

Interim Government supporters who worked for peace and unity from the BRA side, networking with NGOs in other countries (Havini 2004, 71).

In their traditional capacity as 'peacemakers,' women were able to organize and participate in the peace building process. The extent of their success, however, is subject to debate. According to one of the founders of BWPF, Ruth Saovana–Spriggs, one of the reasons they were able to be persuasive was their emphasis on unity. '…women have made it our mission to speak with one voice, a far larger voice than individual women's groups previously achieved, on separate issues of unity, reconciliation, an end to war, and rebuilding our lives and homes' (Saovana Spriggs 2004, 123).

Critics suggest that even when women spoke, they were not necessarily heard, and the actual negotiations and decisions were carried out by men (Garasu 2002). 'Women's public status, condoned male violence, the law – both formal and traditional – and the ways in which it is interpreted and implemented, are crucial elements in the lack of attention paid to women's views and opinions' (Macintyre 2000, 41). Moreover, while some extol the role of women, Macintyre claims that,

> Men listened to women when they finally got sick of fighting–not when their wives died in childbirth because of the lack of hospital facilities; not when women were being routinely raped by soldiers, police and other Bougainvillean men; not when women had to struggle to find food for their families away from their villages. Women had no political presence when so–called peace talks were foundering. Violence by men was constantly met by counter–violence. Rapes were avenged by rapes, killings by killings (Macintyre 2000, 43).

Macintyre goes on to say that in post conflict Bougainville, the reality of women in reconstruction is that 'women's organizations are heavily dependent on outside funding, and that, in projects aimed at reconstruction and development, men are the major decision makers and beneficiaries' (Macintyre 2000, 43).

The Letania Nehan Women's Development Agency, founded in 1992 and recipient of the first UNIFEM Millennium Peace Prize in 2001, is one of the women's organizations working for peace and reconciliation. Letania recognized that the violence experienced by women during and after the crisis did not arise solely as a result of the conflict but rather was related to violence that also existed in peacetime. Moreover, they recognize 'a strong connection between violence against women and militarization of Bougainville society' (Hakena 2005, 165). As a result, they are currently working with entire communities, including men, youth and ex–combatants. The influence of the international development community is visible in Letania's belief that gender mainstreaming needs to be improved and strengthened. They give evidence with such examples as when they began to work

---

they contained information of abuses committed and suffered by all sides in the conflict. <http://www.converge.org.nz/pma/bouwom.htm>, accessed 2 February 2008.

on arms disposal, they were told 'bluntly that arms control was not a women's issue' (Hakena 2005, 168–9).

Letania is facing the dissonance between traditional and transformative roles for women. During the conflict, the success of women in peace making in Bougainville was through use of their traditional gender roles as women, combined with an acknowledgement from outside that women are important in reconstruction and rehabilitation. In other words, women used their gender in a form of cultural governance to promote peace. A feminist analysis of this use of traditional women's roles would conclude that it limits the opportunities for peace making. However, an anti militarist approach to peace 'insists that traditional images of masculinity and femininity reinforce both militarism and sexism', as it fails to challenge the ways these roles contribute to the continuation of patriarchy and militarism (Burguieres 1990, 6, quoted in Bates 2005, 81). Hence, efforts for peace making might be successful, but only if they stay within the confines of established gender roles. Unless the conceptions of masculinity and femininity that sustain systems and structures of domination and oppression are transformed, post conflict society will return to pre–conflict modes of gender expression and domination. Perhaps what we are seeing in Bougainville today is a version of continued oppression due to the inability to totally dismantle and rebuild traditional gender and power relations after the war ended.

Okinawa/Guam (Guahan)

> In times of war, the military takes people's lives. In times of peace, the military takes the dignity – and often lives – of women (Mikanagi 2004, 97).

Militarization is enhanced and exacerbated by actual fighting but it is more a product of preparation for war than of war itself. Preparing for war has enormous economic benefits for weapons' manufacturers but may wreak havoc on the people and environments where the actual preparation takes place. Opposition to the planned relocation of US marines from Okinawa to Guam has created a new site for resistance to US and Japanese cultural governance, as it has brought women of both sides together in a united stand. This has also meant that they address the question of militarization as one of structural violence and has forced them to look at the violent intersection of militarization, gender and racism. The following focuses on how a group of women opposing the bases in Okinawa has changed to incorporate the struggle in Guam/Guahan.

Guam

To fully understand the impact of militarization on Guam and its implications for Okinawa, it is useful to first take a quick look at the history of the US military occupation of that island. Guam came under US administration in 1898 as a result of the Spanish–American War[12] and was occupied by the Japanese Imperial Army in 1941. The US bombardment of Guam beginning on 18 July 1944 was 'the most intense crescendo of conventional firepower ever inflicted on any locality in the Pacific War' (Rogers 1995, 181). It eroded the last vestiges of discipline in Japanese soldiers and policemen. In Agana, 11 Chamoru men, women and young children were bayoneted to death. At a cave near Agat, Japanese soldiers raped more than a dozen teenage girls, and at another cave, Japanese killed an unknown number of Chamoru men (Rogers 1995, 181). US military records show 18,377 Japanese dead on Guam, of whom about two hundred were civilians. An additional 1,250 Japanese surrendered. American casualties numbered 1,747 dead (1,520 US Marines) and 6,053 wounded. During the Japanese occupation about 600 Chamorus were reported as killed (Rogers 1995, 194).

The US Navy quickly reinstated its authority on Guam, and proceeded to use the island as an entry point from which to invade other Mariana Islands and the Japanese mainland. Most of the Chamorus were placed in refugee camps run by the US and their lives were governed by the needs of the US war, although the US provided some education and employment. After the war, the number of military personnel on Guam was greatly reduced, but the island remained under the administration of the US Navy until 1950 when the passage of the Organic Act made Guam an organized unincorporated territory of the United States and the Chamoru population of Guam became US citizens. Guam continues to house important US military, primarily naval, facilities.[13]

What impact has the US military presence on Guam had for the human security of Chamorus? Victoria–Lola Montecalvo Leon Guerrero, of the Guahan Indigenous Collective, offered the following moving testimony to the UN Committee on Decolonization in 2006:

> …Since World War II, the US military presence on Guahan has been devastating to the survival of our language and culture as a Chamoru people, our right to create our own form of government, our right to own the land that was passed down to us by our ancestors, our civil right to vote for all our leaders including the US president that is the Commander in Chief of the military that occupies 30 percent of our island, and our basic human right to survival. The legacy of World War II has led to the toxic pollution of our land and surrounding waters from nuclear and other carcinogenic waste and has increased the amounts of cancers and deaths among Chamoru people. And the legacy of World War II

---

12   The Chamoru people were not consulted in the transfer of sovereignty from Spain to the US, and the ensuing treaty did not recognize indigenous sovereignty nor did it oblige the US to protect indigenous rights, promote their political, economic or social wellbeing or bring them to self government (Rogers 1995, 113).

13   For more on the Marine Corps in Guam, see: <http://usmilitary.about.com/gi/dynamic/offsite.htm?zi=1/XJ/Ya&sdn=usmilitary&cdn=careers&tm=39&f=00&tt=14&&bt=1&&bts=1&&zu=http%3A//www.globalsecurity.org/military/facility/mcas.htm>.

has meant that our Chamoru sons and daughters are forced to leave Guahan, their homeland, because the United States has limited our economic resources to tourism and military spending.

…There is a shortage of competitive jobs for young Chamoru people, who choose to enlist in the US military because they are told it will give them a brighter future. Yet, *in every war the US has fought since World War II – Vietnam, the Gulf War and the current 'War on Terror' more Chamorus have died per capita than any other soldiers*. And what do Chamoru families get when they lose a son or daughter to war? What do we get when we lose a life we poured 21 years and our hopes for the future into? We get a small sum of money, a US flag and a free burial spot to visit at the veteran's cemetery. What about that life? How do we get that back?

How do we get back the lives we've lost, the Chamorus who have been forced off their homeland, and the land we need to build on so that they can return? We do not get these resources back with an increased military presence on our island. But without the right to self–determination, we have no power, no legal recourse in which to stop this military build–up that will further displace the Chamoru people.

…Earlier this year, the US Department of Defense unveiled its plan to move 8,000 Marines and their 9,000 dependents from Okinawa and Japan to Guahan, and to increase the existing population of Navy and Air Force personnel on the island. *By 2014, there will be an estimated population increase of at least 35,000 people*, which will greatly impact the island's current population of 168,000 and change our cultural, political, social and ecological environment…[14] (Emphasis in the original).

The repeated appeals of the Chamoru people for decolonization and self–determination remain unsuccessful and the influx of military and other personnel as a result of the military build–up there has served to further reduce the percentage of Chamoru residents.[15] Today, more Chamorus live on the US mainland than in Guam. The exodus of Chamorus from Guam comes partly as a result of the rising cost of living, making Chamorus unable to afford to live there any longer. This will be further exacerbated by the influx of 8,000 marines and their families, and local residents are concerned about the environmental, healthcare, education and social impact of the population increase. These concerns mirror those of local residents

---

14   <http://blindelephant.blogspot.com/2006/11/un-testimonies-4-this-great-exodus_ 07.html >, accessed 16 November 2006. See also Aguon (2006).

15   In 1980, Chamorus made up 45 per cent of the population but it had fallen to 37 per cent in 2000 and continues to fall. <http://decolonizeguam.blogspot.com/2007/11/question-of-guam-2007.html, accessed 27 December 2007.

in Okinawa, where most of the US bases are located. The Okinawa side of this issue is now considered.

Okinawa

The US presence on Okinawa began with the Battle of Okinawa, the only land battle on Japanese soil during World War II. One out of every three Okinawan civilians died in that battle. US troops remained in Okinawa, even after the Treaty of Peace with Japan entered into force on 28 April 1952. The Okinawan Islands remained under US control until 1970, and still houses 75 per cent of the US forces in Japan. These utilize 10 per cent of the total land area of the Okinawan islands, and 19 per cent of the main island, Okinawa (Chinen 2007, 62). US soldiers stationed on Okinawa have been sent to fight in the Korean, Vietnam, Gulf and Iraq wars, and bases in Okinawa have provided logistical backup. On the main island, the US bases cannot be avoided; the sound of planes taking off and landing interrupts school lessons, military vehicles clog the roads and military personnel roam the streets. Despite the current economic downturn, the bases are surrounded by bars and shops with large signs in English trying to attract military customers. One aspect of those businesses is military prostitution; another is rape and other forms of sexual violence.

Okinawa is home to 12 US Marine Corps installations, including the Marine Corps Air Station Futenma, located in Ginowan City on the main island of Okinawa, and has been a US military airbase since the Battle of Okinawa in 1945. The Futenma Base is located very close to an urban area, and there has been much concern over safety. Air and noise pollution has been a subject of controversy, and these concerns were amplified on 13 August 2004 when a marine helicopter crashed and burned inside the campus of Okinawa International University. Three marines were injured in the crash but no one at the university was hurt.

In 1995 a 12 year old Okinawan girl was kidnapped and repeatedly raped by three American servicemen. This incident brought to the surface the smouldering anger of the people of Okinawa and a month later, an anti–base rally drew 85,000 people.[16] In 1996, in what was initially seen as an attempt to quell the anger of the Okinawan people, the government announced that the Futenma Base was to be returned. It soon became clear that the base was to be relocated to an offshore location in Henoko Bay in the northern part of Okinawa Island (Special Action Committee on Okinawa 1996). The new base was to be built in a beautiful section

---

16   On 18 August 2008, one of the perpetrators of the rape, Kendrick Ledet, committed suicide after strangling a 22 year old co–worker to death (*Japan Times* 25 February 2008). The number of protestors was exceeded on 29 September 2007, when a rally protesting Japanese government plans to take out of textbooks all mention of the role played by Japanese soldiers in the mass suicides in Okinawa, attracted 110,000 people. In February 2008, Japan was shocked by two more accusations of rape, both incidents perpetrated by US military men in Okinawa. The victim in one is a 14 year old girl.

of ocean, rich in marine wildlife and home to the endangered dugong, as well as the Okinawa woodpecker and Okinawa rail. Plans called for filling in a huge section of ocean, 2,500 metres long and 730 metres wide. It would be used for helicopter flight training as well as other activities.

Shortly after plans for the relocation became known, a sit–in began at Henoko, organized by the Henoko 'Society for the Protection of Life.' This sit–in still continues in 2009. In 2004 authorities attempted to begin construction of offshore towers to be used for boring the seabed. Protesters in kayaks and other small craft engaged in non violent resistance, impeding construction of most of the planned towers. Although plans had called for boring in 63 locations, the protestors succeeded in completely preventing it. In 2005 the towers that had been successfully installed were removed.

In October 2005 US and Japanese authorities announced a change in plans. The designated area for the relocation was changed to a section of Henoko that was already included within the area of Camp Schwab, another Marine Corps facility. The reason given for the change was that it would make construction easier, although members of the Society for the Protection of Life attribute the real reason to the success of their protest. By 2008 authorities were engaged in environmental assessments and it is hoped that the presence of endangered species such as the dugong will help to further delay, if not prevent, construction.

Most people in Okinawa desire the relocation of US bases and military forces outside Japan (especially outside Okinawa).[17] US bases may bring some opportunities for employment, tourism and business, but these supposed advantages are off set by the reality of accidents, sexual and other violence, pollution and other hazards. The psychological cost of having US bases on Okinawa is very high Many Okinawan people strongly oppose their forced role in hosting US troops, who provide logistical support for foreign conflict or train on Okinawa, and then leave to kill people elsewhere.

Suzuyo Takasato is one Okinawan who is strongly opposed to US bases. In 1995, after the rape of the Okinawan girl by US soldiers, Takasato and her supporters established 'Okinawa Women Act Against Military Violence' (OWAAMV), an association aimed at stopping military violence and military power. Simultaneously, they opened the 'Rape Emergency Intervention Counseling Centre – Okinawa' to support victims of sexual violence. One of their activities was to compile a list of sexual violence committed against women by US soldiers, and they were surprised to find how pervasive that violence had been. In addition to the many unwanted and forced pregnancies which resulted from frequent raping of women and girls at gunpoint after World War II, they found instances of a nine month old baby who was a victim of sexual violence in 1949 and a six year old girl who was raped and

---

17   A 2005 citizens' referendum on Henoko showed strong opposition to the construction of the new base. For information in Japanese on results of local referenda held in 2005 on US bases see <http://www.geocities.co.jp/WallStreet/1412/rd/news71.html#no3>, accessed 17 December 2007.

killed in 1955. Two to four people were reported to have been strangled to death every year by US soldiers. During the Vietnam War years, it is reported that the violence continued even after Okinawa was returned to Japan in 1972, where rape or attempted rape victims included both a 10 year old and a 14 year old girl.[18]

When the rape of the girl aged 12 years occurred in 1995, Takasato had returned from the Fourth World Conference on Women in Beijing where she had given a presentation with other women from Okinawa on 'Military Violence against Women in Okinawa'. She was furious when she heard the news, and took immediate action to mobilize women to protect themselves and their families, taking the position that the very existence of the military bases on Okinawa was an example of structural and direct violence against women (Takasato 1996).

The initial objectives of OWAAMV were to break the silence surrounding sexual violence by US soldiers and to oust US bases from Okinawa. They soon learned that most Americans knew little or nothing about the sexual violence committed by US soldiers abroad, and so Takasato organized a peace caravan to the US to educate interested American women about the problem. Gradually OWAAMV learned that the problem did not concern just Okinawa and the US, but involved women wherever US bases were located. This awareness led to the formation in 1997 of the 'East–Asia–US–Puerto Rico Women's Network Against Militarism' with women from the Philippines, Korea, US and Puerto Rico. Through this network, the women realized violence against women is not only a violation of human rights, but that it is fundamentally related to the racism, patriarchy, sex discrimination and economic oppression brought by militarism and globalization (Takasato 2003, 185).

After the Seoul Conference in 2002, the OWAAMV network expanded to include Hawaii and Guam. Although there were similarities among the women within different countries, there was not a direct and obvious link with Okinawa. This changed Guam's inclusion into OWAAMV and growing awareness that although the relocation of US soldiers from Okinawa to Guam might mean relief for Okinawan women it could threaten the Chamoru people, because plans for Futenma included the relocation of 8,000 marines and their families from Okinawa to Guam. For OWAAMV, this realization meant that it was no longer possible to simply oppose the presence of the military on Okinawa; they found they could only oppose bases on Okinawa if they were also willing to oppose them on Guam. The OWAAMV subsequently embarked on a campaign to address this issue, calling for security policy based on ridding the military and weapons, rather than being based on military strength (Akibayashi 2003, 175). In January 2008 they initiated a study–tour to Guam to find ways to cooperate.

---

18   In Japanese, refer to <http://www.space-yui.com/koudou.htm>. Also see: 'Outposts of Empire: The case against foreign military bases.' Transnational Institute, March 2007. <http://www.tni.org/detail_page.phtml?andact_id=16374andmenu=11e>, accessed 23 December 2007.

Conclusion

This chapter has examined the intersection of cultural governance, militarization and gendered violence in the Pacific. It has addressed three very different aspects: regional structures for gender mainstreaming and the implementation of Resolution 1325, the role of women in the Bougainville crisis and resistance to presence of US bases abroad and the relocation of US Marines from Okinawa to Guam. These three aspects are linked through hegemonic militarism and its demands for the governance of gender.

One of the underlying issues for all three cases viewed here is the question of development, the quest for sustainable and secure futures. While current international security and development policy recognizes that participation of women is essential for the creation and maintenance of societies free from want and fear, there is tremendous variation in the degree to which women are actually able to participate fully in all aspects of society. In the examples given here, gender mainstreaming and UNSC 1325 are strategies to directly address women's needs, based on experience in the international security and development communities; underlying the struggle in Bougainville is the question of who controls resources and possible futures; both Okinawa and Guam are peripheral regions of their respective states, and lives of people in both places are subject to the whims of patriarchal militarism.

These cases have shown how cultural governance manipulates gender in the pursuit of security and development. For example, traditional roles and gender mainstreaming combine to involve women in every aspect of the conflict resolution process, but in reality, the voices of women are given relatively little notice, even when they play an active and constructive role in bringing armed conflict to an end. Moreover, the establishment of 'peace' does not necessarily include demilitarization or new roles for women. It is suggested that traditional roles of women as 'peace makers' and gender initiatives which fail to recognize the gendered and structural violence upon which they are predicated fall short of truly involving women in the processes of governance and peace building. These processes must redefine the terms of cultural governance, making gendered violence visible, and engaging in demilitarization.

In the Bougainville crisis, women on both sides paved the way for the official peace talks through recognizing the importance of unity and arranging for discussions among Bougainvilleans. In the case of Okinawa and Guam, the requirements of cultural governance from the perspective of Tokyo call for the incorporation of Okinawa into Japan, glossing over its history of colonization and different culture. A similar process occurs with Guam, which Washington treats as being essentially a part of the United States. Opposition to the planned relocation of US marines from Okinawa to Guam has created a new site for resistance to US and Japanese cultural governance, as it has brought women of both sides together in a united stand. They have recognized that the cost of development for their islands will be increased militarization, no doubt accompanied by gender and racial violence.

Women working within international organizations, as well as those on Bougainville, Okinawa and Guam have used their gender identity as an entry point for opposing violence and militarization. In the liberal feminist approach of the international security and development communities, measures such as Resolution 1325 use gender mainstreaming to increase the participation of women and focus on their needs. In its ideal form, gender mainstreaming calls for the transformation of society to include women as actors with opportunities equal to those of men. In practice, however, it often entails merely the addition of numbers of women, without concomitant changes in patriarchal social structures. Moreover, while in theory, measures such as gender mainstreaming seek to address both 'gender violence' and 'gendered violence,' the conflation of gender with women has kept attention on the former to the detriment of the latter, limiting their potential for being transformative. In Bougainville, women used their traditional role as 'peacemakers' to call for unity among the warring parties and pave the way for official peace talks. In so doing, they were able to transcend their allegiance to one side or the other in to recreate and reembody themselves as 'Bougainvilleans.' In the case of Okinawa and Guam, the rape of a 12 year old girl became the catalyst for a growing network in opposition to militarization and military violence, which is calling for a redefinition of the basic concepts of security. In both of these cases, transformation only became possible once they had overcome the binaries imposed by cultural governance. In both cases, 'unity' could not have become a goal without a rejection of militarization and military means to problem solving.

What remains unclear, is the extent to which 'unity' and the rejection of militarization in a particular situation leads to a more generalized stance in opposition to structural violence and ultimately to non violent work for peace. Without such an analysis, the success of 'women's efforts' in such situations may lead to perpetuation of factors underlying the violence in the first place, giving temporary relief without providing a long term solution. This chapter has shown that work to overcome gendered violence must include efforts to address militarization in all its forms, including racism and patriarchy. This involves recognition of various forms of difference, and also acknowledgement that we are both similar to, and different from, both our friends and our enemies. Efforts to resist cultural governance and create alternatives must include such work if they are to be truly transformational. Focusing on women, or gender, or even 'unity' is not enough.

References

Aguon, J. (2006), *The Fire This Time: Essays on Life Under US Occupation* (Tokyo: Blue Ocean Press).

Akibayashi, K. (2003), 'Anzen Hosho no Saiteigi wo Mezasu Josei no Rentai: Higashi Ajia–Beikoku–Puerto Rico Gunjishugi wo Yurusanai Josei Network to ha', *Asojie* 11, 172–178.

Bates, P.A. (2005), 'Women and Peacemaking' in P. Thomas (ed.), *Women, Gender and Development in the Pacific: Key Issues*, Development Studies Network, 81–85, <http://devnet.anu.edu.au/GenderPacific/index.html>, accessed 24 October 2008.

Callahan, W.A. (2006), *Cultural Governance and Resistance in Pacific Asia* (London, New York: Routledge).

Carl, A. and Garasu, L. (eds) (2002), *Weaving Consensus: The Papua New Guinea – Bougainville Peace Process* (special issue of *Accord*, 12).

Chinen, U. (2007) 'Nihon no Yujinyo. Kichi Mottekaette Kara Matann Mensore. Kichi, Senso, Shokuminchi no Okinawa Yori' ('Friends of Japan, Let's meet Again After You Take your Bases Away. From Okinawa, Site of Bases, War and Colonization'), in T. Saito, U. Chinen, S. Numata and C. Hiroiwa, *Anataha Senso de Shinemasuka* (Tokyo: NHK Publishers).

Connell, R.W. (1990), 'The State, Gender and Sexual Politics: Theory and Appraisal', *Theory and Society* 19:5, 507–544.

Enloe, C. (2000), *Maneuvers: The International Politics of Militarizing Women's Lives* (London: University of California Press).

Garasu, L. (2002), 'The Role of Women in Promoting Peace and Reconciliation', *Accord* 12 (special issue, *Weaving consensus: The Papua New Guinea – Bougainville Peace Process*), 28–11, <http://www.c-r.org/our-work/accord/png-bougainville/women-peace-reconciliation.php>, accessed 18 December 2007.

Hakena, H. (2005), 'Papua New Guinea: Women in Armed Conflict', in R. Baksh, L. Etchart, E. Onubogu and T. Johnson (eds), *Gender Mainstreaming in Conflict Transformation: Building Sustainable Peace* (London: Commonwealth Secretariat), 160–170.

Hau'ofa, E. (1993), 'Our Sea of Islands', in E. Waddell, V. Naidu and E. Hau'ofa (eds), *A New Oceania. Rediscovering Our Sea of Islands* (Suva: School of Social and Economic Development, University of the South Pacific in association with Beake House), 2–14.

Havini, M.T. (2004), 'Prologue: Women in Community During the Blockade' in Sirivi, J.T. and Havini, M.T. (eds), *…as Mothers of the Land: The Birth of the Bougainville Women for Peace and Freedom* (Canberra: Research School of Pacific and Asian Studies, ANU, Pandanus Books), 69–72.

Kaplan, L.D. (1994), 'Woman as Caretaker: An Archetype That Supports Patriarchal Militarism', *Hypatia* Special Issue: Feminism and Peace 9:2, 123–132.

Macintyre, M. (2000), 'Violence and Peacemaking in Papua New Guinea: A Realistic Assessment of the Social and Cultural Issues at Grassroots Level,' *Development Bulletin* 53, 34–37.

McCutchan, A. (1997), 'The Bougainville Experience', *Pacific Women's Network Against Violence*, September, 1.

Mikanagi, Y. (2004), 'Okinawa: Women, Bases and US–Japan Relations', *International Relations of the Asia–Pacific* 4:1, 97–111.

Miriori, S.R. (2004), 'Occupation. Rape, A Weapon of War', in Sirivi, J.T. and Havini, M.T. (eds), *...as Mothers of the Land: The Birth of the Bougainville Women for Peace and Freedom* (Canberra: Research School of Pacific and Asian Studies, ANU, Pandanus Books), 63–65.

Nayak, M. and Suchland, J. (2006), 'Gender Violence and Hegemonic Projects', *International Feminist Journal of Politics* 8:4, 467–485.

O'Callaghan, M. (2002), 'The Origins of the Conflict', *Accord* 12 (special issue), *Weaving consensus: The Papua New Guinea – Bougainville Peace Process*, 6–11.

Onubogu, E. and Etchart, L. (2005), 'Achieving Gender Equality and Equity in Peace Processes', in R. Baksh, L. Etchart, E. Onubogu and T. Johnson (eds), *Gender Mainstreaming in Conflict Transformation: Building Sustainable Peace* (London: Commonwealth Secretariat), 34–55.

Pacific Islands Forum Secretariat (2006), 'Regional Workshop on Gender, Conflict Peace and Security June 15–17 2006, Draft Outcomes Document', <http:// www.forumsec.org.fj/_resources/article/files/List%20of%20Participants1. pdf>, accessed 24 October 2008.

Pacific Women's Bureau (2004), 'Revised Pacific Platform of Action on the Advancement of Women and Gender Equality 2005–2015', <http://www.spc. int/Women/PDF%20files/9th%20Triennial%20Volume%201.pdf>, accessed 14 January 2009.

Pacific Women's Bureau (2005), 'Pacific Women's Bureau Strategic Plan 2006–2009', <http://www.spc.int/Women/Publications/Pdf/PWB%20SPP%202006-09.pdf >, accessed 24 October 2008.

Reardon, B. (1985), *Sexism and the War System* (New York: Teacher's College Press).

Rogers, R.F. (1995), *Destiny's Landfall: A History of Guam* (Honolulu: University of Hawaii Press).

Saovana Spriggs, R. (2004), 'Prologue. Unity and the Peace Process', in Sirivi, J.T. and Havini, M.T. (eds), *...as Mothers of the Land: The Birth of the Bougainville Women for Peace and Freedom* (Canberra: Research School of Pacific and Asian Studies, ANU, Pandanus Books), 121–124.

Special Action Committee on Okinawa (SACO) Final Report, 2 December 1996   <http://www.mofa.go.jp/region/n-america/us/security/96saco1.html>, accessed 24 October 2008.

Takasato, S. (1996), *Okinawa no Onnatachi – Josei no Jinken to Kichi* (Tokyo: Akashi Shoten).

—— (2003), 'Okinawa no Kichi, Guntai no Genjou to Undo – Dai 4 kai Higashi Asia–Beikoku–Puerto Rico Gunjishugi wo Yurusanai Josei Network 2002.8.15–20 Seoul Kaigi de no Okinawa Hokoku.' *Asojie* 11, 9–185.

Thomas, P. (2005a), 'The Pacific: Gender Issues in Conflict and Peacemaking', in R. Baksh, L. Etchart, E. Onubogu and T. Johnson (eds), *Gender Mainstreaming in Conflict Transformation: Building Sustainable Peace* (London: Commonwealth Secretariat), 155–159.

—— (2005b), 'Introduction: Conflict and Peacemaking: Gender perceptions' in P. Thomas (ed.), 'Women, Gender and Development in the Pacific: Key Issues', *Development Studies Network*, 3–6, http://devnet.anu.edu.au/GenderPacific/index.html, accessed 24 October 2008.

UNSC Resolution 1325 (2000), <http://www.unfpa.org/women/docs/res_1325e.pdf>, accessed 13 November 2007.

Volker, B. and Garasu, L. (2004), 'Papua New Guinea: A Success Story of Post–conflict Peacebuilding in Bougainville', in A. Heijmans, N. Simmonds and H. van de Veen (eds), *Searching for Peace in Asia Pacific: An Overview of Conflict Prevention and Peacebuilding Activities* (Boulder: Lynne Reinner Publishers), 564–580.

Chapter 7

Development and Security: Aotearoa/ New Zealand and the Millennium Goals[1]

Phil Goff

Security and development

The theme brings together two of the greatest challenges facing the world: security and development. United Nations (UN) Secretary General, Kofi Annan (2005), has emphatically reminded us of this in his challenging report, *In Larger Freedom*: 'We will not enjoy development without security, we will not enjoy security without development, and we will not enjoy either without respect for human rights.' Annan's report addresses security and development challenges, and the reformation of some of the principal organs of the UN, including the Security Council.

This year (2005) should be a watershed year for the UN and the global system. Five years on from the Millennium Summit and the establishment of the Millennium Development Goals (MDGs) we are at risk of failing to meet the 2015 targets in too many countries and regions, including the Pacific. In a post 9/11 environment we have been mesmerized, not unreasonably, by global security issues. Terrorism is an important issue but addressing its causes is as important as suppressing its symptoms. One cause is the alienation of those deprived of decent living standards and of hope. Meeting the poverty gap and development challenges is complimentary to realizing the challenges of political security. The UN Secretary–General's Report (Annan 2005) indicated that:

- One billion people, one–fifth of the world's population, live in extreme poverty, and 800 million are under nourished;
- One hundred million primary school children, 60 per cent of whom are girls, are not at school;

---

1 This chapter reproduces Phil Goff's keynote address to the 2005 Otago Foreign Policy School in his position as New Zealand's Minister of Foreign Affairs and Trade. It is an official governmental stance on the MDGs and security with respect to New Zealand's external aid partners. Goff's speech indicated the proactive stance New Zealand took in supporting the MDGs but also indicates how already by 2005 serious doubts were being raised at governmental levels over whether the MDGs could be attained in an insecure world. This chapter also summarizes UN Secretary General, Kofi Annan's assessment of the MDGs.

- Eleven million children under five die each year of preventable causes;
- Life expectancy in the poorest countries is as low as 40, nearly half that of the life expectancy in our country.

The existence of the poverty gap is a moral affront as well as a contributor to insecurity and a lost economic opportunity for masses of people. In September 2000, the UN General Assembly ended on a historic note, with the adoption of the UN Millennium Declaration. The Declaration, covering human rights, security, peacekeeping, the rule of law, and the environment, also collectively committed governments, including New Zealand, to work towards freeing the world of extreme poverty and international development goals.

The MDGs reflect unprecedented international consensus to close the poverty gap. Never before has the global system set goals and timelines to address poverty in its many manifestations. These specify:

- Halving the number of people living on less than $1 per day;
- Halving the number of people suffering hunger;
- Achieving universal primary education and gender equality in education;
- Reducing infant mortality by two thirds;
- Reducing maternal mortality by three quarters;
- Halting and rolling back HIV/AIDS and malaria and other major diseases;
- Addressing key environmental sustainability issues; and,
- Developing a 'Global Partnership for Development', including freer, fairer and more open trade, more and better Official Development Assistance (ODA) and debt relief, and recognizing the special needs of small states and the poorest.

The MDGs have considerable strengths, which include offering a consensus vision of a better world, and collectively motivating the attainment of that vision. The MDGs are poverty and results oriented. They are also based on quantitative measures, which helps countries and aid agencies evaluate and then change their policies and activities.

Limitations to the MDGs: The need for local ownership

Although the MDGs provide clear and simple directions as to where we should be heading, the future is not straightforward or easy. The MDGs are not comprehensive. For example, sexual and reproductive health and rights are a vital area within the goals of child and maternal health that require attention. The achievement of the MDGs will depend on a complex of factors, and a multiplicity of actors: such as global economic performance, the international trading environment, the quality of governance and of policy in developing countries, and the volume and effectiveness of ODA. There also remain challenges about priorities.

While the MDGs are all interrelated, development experience suggests a first priority is basic education, especially for women, as that makes an essential contribution to improved health status for families and children. Education is also essential for progress on reducing income poverty. New Zealand is prioritizing the rebuilding of the basic education system in Solomon Islands, for example, for these very reasons. New Zealand has reprioritized basic education as a component of overall educational aid, moving it from five per cent of expenditure in 1999 to 31 per cent in 2005.

The right approaches are also essential to achieving the MDGs. No development is effective, or sustainable in the long run, unless it is locally owned. The development strategies for setting priorities and achieving the MDGs at country level must be nationally led and nationally owned to be effective. Where there is a regional dimension, for example in the Pacific, good regional cooperation is essential. That is one of the reasons why New Zealand is a strong promoter of the Pacific Plan being devised by Pacific Island Forum countries for greater cooperation and integration.

Another vital area is governance, which while not a MDG, is critical to their achievement. Governments that have the interest of their people at heart, and which avoid the cancer of corruption, will emphasize such matters as the provision of basic services to the people, and the creation of a policy environment that encourages economic activity and attracts investment. Poor governance is generally a rapid route backwards into poverty, especially if civil conflict is also a factor, as recently indicated in Papua New Guinea, Solomon Islands and Afghanistan. However, New Zealand does not consider that poor governance is a reason to disengage from assisting fragile states. Rather, we should be tailoring our engagement to address the problem, for example by focusing on strengthening the capacity, transparency and accountability of government systems. This type of approach is highly relevant to some of the fragile states in New Zealand's own neighbourhood.

Jeffrey Sachs' Millennium Project Report released in January provided a useful account on progress of the developing world against the MDGs (UN Millennium Project 2005). East Asia is largely on track for most goals; with the economic growth rates following adoption of market economies, and policies targeting poverty in India and China, millions of people have been lifted out of poverty. That is the main contributor to the world already having halved the 1990 level of income poverty, on a population basis. However sub–Saharan Africa is off track against most goals.

Development aid in the Pacific: A New Zealand perspective

After sub–Saharan Africa, the region most off track against meeting the MDGs is the Pacific. Statistics from some of New Zealand's neighbours in the Pacific paint a grim picture:

- In Vanuatu more than 66 per cent of adults are illiterate;
- Over 16 per cent of people in Kiribati are not expected to survive to the age of 40;
- Papua New Guinea has the lowest living standards, the lowest average life expectancy, and the highest maternal and infant mortality rates of any country in the Pacific;
- An increasing number of Pacific nations are beginning to live in the shadow of HIV/AIDS.

The Pacific is a region that New Zealand knows well and where a real difference can be made. NZAID, the government's international aid and development agency, implements major bilateral and regional programmes there. The recently announced increase in our ODA funding is predicated on New Zealand aiming, in cooperation with partner governments, and donor agencies, at:

- Ensuring every Pacific child has access to a good education;
- Helping reverse the growing incidence of lifestyle diseases and HIV/AIDS in the Pacific;
- Meeting the basic needs of Pacific communities through the provision of access to clean water, good sanitation and adequate healthcare;
- Improving the skills and knowledge of Pacific leaders and their officials;
- Fostering sustainable economic growth and improved livelihoods across the Pacific and Asia, including through trade and development;
- Contributing to regional and multilateral management of common challenges such as preparation and protection against natural disasters, and the pursuit of security and prosperity.

The following are a few specific examples of practical actions of New Zealand's contribution to aid, development and security. I have referred briefly to Solomon Islands. Rebuilding the education system, in partnership with the government and the European Union, involve New Zealand contributing $30 million over three to five years. We will be implementing a similar process in Tonga, where there are better foundations than in Solomon Islands but issues of access and quality of education remain – this time with the government and the World Bank. In Papua New Guinea, we have been appointed a lead donor, not in volume of aid, but for policy coordination for the combined donor input to the health sector.

I mentioned the importance of governance. We continue to make major contributions in the areas of improved policing and corrections, judicial and prosecutorial capacity, public sector reform and strengthening and educating leaders. In July 2005 we will cohost with the Univerity of the South Pacific, a major symposium on Pacific leadership: What is leadership, what state is it in and how can it be improved? The participants will be Pacific Islanders, not expatriates.

The New Zealand government contributes significant funding and expertise in areas such as trade facilitation and management of fisheries resources. We also recently provided $2 million to the United Nations Children's Fund (UNICEF) to help prevent HIV/AIDS affecting children in the Pacific through mother to child transmission.

New Zealanders, as revealed in a 2004 NZAID/UMR survey, strongly support New Zealand's contributions to development in the Pacific. They recognize it is our home region and deserves our support. To do that, and much else in other regions where we are active – Asia, Africa and Latin America as well as support for the UN system – the government recognizes that increased funding is required. The longstanding international target of wealthy countries assigning 0.7 per cent of Gross National Income (GNI) to ODA has been repeatedly reaffirmed, at the Millennium Summit and the Monterrey Conference on Financing for Development in 2002. Many of the OECD donor countries have committed to significant increases in ODA, including interim targets on the way to 0.7 per cent. Total ODA projected for 2006 will be 28 per cent up on 2003 (US$66–83 billion). In keeping with the government's commitment to move to the 0.7 per cent as our resources permit; the 2005 budget contains an increase of approximately $60 million to development assistance. This increase, of 23 per cent, will take New Zealand from 0.23 per cent to 0.27 per cent of GNI and a total ODA contribution of $380 million. This is a small but significant step towards the target of 0.7 per cent of GNI. We will ensure that we hold at 0.27 per cent in 2006/07, and lift ODA to 0.28 per cent the following year. On current GNI estimates, that will be around $440 million per annum.

Debt relief and development

The MDGs also call for the international community to address the debt position of many of the world's poorest countries. The cost of servicing many unsustainable debt levels is a huge barrier to achieving the MDGs. Although New Zealand has no bilateral debts to write off, it continues to play a constructive role in multilateral debt relief initiatives. New Zealand has contributed over $6 million to the Heavily Indebted Poor Countries initiative.

I have welcomed the recent G8 Finance Ministers' agreement on a new package of debt relief, effectively cancelling the multilateral debts of all eligible Heavily Indebted Poor Countries. New Zealand will be shouldering our share of the burden in respect of debt relief to poor countries owing debt to the World Bank and the Asia Development Bank. Increased and effective ODA, and effective and sustainable debt relief are two of the key requirements if the MDGs are to be met.

Trade and development

Trade is a third pillar in development. A key priority is improving market access. To quote Kofi Annan (2005): 'No single change could make a greater contribution to eliminating poverty than fully opening the markets of prosperous countries to the goods produced by poor ones.' New Zealand has a proactive record with this unlike some of the major members of the OECD. Developed countries are distorting the opportunities for developing countries to trade in an area of their comparative advantage, agricultural products, by keeping markets closed and/or subsidising their own exports.

A recent Oxfam (2005) paper used rice as an example. Rice affects the livelihoods of two billion people – one third of the world's population. Smallholder farmers grow around 90 per cent of the world's rice. Rice is vital for food security and rural livelihoods in many developing countries. Unfortunately, the global trade in rice is highly distorted by subsidies paid to developed country farmers. The US is currently the third largest rice exporter in the world but each tonne costs an average of US$188 to produce, two and a half times as much as in Thailand and Vietnam. In 2003 US farmers remained in business because their government paid US$1.3 billion in subsidies to the sector. This subsidized rice is then 'dumped' on markets in countries like Haiti and Ghana with devastating consequences for the livelihoods of rice growers in those countries, particularly women who tend to be more involved in the cultivation of food crops. While the report focuses on rice, the same arguments apply to crops such as cotton, soybeans and wheat. The European Union, as well as the US, has been a major contributor to this problem. OECD countries currently expend around $280 billion a year on subsidising agricultural exports. This is more than three times the level of development assistance, around $80 billion a year, which these countries provide to the developing world. The WTO Doha Development Round is critical to addressing this situation and New Zealand is playing a crucial role. New Zealand needs to secure improved market access, including that for developing country products, and needs to see export subsidies eliminated. I applaud the European Union's agreement last year to eliminate export subsidies on agriculture.

Conclusion

I have touched on the three main inputs of aid, trade and debt relief towards achieving the MDGs but there are other issues. Remittances, estimated at US$126 billion in 2004, are very important for some countries such as India and the Philippines. Within the Pacific Samoa and Tonga gain 21 per cent and 41 per cent respectively of their GNI from remittances. The challenge is to harness some of these flows for development purposes. Private capital flows, much of it as investment, is also a large element, globally estimated at US$301 billion in 2004. In particular, opportunities to increase spending on development from any reduction in military spending are forgone when globally, the latter is currently estimated at US$997 billion per year.

In September 2005 world leaders will return to New York for the Millennium plus 5 Summit. They will be looking at more than progress on the MDGs. They will be debating proposals to reform the UN and at strengthening aspects of security and human rights. While substantial UN reform is uncertain, we need to make progress on some of Kofi Annan's key proposals such as the Peace Building Commission and updating the Security Council. Above all, world leaders must reaffirm the vital importance of an effective multilateral system, with a strong United Nations at its core. Only then can we hope to address effectively the challenges and threats confronting us in this century, and to achieve progress in the interconnected areas of development, security and human rights. Only then can we hope to succeed in tackling world poverty and enabling millions of poor people to be able to reach their full potential.

References

Annan, K. (2005), *In Larger Freedom: Towards Development, Security and Human Rights for All. Report of the Secretary–General* (New York: United Nations Publications).

Oxfam (2005), *Kicking Down the Door*, Oxfam Briefing Paper, 72 (April) <http://www.maketradefair.com/en/assets/english/kickingreport.pdf>, accessed 13 April 2009.

UN Millennium Project (2005), *Investing in Development: A Practical Plan to Achieve the Millennium Development Goals. Overview* (New York: United Nations Development Programme).

Chapter 8

Gender Security and Trade: The Millennium Development Goals in the Pacific

Terence Wood and Vijay Naidu

Introduction

Within the Pacific region, the increasingly short journey from the travel pages to the international section of any New Zealand newspaper feels like a voyage between two different parts of the world. The travel pages still reveal the Pacific of popular imagination: warm, welcoming and peaceful. The world pages, alternatively implode with a Pacific of much less cheerful images; corruption, poverty, ill health, instability and armed conflict. It seems implausible that these two Pacifics could exist in the same ocean, much less within the same newspaper. Part of the reason for this contrast is simply that the Pacific of popular imagination never really existed. Marketing campaigns and exclusive resorts insulated from the countries they are situated in have long kept issues of Pacific development out of the sight of tourists. Likewise, the media has, until relatively recently, tended to under report Pacific issues, while now it is arguably guilty of over–sensationalizing them. It is difficult to escape the conclusion that the Pacific region is currently facing a series of challenges – some new, some the result of previously unaddressed issues coming to a head – that pose a major threat to the region's development and most importantly to its people.

Simultaneously as issues of Pacific development are coming to the fore, increasing emphasis has been placed on a major international development initiative, the Millennium Development Goals (MDGs). These are a set of internationally agreed development targets that have become the major focus for international development efforts.

This chapter examines the state of Pacific development through the lens of the MDGs. It assesses progress towards meeting the MDGs and outlines the major obstacles to meeting the Goals and by inference, to development in the Pacific. It then considers potential solutions to the challenges confronting the region. Particular attention is paid to gender and conflict. Gender is not only a key area where the MDGs have been strongly critiqued but is also a key area where the Pacific region's outcomes are of concern. Conflict is also highlighted because this has considerable potential to derail the achievement of the MDGs.

The Millennium Development Goals and critics

The eight MDGs are divided into more specific targets and indicators. All of the targets have 1990 as a baseline year and most of the targets should be delivered by 2015. The indicators may be adjusted for particular countries and regions and are intended for use in monitoring progress towards each of the targets (Asian Development Bank 2003). The eight MDGs are shown in Table 1.1 and a complete list of the Goals, Targets and Indicators are on the official United Nations MDGs Indicators' page (United Nations Statistics Division n.d.). In January 2008 the United Nations updated the official list of MDG targets and indicators to reflect commitments made in the years after the original MDG list was drawn up. Most of the changes made in the update are relatively minor and because data for the Pacific is not yet fully collated for the new targets and indicators, this chapter is confined to discussing progress against the original set of targets and indicators.

While the first seven MDGs are measures of progress rather than policy prescriptions, the goals are not intended to be used simply as a development yardstick. Goal 8 outlines elements of a development partnership between the developed and developing worlds. Moreover, development agencies and governments are expected to design policies around the objective of achieving the Goals. The Goals are intended to serve as a form of 'soft law' or moral imperative against which nations can be held to account, particularly by their own people (Asian Development Bank 2004).

Although the MDGs have become a central figure of the development landscape, their worth is far from uncontroversial. Since their development, the Goals have been subjected to considerable critique. They have been decried both as under ambitious (Gold 2005), and as overly ambitious (Clemens, Radelet and Bhavnani 2004), although both these critiques appear to miss the point that the MDGs can be tailored to a country's specific circumstances.

More substantively, some critics of the MDGs have highlighted that these make no reference to indigenous and other minority groups within countries, or mandate the collection of separate statistics on these groups (Minority Rights Group International 2003). This omission is cause for considerable concern as in many developing and developed countries, various different minority groups have substantially worse human development outcomes than the national average (Minority Rights Group International 2003).

In addition, the MDGs (unlike the Millennium Declaration which they are based upon) make no specific reference to human rights (United Nations General Assembly 2000; Barton 2005; Gold 2005). This leads to the paradoxical situation where potentially a country that suppresses free speech, and detains and tortures dissidents can appear to have done more to improve human development, as measured by the Goals, than a neighbouring country that is democratic, and which respects human rights, but which has had a slightly lower reduction in poverty.

Some of the most trenchant critiques of the MDGs have come from those working with gender and development related issues. One area that elicited strong critique was the initial exclusion in the Goals of any mention of women's sexual and reproductive rights. To Peggy Antrobus, from Development Alternatives with Women for a New Era (DAWN), the absence of direct reference in the original MDGs to women's sexual and reproductive rights was:

> ...inexcusable given that women's sexual and reproductive rights is not only a goal but a crucial target and/or indicator of progress under at least 3 Goals – Goal number 3 (women's equality and empowerment), Goal number 4 (child mortality), Goal number 5 (maternal health) and Goal number 6 (combating HIV/AIDS) (Antrobus 2003, 1).

Antrobus, and many other members of gender and development focused organizations, considered not only the exclusion vexing because it undermined the other Goals, but also because it represented retrogression from previous international agreements on gender such as the Beijing Platform for Action which had included references to these rights (Antrobus 2003; Barton 2005).

The campaign to include women's sexual and reproductive rights to be measured in the Goals began before the release of the original list of MDGs. By 2008 it appears that this campaign has been successful. At the 2005 UN world summit a commitment was made to recognizing the importance of sexual and reproductive rights. In 2006 Kofi Annan announced that a new MDG target of universal access to reproductive health would be included under MDG 5 (International Planned Parenthood Foundation n.d.). By 2008 the official online list of MDG Goals, Targets and Indicators was finally updated to reflect this commitment (United Nations Statistics Division n.d.).

Even with the inclusion of a target on sexual and reproductive health, there are still significant shortcomings in how the MDGs treat issues of gender. While MDG 3 relates specifically to gender, many critics of the Goals have noted that the indicators associated with this Goal provide a very limited snapshot of the state of gender relations within societies (Antrobus 2003; Barton 2005). The Indicators associated with Goal 3 are:

- Indicator 9 – the ratio of girls to boys in primary, secondary, and tertiary education,
- Indicator 10 – the ratio of literate females to males in 15–24 year olds,
- Indicator 11 – the share of women in wage employment in the non agricultural sector,
- Indicator 12 – the proportion of seats held by women in the national parliament.[1]

---

1   The 2008 update of the MDG indicators has a new numbering system. Indicator 9 becomes Indicator 3.1, Indicator 10 is included under Indicator 2.3, Indicator 11 becomes indicator 3.2, and Indicator 12 becomes Indicator 3.3.

To these critics, Indicator 9 says nothing about the quality of education, while Indicator 11 gives equal value to a woman working in a sweatshop as to a female heading a major organization. Critics also identify missing indicators measuring violence against women, female infanticide and other social characteristics that indicate much about the status of women (Barton 2005).

Are the MDGs worth engaging with?

The limitations of the MDGs, most apparent in how they treat issues of gender and development, provide a potential reason for disregarding the Goals altogether. Instead three key reasons as to why the MDGs must be addressed are presented here. First, as the experience of campaigns to have women's sexual and reproductive rights included in the Goals has shown, those who are willing to engage with the MDGs may potentially succeed in improving the measures. Secondly, while the MDGs have limitations, they are an improvement on the reductionist approaches to quantifying development (in which development was often equated only with economic growth) that were prevalent in the 1980s and 1990s. The MDGs are not a perfect set of measures for progress in human development but they are a starting point for a more holistic take on development progress. Thirdly, the MDGs have become a central focus in the rhetoric and practice of most multilateral and national development agencies. This means that those who wish to engage with these agencies also need to engage with the MDGs. We consider that the best approach to the MDGs is one of careful engagement. In places where the Goals are not being met, it can be assumed that human development quantified in broader terms is also not taking place. The countries that are meeting the Goals indicate ground for optimism although further investigations are necessary to ensure that human rights are not being violated and that the needs of women and minorities are being met as part of overall progress.

Progress in the Pacific

This discussion of the Pacific Island Countries' (PICs)[2] progress towards meeting the MDGs begins with two caveats. The first is that measurement of the Goals is fraught with issues, particularly where aspects of the measures need to be estimated or derived from other observations (Vandemoortele 2004). The second is that for many PICs there is insufficient time–series data to accurately discuss MDG progress (Secretariat of the Pacific Community 2004). Despite this caution, Figure 8.1 reports the PICs' progress with the MDGs.

---

2   Cook Islands, Federated States of Micronesia, Fiji Islands, Kiribati, Marshall Islands, Nauru, Niue, Palau, Papua New Guinea, Samoa, Solomon Islands, Tokelau, Tonga, Tuvalu and Vanuatu (Timor–Leste is sometimes also grouped as part of the Pacific).

- Papua New Guinea and Solomon Islands lag behind other PICS in almost all areas where there is data.

- Several other PICs such as Kiribati, Tuvalu and Vanuatu exhibit worrying trends or poor absolute performance in many but not all indicators.

- Cook Islands, Tonga and Samoa are the best overall MDG performers. In these states performance is strong across a majority of the MDG Indicators.

- In the education–related indicators many of the PICs are performing very well by developing country standards. However, these measures may be misleading as they report on enrolment rates and years of schooling but offer no information about the quality of education received.

- Most PICs have good absolute performance levels in education and reducing child and maternal mortality. Some PICs have recently shown a downward trend. This should be cause for concern even if absolute performance remains high.

- Although data is insufficient to accurately quantify the trend, the general perception is that poverty is worsening around the Pacific region. Poverty statistics indicate that this is a significant issue for the region (Abbott and Pollard 2004).

- HIV/AIDS (covered under MDG 6) is a major issue in Papua New Guinea, but not yet for the rest of the Pacific. Evidence suggests that this may change in the future.

- Malaria remains a long–standing scourge in Papua New Guinea (10 – 50 per 1000), Vanuatu (10 – 50 per 1000) and Solomon Islands (100 – 200 per 1000) and tuberculosis is on the rise in many PICs.

Figure 8.1   Pacific Islands Countries' progress with the Millennium Development Goals by 2004

Source: Unless indicated, Secretariat of the Pacific Community (SPC) data (2004).

Progress in gender related indicators

At a cursory glance there appears to be something paradoxical about the PICs' progress on the MDG indicators related to gender: in two of the indicators (Indicators 9 and 10) the PICs perform well; in another (Indicator 11), their performance is relatively poor; and in the fourth (Indicator 12) the Pacific's results are egregious.

MDG Indicator 9 is based on the ratio of girls to boys in primary, secondary and tertiary education. In primary education no PIC has a boy to girl enrolment ratio of less than 0.8 and the majority have an enrolment ratio of 0.9–1.0 with Nauru having more girls than boys enrolled in primary school (SPC 2004, 47). Similarly, at a secondary level only Solomon Islands and Papua New Guinea have ratios of less than 0.8, while six PICs have ratios of greater than 1.0 (more girls than boys enrolled) (SPC 2004, 47). At a tertiary level, ten of the PICs have a ratio of one or better (in Niue the ratio is higher than 3 to 1) (SPC 2004, 47).[3] There are still some PICs that stand apart from the positive results, most notably Solomon Islands and Papua New Guinea, but in general, the Pacific is doing much better than many developing regions in achieving gender parity in education. Data for Indicator 10 (literacy ratios) needs to be treated with caution as in many PICs literacy rates are inferred only from primary school enrolment rates. If the quality of schooling is poor, the relationship between primary school enrolment and literacy may be tenuous. Data suggests that many PICs have as many literate women as men (SPC 2004, 51).

MDG Indicator 11 is less positive as data indicates that the share of women in wage employment is near static or even decreasing in nearly half of the PICs for which there is available information. Moreover, Indicator 11 is a highly inadequate measure of gender parity in employment as it equates a woman employed in a sweatshop with a corporate manager (Barton 2005). Other data indicates considerable inequality and discrimination against women within the paid workforce of most PICs (SPC 2004; Narsey 2007)

MDG Indicator 12 provides further cause for concern. The SPC's 2004 report uses 2000 (or closest available year) data in its table for this indicator. This shows three PICs as having no female members of parliament, while in only two; over 10 per cent of MPs were women. In 2000 Fiji was the PIC with the highest level of female parliamentary representation, with 15.5 per cent of parliamentary seats held by women. Later coups have seen this number drop, as gender equality has suffered from political insecurity. Overall, the Pacific's results for Indicator 12 have fluctuated between being the worst (during 1990, 2008) and second worst (in 2004) of any global region (United Nations 2008, 19).

The apparent paradox between the PICs strong performance in Indicators 9 and 10 and their considerably poorer results in Indicators 11 and 12 is illustrative of the limitations of MDG gender indicators. While education is empowering and a critical capability, much lies between having an educated female population and social conditions where women have equal voice in how they live their lives and societies are shaped. A broader set of MDG indicators could offer a more detailed picture of gender relations in the PICs, showing whether the impact of education

---

3   Some care needs to be taken with tertiary rates as many are based on incomplete data or on estimates.

was 'trickling up' through society and where obstacles to progress might lie. Further examination of the status of women in the PICs, beyond that measured in the original set of gender related MDG indicators, suggests that there is cause for concern in the region. Domestic violence rates are high (SPC 2004) while other goals such as universal access to sexual and reproductive health services are unlikely to be met in the near future (House 2000).

Nevertheless, the state of Pacific gender relations are not entirely bleak. The majority of PICs have ratified the Convention on the Elimination of all Forms of Discrimination Against Women (CEDAW) and all have endorsed the Pacific Plan for Action, which calls for Pacific–wide recognition of CEDAW (SPC 2004). Some progress has been made in legislation around gender issues as indicated in a review of Pacific progress in implementing the Beijing Platform for Action (Young Women's Christian Association 1999). House (2000, 63) details this:

> ...many governments seem to have made changes to national legislation or policies in order to improve the status of women and the pace of change has accelerated since 1995. New legislation or national policies have entailed changes in family law and implementation of procedures to punish gender violence, as well as policies to raise girls' and women's access to education and training.

These legislative changes must be continued, consolidated, enforced and extended across the region. Legislative progress needs to be reflected in tangible changes in the attitudes and actions of decision makers and men in general.

The challenges ahead

The mixed progress of the PICs in meeting the MDGs is cause for concern but the region is still confronted by several challenges, which if not surmounted will further reduce chances of meeting the Goals and sustaining broad–based human development.[4]

Non communicable diseases and HIV/AIDS

A key challenge to Pacific MDG progress is that of the rising incidence of Non Communicable Diseases (NCDs) and HIV/AIDS. NCDs are not specifically mentioned in the MDGs, yet for many PICs, particularly within the more affluent ones, they pose a major challenge. Nauru already has the world's highest incidence

---

4   Climate change is a significant challenge not addressed here. This is primarily because this is a global issue – requiring global solutions – as opposed to the other specific issues concerning the region. The issue of climate change stands as a huge challenge to human development in the Pacific. If no action is taken to remedy the problem, then the outlook for human development in the Pacific will be bleak.

of diabetes mellitus per capita (International Diabetes Foundation 2003, 1) and several other PICs also have very high incidences of not only diabetes but also heart disease. More troubling is that the available evidence on NCD risk factors suggests that NCDs may become more prevalent across the region in the future (SPC 2004). The threat posed by NCDs is two–fold. These diseases have a direct impact through substantially increased morbidity and mortality. The treatment of NCDs threatens human development and attaining the MDGs through diverting government resources from other areas. Treatment costs for NCDs account for 11 per cent of the Fiji government's health spending, 18 per cent of the total in Tonga, and 27 per cent in Samoa (SPC 2004, 79). Unless the trends in NCDs are reversed, costs are likely to increase in the Pacific in the future (Khaleghian 2003).

HIV/AIDS prevalence across the Pacific region remains significantly lower than the prevalence of NCDs yet the illness has as a potential to derail development progress in the region. Papua New Guinea is currently the only Pacific Island country experiencing a generalized HIV/AIDS epidemic but the rapid spread, and impact, of the disease provides a sobering warning for the rest of the region. In 1987, there were only six reported cases of HIV/AIDS infection in Papua New Guinea; by the end of 2003 an estimated 0.6 per cent and possibly as many as one per cent of Papua New Guinea's population were estimated to be HIV/AIDS positive (Centre for International Economics 2002, 81; UNAIDS 2004, 1). Not only has the illness spread rapidly in Papua New Guinea but direct implications such as loss of life and incapacitation), as well as indirect effects on economic and health resources are significant (Centre for International Economics 2002). The situation in Papua New Guinea may become significantly worse, with the epidemic potentially becoming as severe as that in some Sub–Saharan African countries. An epidemic of this extent has major development implications beyond the immediate impact of the illness (UNAIDS n.d.). Economies may stagnate, and social structures may unravel (UNAIDS n.d.).

Unless action is taken, many other PICs may have to address rising HIV/AIDS levels. There are several reasons for believing that such a spread is a real risk. First, current statistics measuring HIV/AIDS incidence in the Pacific underestimate the prevalence of the disease. This is because many PICs do not currently have adequate HIV/AIDS testing programmes and also because the stigma associated with HIV/AIDS discourages people from being tested for the illness (AIDS New Zealand 2005). Second, at present, across much of the Pacific there are high incidences of teenage pregnancies and incidence of sexually transmitted infections. The World Bank has recently estimated that Papua New Guinea 'generates over one million new cases of curable sexually transmitted infections (STIs) every year' (*Fiji Times*, 20 March 2008, 17). This is significant not only because pregnancies and the incidence of sexually transmitted infections is indicative of unsafe sex practices, but also because existing sexually transmitted infections can facilitate the transmission of HIV/AIDS (AIDS New Zealand 2005; UNAIDS 2004). Finally, the incidence of religious beliefs and other cultural practices in many PICs make the discussion of sexual matters taboo. Such taboos impede safe sex and other illness awareness programmes that will be required to stop HIV/AIDS from spreading (AIDS New Zealand 2005; UNICEF, UNESCAP and ECPAT 2006).

The rise of HIV/AIDS in the Pacific has consequences for the region's women. Virus transfer mechanisms mean that women are much more likely to contract HIV/AIDS through heterosexual sex than men. Gender norms, as well as economic factors (in particular, men travelling for work as well as some of them having large disposable incomes) may lead to men having multiple sexual partners, thus increasing the risks of disease contraction for these women. Within relationships, gender power imbalances may mean that women are unable to request their partners to use condoms. Women are also often required to take on a disproportionate burden of care giving roles when a family member contracts HIV/AIDS (WHO n.d.).

Similarly, HIV/AIDS and conflict are interrelated. Due to its forced nature, sexual violence associated with conflict is more likely to lead to HIV/AIDS infection than consensual sex (WHO n.d.). Conflict situations can also prevent HIV/AIDS positive people from receiving the treatment they need. The likelihood of the spread of HIV/AIDS through the Pacific and the destructive impacts of the disease lead us to conclude that it represents a major development challenge to the region.

The imposition of inappropriate economic policies

In its geography, culture, institutional structures and history, the Pacific is like no other region on earth. Not only is it unique, but also the region is diverse, with much variation between countries. It would seem apparent that a pragmatic, contextually specific approach to economic policy would be the most fruitful means to fostering economic development in the region. However, the past two decades have seen the opposite occur: neoliberalism, an economic ideology with a questionable record elsewhere in the developing world (Stiglitz 2002; Hardstaff 2005) has been applied in a cookie–cutter fashion across the Pacific, usually at the behest of donor agencies, multilateral organizations, and foreign governments (ACFOA 2002; Coates and Lennon 2005; Kelsey 2004; Lennon 2005; Slatter 2006; Storey and Murray 2001).

Neoliberalism is typically associated with a laissez–faire approach to both domestic and international economics. In most PICs this has meant a shrinking of the state, where applied on the domestic front. This is not invariably negative: overly restrictive legislative regimes can stifle business development while oversized inefficient bureaucracies can drain money that could be best spent elsewhere. However, neoliberalism in the Pacific has not simply been restricted to these types of changes. Instead, its advocates have pushed for across the board policy change. In the Cook Islands, for example, neoliberal reforms led the education budget being almost halved in the mid–1990s while the budget for housing and community services was reduced from $9 million to $1 million over the same period (ACFOA 2002, 11). In Tonga, neoliberal reforms led to increased prices for services such as electricity (ACFOA 2002). In Vanuatu neoliberal reforms precipitated increased urban unemployment (Lennon 2005), while in Fiji reforms raised costs for basic services such as water and the introduction of Value Added Tax (VAT), leading to a rise in the cost of foodstuffs (ACFOA 2002; Barr 2004). The 1990s, when most of the reforms were introduced in Fiji, were a period of increased income poverty (Abbott and Pollard 2004), partly attributable to neoliberal economic policies (Naidu 2002). The social costs of such reforms are extremely unlikely to aid the MDGs being met.

The neoliberal prescription for the domestic economies' interface with the international economy is trade liberalization: lowering tariffs, reducing other barriers and increasing international trade. Although the goal of increased international trade is broadly laudable, the neoliberal approach to international economics is as counter–productive to human development as its approach to domestic economics. Much of the problem is that neoliberalism tends to equate increased trade with simply reducing formal barriers while paying no attention to less visible impediments along with countries' capacity to trade. Yet capacity is crucial and, importantly, the creation of such capacity does not appear to simply follow reduced trade barriers (Rodrik 2001). Most of today's developed countries achieved this status through various means, such as tilting the economic playing field in favour of their own domestic industries (Chang 2002). Requirements that the PICs abandon such tools indicate that advocates of neoliberalism will significantly impede PICs' development opportunities.

Neoliberalism also elevates increased trade from being a development strategy to be pursued, among others, to being the development strategy to be pursued at all costs. In the Pacific these costs are significant. For example, trade liberalization entails the removal of tariffs; yet in many PICs, tariffs are a major source of government income. In 2001, they comprised as much as 64 per cent of state revenue in Kiribati (Scollay 2001, 11). The International Monetary Fund (IMF) forecasted that with the adoption of the regional free trade agreements, countries like Fiji are likely to lose over US$100 million each year (*Fiji Times*, 21 March 2008, 16). Given this, it is highly likely that large scale tariff reduction will entail either reduced state spending (often social spending) or the raising of revenue from alternative sources by PIC governments, In the case of reduced government spending, when it comes from social services the consequences of this for meeting the MDGs are clear. However, the raising of revenue from alternative sources is also problematic, primarily because alternative revenue is typically raised via indirect taxation (such as VATs) with the flow on effect of increased costs for basic foodstuffs, that harms the poor[5] (Barr 2004; Coates and Lennon 2005).

---

5   Theoretically, price rises associated with VATs should offset price reductions resulting from tariff reductions; however, in the case of Vanuatu, this did not happen (Lennon 2005). Moreover, in many PICs staple produce is often grown locally (and thus not impacted on by tariffs) while it is 'luxury goods' (of little relevance to the poor) which are imported.

Another cost associated with trade liberalization is the destruction of existing industries with increased competition. Typically such 'creative destruction' is not seen as a problem by advocates of neoliberalism who argue that industries destroyed in the short term will be replaced in the medium to long term by newer, more efficient businesses. However, in the Pacific context of very small economies, such restructuring may not occur or restructuring may have considerable adverse effects on human development (Coates and Lennon 2005; Firth 2005).

Neoliberalism and the economic change it brings also have gendered consequences. The destruction of traditional sources of income can lead to men travelling long distances from their homes for work, and marginalize women from traditional productive activities in small scale production for household consumption and for the domestic market. Equally employment opportunities, in both export production sectors such as the garments and fish cannery industries and the service industries may favour female employment (e.g., Emberson–Bain 1994; Harrington 2004). Urbanization may also induce the disruption of traditional social networks that can lead to an increased burden of domestic work for women. The reduced government spending on health and education described above may also be borne most heavily by women (Willis 2005).

The rising tide of neoliberalism has stemmed somewhat since its peak in the 1990s yet it has not yet reversed in the region and there remains considerable pressure from the regional powers and some donors on the PICs to adopt neoliberal policy, particularly with respect to trade liberalization (Kelsey 2004; Oxfam New Zealand 2005). Until this is reversed and a more practical context–specific approach to economics adopted across the region, neoliberalism will remain a hurdle to the meeting of the MDGs.

Regional powers, power imbalances and inappropriate engagement

The promotion of neoliberalism is not the only area where the regional powers are having an impact on the Pacific. Indeed, given the vast disparity in size and political clout between the PICs and countries such as New Zealand, Australia, Japan, China, Taiwan, France and the United States, it is unsurprising that these countries continue to have a major influence on patterns of development in the Pacific. The European Union (EU) has also become a significant player as the partner of ACP countries in the region. Such influence is not always negative. Well given aid, for example, can enhance the PICs' development as can well planned peacekeeping missions. Yet too much of the engagement that these larger powers have with the Pacific is guided by self interest. Because of the power imbalance involved, self interested actions on behalf of the larger regional players have the potential to significantly impede Pacific development.

One example of the problematic interaction between the regional powers and the PICs is the vying for influence between China and Taiwan for political representation, through embassies and access to Pacific resources (Perlez 2006; Shie 2006). This striving for embassies and influence has led to large 'no strings attached' aid packages being offered to some PICs (Perlez 2006; Shie 2006). Such aid is not invariably bad but it is potentially counterproductive as it is given with little conditions or concern for how it is used. This increases the potential for corruption and can even have a destabilizing influence as the Chinese and Taiwanese governments exert pressure on PIC governments and political parties (Moore 2008). The race for resources is also not necessarily destructive – expanding markets for Pacific goods ought to aid development. Unfortunately, at present much of the economic activity is extractive, centred around natural resources, and unsustainable.[6] The long term impact on human development is likely to be more harmful than beneficial (Moore 2008).

There are numerous other examples (such as past nuclear testing by France and the US, and 'arm twisting' on WTO accession committees) where regional powers act with little regard to the interests of the PICs. There seems little evidence of this abating. For this reason and because of the sheer scale of the power imbalance between the regional powers and the PICs the actions of the regional powers will continue, in many instances, to be a challenge to meeting the MDGs in the region.

Governance

Issues of power and development are not limited to interactions between states: political power and its use and abuse within states also has the potential to dramatically influence development outcomes. Issues such as corruption and weak institutions can significantly impede not only economic development (Acemoglu 2003) but also social, environmental and other components of the development process (Eigen–Zucchi, Eskeland and Shalizi 2003). The development community is aware of this and internationally governance has become central to development discourse. The Pacific has embraced this trend especially with recent examples of bad governance in the region (see for example, Moore 2004; Naidu 2002).

The importance of improving governance in the PICs is now being taken seriously by many of the regional development actors. However, taking action and successful outcomes are not the same, and it is our view that the good governance agenda has problems. Too often, it tends to be reductionist and poorly suited to the complex reality of the Pacific (see for example, Hughes 2003). In particular, it appears blind to the need for successful institutions to be context–specific. Models that have succeeded elsewhere may be prone to failure in the PICs. Moreover, there is a strong tendency to view good governance as solely an internal issue for the PICs. Yet corruption in developing nations is partly the result of external forces,

---

6   Chinese and Taiwanese firms are not the only ones engaging in environmentally damaging extractive industries. Korean and Malaysian firms have also been involved in several countries.

> ...corruption has two sides – demand and supply. For every leader who demands
> a bribe, there is usually a multinational company or a Western official offering
> to pay it. For every pile of illicit wealth, there is usually a European or American
> financial institution providing a safe haven for the spoils (Birdsall, Rodrik and
> Subramanian 2005, 148),

In the Pacific, recent history is rife with examples of business and other interests from outside the region acting to undermine governance (Firth 2005; Kabutaulaka 1998; Kahn 2000; Larmour 1998; Moore 2004; Naidu 2003). If the regional powers are serious about improved governance in the Pacific then they will also need to tackle those problems that stem from within their own borders. At present, this side of governance is mostly neglected.

Such shortcomings associated with the 'Good Governance in the Pacific' agenda lead us to be much more pessimistic about the potential for improved governance in the region. Despite the attention that is being paid to the problem, the obstacle of governance in many PICs seems set to remain as an obstacle to currently meeting the MDGs.

Conflict

The risk of significant conflict does not exist in all PICs, but where there is conflict or the potential for conflict, the issue is of central concern. Significant conflict is certain to derail sustained human development and progress in meeting the MDGs in the countries where it occurs.

The most direct development impact of conflict is simply the loss of life and harm associated with the violence itself. As the examples of the Bougainville conflict and Solomon Islands (Alexander 2006; Amnesty International 2004; Finnin and Wesley–Smith 2000) show, such impacts can be tragic and a significant impediment to human development. However, in the Pacific, as elsewhere, the indirect impacts of conflict on development spread far further than the actual fighting. Damage associated with rioting and fighting is often significant, as in the case of riots in Solomon Islands and Tonga during 2006, and the impact of this on businesses as providers of both employment and goods. In addition to destruction of physical capital, conflict, particularly where it has an ethnic dimension, can lead to human capital depletion associated with emigration. In Fiji and elsewhere, conflict has contributed to overall economic malaise (Naidu 2005). Conflict's indirect impact on human development also extends beyond the economic sphere by impacting on government functioning and the government's ability to provide social services. Conflict in Bougainville led to political resignations and significantly diminished government revenues (O'Callaghan 2002), while the conflict in Solomon Islands led to near complete government collapse (Moore 2004). As indicated in Solomon Islands, conflict can be particularly harmful to the wellbeing of women, with sexual violence against women rising dramatically during the period of fighting (Amnesty International 2004).

While conflict is often a cause of failure in human development, it is important to note that stalled human development is also often a contributing factor to conflict. High unemployment, for example, is both a common symptom of stalled development and a significant contributing factor to conflict (Sardesai and Wam 2002). In Solomon Islands recent research suggests that high male unemployment has been a key contributing factor to ongoing tension (Romer and Renzaho 2007). The same study also found that corruption was also perceived to be a key contributing factor to conflict.

Domestic issues are not the only potential source of conflict within the region. In many cases the actions of outside interests have served as catalysts for outbreaks of violence. With the Bougainville conflict (see Chapter 6), the Australian run Panguna mine was a major contributing factor in the outbreak of violence (O'Callaghan 2002). Similarly, there is evidence that external business interests may have played a role in sparking the Fijian coup of 2000 (Naidu 2003). The corruption of some sectors of the Chinese business community appears to have been one of the contributing factors in recent riots in Solomon Islands (Moore 2008). Misguided development strategies can serve as catalysts to conflict. In the wake of the 1997 Asian Financial Crisis, International Monetary Fund (IMF) imposed structural adjustment programmes led to conflict and unrest in several Asian countries as well as in Argentina (Stiglitz 2002). Public sector reform in Solomon Islands coincided with tensions and the outbreak of open conflict in 2000.

We stress that conflict is a critical issue for the affected PICs. Unless further conflict can be prevented it is extremely unlikely that the MDGs will be met in these countries. The nexus of conflict's causes and effects is revisited in the next section.

Future pathways: Overcoming challenges meeting the MDGs

Although we have noted the Pacific's patchy progress in meeting the MDGs and detailed the major challenges we see confronting the region, we advise against pessimism. Pacific people have faced and adapted to challenges throughout their history and we are confident that they will do so again. None of the challenges facing the region are insurmountable and there are several key actions that could be taken to greatly enhance the chance of the MDGs being met and sustained human development occurring.

International engagement guided by enlightened self interest

As noted above, the scale of differences in political power between most of the PICs and the regional powers means that relatively minor decisions made by the regional powers can have significant repercussions in the PICs. However there is a positive flipside to this argument. The 'costs' for the regional powers of pursuing policies in the region that are guided more by enlightened self interest rather than self interest alone are typically small.

There are four major areas where a more enlightened approach from the regional powers to engagement with the PICs should significantly enhance regional development prospects. Two of these, aid and peace building, are dealt with separately. The other two – trade policy and monitoring of business interests – are covered here.

The need for a different approach to trade policy requires particular attention from the Australian and New Zealand governments and the EU. In recent years the governments of these nations as well as EU trade negotiators (sometimes accompanied by multilateral agencies) have pressured the PICs to reduce tariff and other formal barriers to international trade. Pressure has been exerted through the creation of the Pacific Island Countries Trade Agreement (PICTA) and Pacific Agreement on Closer Economic Relations (PACER) trade blocks (Kelsey 2004; Chapter 9), the signing of Economic Partnership Agreements (EPAs) with the EU, and also through the World Trade Organization (WTO) Accession processes that several PICs are undertaking or have undertaken (Oxfam New Zealand 2005). Presumably motivated both by misplaced ideology and potential benefits to domestic interests, the drive for trade liberalization in the Pacific has mostly been pursued with little concern for context and the potential adverse impacts of wholesale liberalization. As detailed above, such impacts are potentially major. This has been pointed out to trade officials, not only by civil society organizations and academics, but also by PIC governments, yet it continues to be ignored. Indeed, the demands placed on Tonga during its recent WTO accession were some of the most severe of any accession (Oxfam New Zealand 2005),[7] while recent EU EPAs were particularly aggressive in their demands. Simultaneously, with the small size of most PIC markets, the benefits to the EU, Australia and New Zealand of pursuing such liberalization are not huge but neither are the costs of relaxing their position. If they were willing to take a more pragmatic approach to regional trade, these powers would be more likely to increase the PICs' possibilities of achieving the MDGs.

In addition to the EU, Australia and New Zealand changing their approach to trade liberalization and trade agreements in the region, almost all of the regional powers could contribute to enhancing the PICs' chances of meeting the MDGs through the simple act of scrutinizing their own business interests. As noted, business interests based in the various regional powers have contributed to conflict in Bougainville, Solomon Islands and possibly Fiji, as well as corruption and poor governance in almost all PICs. Accordingly, a concerted effort by the regional powers to tackle unsavoury business practices by their nationals should aid governance and reduce the risk of issues such as conflict and, in turn, increase the chances of the MDGs being met.

---

7   After a process spanning more than ten years Tonga became a formal member of the WTO in 2007.

More and better Official Development Assistance

The potential for Official Development Assistance (ODA) to aid in meeting the MDGs in the Pacific is clear. ODA can pay for provision of health care and education, fund increased capacity in government ministries, facilitate the flourishing of civil society and assist pro–poor economic development. However, in the absence of ODA, it is hard to see how PICs will be able to afford the social services necessary for meeting many of the targets let alone tackle challenges such as the HIV/AIDS epidemic.

ODA will only assist the PICs in meeting the MDGs if it works. Indeed, the argument that aid does not work is commonly heard from opponents of aid giving (for example, Hughes 2003). Typically, opponents of ODA cite one of two types of evidence as example of its supposed ineffectiveness: cross country econometric regressions that 'show' a negative or insignificant relationship between ODA levels and economic growth (for example Hughes 2003) or examples of failed aid projects which are given as evidence that all aid fails. Such 'evidence' can appear convincing at first. Further investigation reveals a significantly more complex picture. Although some econometric studies provide evidence that ODA has an insignificant impact on development (see for example Easterly, Levine and Roodman 2004), many other studies find a positive relationship (Clemens, Radelet and Bhavnani 2004; McGillivray, Feeny, Hermes and Lensink 2005). Moreover, cross country regressions, blunt instruments at best, suffer from constraints, which limit their usefulness in evaluating aid effectiveness. For example, most studies quantify results in terms of economic growth, yet this is far from the only reason for which ODA is given. Entirely desirable aid project outcomes may never show up in growth statistics or only many years after the aid has been given (for instance, projects to improve health, projects to improve gender relations in a society, projects to strengthen civil society). One recent study which attempted to overcome this limitation by regressing ODA against a wider variety of human development indicators (Fielding, McGillivray and Torres 2005) found positive correlations between increased aid levels and improved outcomes in areas such as sanitation, child health and basic household assets.

A further problem with cross country regressions investigating aid effectiveness is that most regression analyses make no attempt to distinguish well given ODA from that which is given poorly. A recent attempt at tackling such limitations found a clear positive result between ODA and economic growth (Reddy and Minoiu 2006). There is some doubt over the robustness of this finding (Raghuram and Subramanian 2008), and the analysis still uses blunt tools for determining good from bad ODA, but it appears suggestive of a broader point: well given ODA can work.

This is certainly the conclusion that is most apparent from an unbiased assessment of the results of individual aid projects. While ODA's critics often point to the failures of particular projects as being evidence of ODA always failing, there are also numerous examples of ODA programmes that have succeeded. Birdsall

Rodrik and Subramanian (2005, 142), while mindful of the limitations of ODA, provide a useful list of some of its successes:

> Aid has accomplished some great things. On the health front, smallpox has been eradicated, infant mortality rates have been lowered, and illnesses such as diarrhoea and river blindness have been widely treated. Aid programs have improved women's access to modern contraception in Bangladesh and Egypt and helped increase school enrollment in Uganda and Burkina Faso. Aid also pays for much of the (still–limited) access to AIDS medicines in poor countries. In the last decade, aid has helped restore peace and order after conflicts in places including Bosnia, East Timor, and Sierra Leone.

If ODA is critical to the MDGs being met in the PICs and ODA is most effective when it is given well, the next question must be what constitutes good aid? We emphasize four salient points.

The first is that good ODA needs to be genuinely given. Many of the worst aid failures stem from the cold war era when money was given to despots, regardless of how they spent it, simply to keep them 'on our side'. Similarly, ODA which is tied to purchases in the donor country (given as a form of domestic business subsidy) is less likely to be effective than ODA accompanied by the freedom to purchase appropriately (Greenhill and Watt 2005). The second key element of good ODA is that it needs to be given free of harmful conditionalities which tie it to inappropriate economic reforms (Greenhill and Watt 2005; Stiglitz 2002). Thirdly, ODA should be given in a manner that pays concern to intersecting issues and in particular, gender. From power to poverty, gender issues cut across development and development projects (Willis 2005), and if insufficient attention is paid to gender, ODA will fail to live up to its promise and may leave women worse off. The fourth key element of effective ODA involves giving aid as an honest and open learning process. While we have some ideas as to what constitutes good ODA, not all of the contributing factors to successful ODA are clear. The monitoring and evaluation processes that have become omnipresent in recent ODA programmes should provide some of the required information, yet these are often limited. Existing monitoring evaluation needs to be complemented with systematic investigations of aid effectiveness, which examine not only individual projects and programmes but also the combined influence of aid undertakings on regions and countries. If these four key elements are adopted – and some progress is being made on these – then ODA could fulfil its potential in assisting the realization of the MDGs.

Strengthening progressive civil society

The role of civil society in fostering better governance and through this, improved development is increasingly recognized in development circles (Edwards 2004; McNeil and Mumvuma 2006; Siri 2000). The UN Millennium Project explains the importance of civil society to human development:

> Strong civil society engagement and participation are crucial to effective governance because they bring important actors to the fore, ensure the relevance of public investments, lead to discussions that best address the people's needs as they perceive them and serve as watchdogs for the development and implementation of government policies (UN Millennium Project 2005, 32).

In addition to the rationale listed by the UN Millennium Project, civil society is important because it gives citizens the ability to speak with a collective voice, and it can act as a 'countervailing force' to the manipulation of the democratic process by vested interests.

Civil society is not a homogenous sector, uniformly dedicated to improving human development (Edwards 2004). Within the Pacific, some civil society organizations have played strongly counterproductive roles (such as when some church groups have hindered sexual and reproductive health). Yet throughout the Pacific there are increasing numbers of new civil society organizations arising, which do have a strong human development agenda (Naidu 2002; Tate 2005).

These 'new' civil society organizations, along with the more progressive elements of traditional civil society groups, have the potential to become a strong force working in favour of the MDGs in the Pacific. However, many of these organizations suffer from capacity and resource constraints. Overcoming these constraints will be a long term process. Meanwhile, one important contribution that external actors can make towards MDG progress in the region is funding, via ODA and private aid, civil society organizations. The fostering of the development of civil society organizations, that can hold governments to account, means that aid can become a tool for promoting good governance and healthy democracy (Greenhill and Watt 2005).

While civil society can facilitate improved governance, the relationship between civil society organizations and governments is not all one way. Governments can do much to aid the development of civil society but can also simultaneously stifle it (Edwards 2004). For this reason it is critical that the governments of the PICs allow space for civil society to develop. It is also critical that, when this space is not provided other regional actors (including governments, international Non Governmental Organizations and development agencies) engage in constructive action to stop such repression.

Peace building in the Pacific

Conflict, as noted, poses a major development challenge to the affected PICs. The challenge of conflict is compounded because it is much harder to stop than prevent. Conflict prevention should be a primary concern of the region's development actors.

There are several mechanisms through which such concern could be translated into tangible action. One area of improvement, already touched on, would be the region's powers making sure that their business interests are not sowing the seeds of conflict through corrupt and destructive practices. If they are serious about preventing conflict in the Pacific, the regional powers will need to further clamp down on such practices.

In addition to monitoring the actions of their business interests, the regional powers need to pay careful attention to domestic policies, such as criminal repatriation, that may serve to spark unrest within the PICs. Donor agencies and multilaterals should also consider the value of preempting conflict when designing development strategies. Public sector employment creation schemes may be problematic and not mesh well with economic orthodoxy, but when considering the large concentrations of unemployed young men in conflicts around the region (Romer and Renzaho 2007) such schemes may be worthwhile. Similarly, seasonal migrant labour schemes, as have recently been discussed in Australia and implemented in 2007 in New Zealand, have the potential to relieve labour market pressures and when applied in post conflict situations, could be considered a potential peace building tool.

Economic reforms that lead to high levels of unemployment (even if only short term), in potential conflict areas, need to be avoided. Once conflict has started the issue of outside intervention arises. Such interventions are never easy and should only be embarked upon if there is a reasonable chance of success – best exemplified by the peace keeping mission in Bougainville (Fraenkel 2006). The recent Regional Assistance Mission to Solomon Islands (RAMSI) is an example of an initially successful intervention that has subsequently encountered problems.[8] The success of RAMSI was because this intervention was needed and strongly supported by most Solomon Islanders (Maclellan 2006). Subsequent problems encountered by the initiative have partly reflected the unavoidable differences of peace building and development, but also an approach that has been heavy–handed, particularly in its initial phases (Maclellan 2006). Interventions can help diffuse conflict in the PICs and should occur where they are locally supported, practical and necessary. However, if they are to succeed, they need to be holistic with the scope of development, pragmatic, and enter into in partnership with recipient countries.

---

8   The RAMSI mission to the Solomon Islands commenced in 2003 and was initially designed to restore peace and security after several years of instability and armed conflict primarily on the islands of Guadalcanal and Malaita. The mission commenced with the support of the parliament and people of Solomon Islands. While its name suggests a regional initiative and officially, 15 countries are contributing to the initiative, RAMSI draws much funding and personnel from Australia and to a lesser extent, New Zealand. RAMSI's initial focus was on restoring stability but the mission now works considerably in areas such as governance.

Conclusion

If the average New Zealander is troubled by the problems of the Pacific as they read the world pages of their local newspaper, they can simply turn the page. Policy makers, development professionals and the people of the Pacific do not have this luxury. The problems that confront the region are real and pressing, and wishful thinking and a business as usual approach will not bring about resolution. In the absence of concrete action, there is a very real chance that many of the PICs will fail to achieve the MDGs and fail to deliver sustained human development. This chapter has highlighted mixed PIC progress on the MDGs and critically, the key challenges to the Goals being met. It has outlined the risks posed by disease, inappropriate economic policy prescriptions, poor governance, conflict, and the self interest of regional powers.

These challenges are especially pressing because they are reinforcing. For example, disease burdens can contribute to economic problems, while inappropriate economic prescriptions can lead to worsening health situations. Worse still, political power imbalances and the external imposition of economic orthodoxies mean that decisions are often taken away from Pacific Islanders. Even where good policies are implemented, poor governance can lead to their failure. Within many of the challenges, gender – all too inadequately dealt with by the MDGs – is a critical cross cutting issue. From neoliberalism to HIV/AIDS the burdens of the problems facing the PICs will fall hardest on women.

If these challenges are not addressed, the worse scenario is conflict, as already painfully realized in several PICs. The histories of the Bougainville and Solomon Islands conflicts reiterate how destructive conflict is to both development and human wellbeing. Even for those who choose to ignore measures such as the MDGs, the rise in conflict in the Pacific over the last two decades should serve as a wake up call: action needs to be taken.

The challenges facing the Pacific may be significant and the causes for concern real but they are not insurmountable. In most instances they could potentially be overcome through the adoption of the solutions we have described. If the regional powers were to act to minimize the destabilizing actions of their business interests, this would help reduce corruption, environmental degradation and the risk of conflict. Increased and improved ODA could help the attainment of education and health goals as well as strengthening civil society. An approach to trade agreements and economic policy that moves from neoliberalism to pragmatism could provide crucial development space. A similarly pragmatic approach to issues of governance and conflict – which also pays attention to gender issues – will enhance development work. None of these solutions are particularly radical; all that would be required to put them in place would be for governments involved to be guided by the principal encapsulated by MDG 8: a partnership for development.

References

Abbott, D. and Pollard, S. (2004), *Hardship and Poverty in the Pacific* (Manila: Asian Development Bank).

Acemoglu, D. (2003), 'Root Causes: A Historical Approach to Assessing the Role of Institutions in Economic Development', *Finance and Development* June 2003, 27–30.

ACFOA (2002), 'Inquiry into Australia's Relationship with Papua New Guinea and Other Pacific Island Countries: Submission to the Senate Foreign Affairs, Defence and Trade References Committee' (Canberra: Australian Council for Overseas Aid).

AIDS New Zealand (2005), 'Update on HIV/AIDS/AIDS in the Pacific Region', *AIDS New Zealand* 56, 1–6.

Alexander, R. (2006), 'Political Violence in the South Pacific: Women after the Coups in Fiji', *Journal of International Cooperation Studies* 4:1, 1–31.

Amnesty International (2004), 'Solomon Islands: Women Confronting Violence', Amnesty International Report No.: ASA 43/001/2004.

Antrobus, P. (2003), 'Presentation to Working Group on the Millennium Development Goals and Gender Equality', Presentation given as part of the UNDP Caribbean Regional Millennium Development Goals Conference, Barbados, 7–9 July 2003.

Asian Development Bank (2003), *Millennium Development Goals in the Pacific: Relevance and Progress* (Manila: Asian Development Bank).

Barr, K. (2004), 'Fiji and the Pacific: Competing Paradigms of Good Governance, Human Rights and Democracy', in J. Randel, T. German and D. Ewing (eds), *The Reality of Aid 2004: An Independent Review of Poverty Reduction and Development Assistance: Focus on Governance and Human Rights* (London: Zed Books), 85–99.

Barton, C. (2005), 'Women's Movements and Gender Perspectives on the Millennium Development Goals', in *Civil Society Perspectives on the Millennium Development Goals* (United Nations Development Program Civil Society Unit), 1–27, <http://www.choike.org/documentos/mdgs_cso_barton.pdf>, accessed 30 October 2009.

Birdsall, N., Rodrik, D. and Subramanian, A. (2005), 'How to Help Poor Countries', *Foreign Affairs* 84:4, 136–152.

Centre for International Economics (2002), *Potential Economic Impacts of an HIV/AIDS Epidemic in Papua New Guinea* (Canberra: AusAID).

Chang, H. (2002), *Kicking Away the Ladder: Development Strategy in Historical Perspective* (London: Anthem Press).

Clemens, M., Radelet, S. and Bhavnani, R. (2004), 'Counting Chickens When They Hatch: The Short–term Effect of Aid on Growth', Centre for Global Development, Working Paper 44.

Coates, B. and Lennon, S. (2005), *Re–visioning Trade and Development in the Pacific* (Auckland: Oxfam New Zealand).

Easterly, W., Levine, R. and Roodman, D. (2004), 'New Data, New Doubts: A Comment on Burnside and Dollar's "Aid, Policies, and Growth"', *American Economic Review* 94:2, 253–259.

Edwards, M. (2004), *Civil Society (Themes for the 21st Century)* (Cambridge: Polity Press).

Eigen–Zucchi, C. Eskeland, G. and Shalizi, Z. (2003), 'Institutions Needed for More than Growth', *Finance and Development* 40:2, 40–3.

Emberson–Bain, A. (1994), 'Backbone of Growth: Export Manufacturing and Fiji's Tuna Fish Wives', in A. Emberson–Bain (ed.), *Sustainable Development or Malignant Growth?* (Suva: Marama Publications) 149–172.

Field, M. (2007), Interview on Radio New Zealand 'Nine to Noon' show, 2 February 2007.

Fielding, D., McGillivray, M. and Torres, S. (2005), *Synergies Between Health, Wealth, Education, Fertility and Aid: Implications for Achieving the Millennium Development Goals*, <http://www.wider.unu.edu/research/2004-2005/2004-2005-1/mdg-papers/fielding-mcgillivray-torres-160805.pdf>, (accessed 25 February 2007).

Fiji Times (2008), 'NGO: Pacific States Pressed to Sign Agreements', 16 March, 16.

Fiji Times (2008), 'PNG Records High STI Cases', 20 March, 17.

Finnin, G. and Wesley–Smith, T. (2000), 'Coups, Conflicts, and Crises: The New Pacific Way?' East West Centre Working Papers – Pacific Islands Development Series, Number 13, June 2000.

Firth, S. (2005), 'The Impact of Globalization on the Pacific Islands', Briefing paper for the 2nd South–East Asia and the Pacific Subregional Tripartite Forum on Decent Work, 5–8 April 2005, Melbourne, Australia.

Fraenkel, J. (2006), 'Pacific Democracy: Dilemmas of Intervention', *Open Democracy*, <http://www.opendemocracy.net/globalization-institutions_government/pacific_democracy_4135.jsp>, accessed 25 February 2007.

Gold, L. (2005), 'More than a Numbers Game: Ensuring that the Millennium Development Goals Address Structural Injustice', *Center Focus* 168.

Greenhill, R. and Watt, P. (2005), *Real Aid: An Agenda for Making Aid Work* (United Kingdom: ActionAid).

Hardstaff, P. (2005), 'WDM Media Briefing on the UN Millennium Project Report, in J. Sachs (ed.), *World Development Movement*, <http://www.wdm.org.uk/news/sachsbrief.doc>, accessed 13 October 2005.

Harrington, C. (2004), '"Marriage" to Capital: The Fallback Positions Of Fiji's Women Garment Workers,' *Development in Practice* 14:4, 495–507.

House, W.J. (2000), 'ICPD Goals and Thresholds: How Well have the Pacific Island Countries Performed?', *Development Bulletin* 51, 61–65.

Hughes, H. (2003), 'Aid has Failed the Pacific', *Issue Analysis* (the Centre for Independent Studies) 33, 7 May 2003, 1–32.

International Diabetes Foundation (2003), *Diabetes Atlas*, <http://www.eatlas.idf.org/Prevalence/All_diabetes/>, accessed 13 September 2005.

International Planned Parenthood Foundation (n.d.), *MDG Timeline*, <http://www. ippf.org/en/What-we-do/MDG+timeline.htm>, accessed 23 September 2007.

Kabutaulaka, T. (1998), 'Deforestation and Politics in Solomon Islands', in P. Larmour (ed.), *Governance and Reform in the South Pacific* (Canberra: National Centre for Development Studies, Australian National University), 121–153.

Kahn, J. (2000), 'The Mahogany King's Brief Reign; Business Interests Lurked Behind Fiji's Haphazard Coup', *The New York Times*, 14 September 2000.

Kelsey, J. (2004), *Big Brothers Behaving Badly* (Auckland: Pacific Network on Globalization).

Khaleghian, P. (2003), *Non–Communicable Diseases in Pacific Island Countries: Disease Burden, Economic Cost and Policy Options* (Noumea: Secretariat of the Pacific Community).

Larmour, P. (ed.) (1998), *Governance and Reform in the South Pacific* (Canberra: National Centre for Development Studies, Australian National University).

Lennon, S. (2005), 'Make Extortion History: The Case for Development–Friendly WTO Accession for the World's Poorest Countries', *Oxfam Briefing Paper*.

Maclellan, N. (2006), *Bridging the Gap between State and Society: New Directions for the Solomon Islands* (Fitzroy: Oxfam Australia).

McGillivray, M., Feeny, S., Hermes, N. and Lensink, R. (2005), 'It Works; It Doesn't; It Can, But That Depends', United Nations World Institute for Development Economics Research, Research Paper 2005/54.

McNeil, M. and Mumvuma, T. (2006), *Demanding Good Governance: A Stocktaking of Social Accountability Initiatives by Civil Society in Anglophone Africa* <http://siteresources.worldbank.org/WBI/Resources/Demanding_Good _Governance-FINAL.pdf>, accessed 25 February 2007.

Minority Rights Group International (2003), *Minority and Indigenous Peoples' Rights in the Millennium Development Goals* (London: Minority Rights Group International).

Moore, C. (2004), *Happy Isles in Crisis: The Historical Causes for a Failing State in Solomon Island 1998 – 2004* (Canberra: Asia Pacific Press).

—— (2008), 'No More Walkabout Long Chinatown: Asian Involvement in the Solomon Islands Economic and Political Processes', in S. Dinnen and S. Firth (eds), *Politics and State Building in Solomon Islands* (Canberra: Asia Pacific Press), 64–95.

Naidu, V. (2002), The Millennium Development Goals and the South Pacific, *DevNet*, <http://www.devnet.org.nz/conf2002/papers/Naidu_Vijay.pdf>, accessed 20 September 2004.

—— (2003), 'A White Shark Among Minnows? Australia's Changing Role in the Pacific', Paper presented the Australian Council for Overseas Aid Forum: 'Shifting Tides in Pacific Policy', 18 September, Canberra, Australia.

—— (2005), 'Underdevelopment and Conflict' in J. Henderson and G. Watson (eds), *Securing a Peaceful Pacific* (Christchurch: University of Canterbury Press), 370–375.

Narsey, W. (2007), *Gender Issues in Employment, Underemployment and Incomes in Fiji* (Suva: Vanuavou Publications).

O'Callaghan, M. (2002), 'The Origins of the Conflict', *Accord: An International Review of Peace Initiatives*, Issue: The Papua New Guinea – Bougainville Peace Process.

Oxfam New Zealand (2005), 'Blood from a Stone', Oxfam < http://oxfam.intelli-direct.com/e/d.dll?m=235&url=http:// www.oxfam.org/en/files/bn051215_tonga_bloodfromastone/download>, accessed 23 September 2007.

Perlez, J. (2006), 'China Competes with West in Aid to its Neighbors', *The New York Times*, 18 September 2006.

Reddy, S. and Minoiu, C. (2006), 'Development Aid and Economic Growth: A Positive Long–Run Relation', United Nations Department of Economic and Social Affairs Working Paper No. 29.

Raghuram, R. and Subramanian, A. (2008), 'Aid and Growth: What Does the Cross–Country Evidence Really Show?', *The Review of Economics and Statistics* 90:4, 643–65.

Rodrik, D. (2001), *The Global Governance of Trade as if Development Really Mattered*, United Nations Development Programme, <http://system2.net/ukpgh/wp-content/uploads/rodrikgovernance.PDF>, accessed 31 October 2009.

Romer, K. and Renzaho, A. (2007), 'Re–emerging Conflict in the Solomon Islands? The Underlying Causes and Triggers of the Riots of April 2006', *Journal of Peace Conflict and Development* 10, 1–23.

Sardesai, S. and Wam, P. (2002), *The Conflict Analysis Framework (CAF) Identifying Conflict–related Obstacles to Development*, <http://lnweb18.worldbank.org/ESSD/sdvext.nsf/67/ByDocName/TheConflictAnalysisFrameworkCAFIdentifyingConflict-relatedObstaclestoDevelopment/$FILE/CPR+5+final+legal.pdf>, accessed 23 September 2007.

Scollay, R. (2001), 'Regional Trade Agreements and Developing Countries: The Case of the Pacific Islands' Proposed Free Trade Agreement', UNCTAD – Policy Issues in International Trade And Commodities Study Series No. 10.

Secretariat of the Pacific Community (SPC) (2004), *Pacific Islands Regional Millennium Development Goals Report 2004*, (Noumea: SPC).

Shie, T.R. (2006), 'China Woos the South Pacific', *PacNet*, 10a, 17 March.

Siri, G. (2002), *The World Bank and Civil Society Development: Exploring Two Courses of Action for Capacity Building*, (Washington, D.C.: The World Bank).

Slatter, C. (2006), 'Treading Water in Rapids? Non–Governmental Organizations and Resistance to Neo–liberalism in Pacific States', in S. Firth (ed.), *Globalization and Governance in the Pacific Islands* (Canberra: Australian National University E–Press), 23–42.

Stiglitz, J. (2002), *Globalization and Its Discontents* (London: Allen Lane, Penguin Press).

Storey, D. and Murray, W. (2001), 'Dilemmas of Development in Oceania: The Political Economy of the Tongan Agro–Export Sector', *The Geographical Journal* 167: 4, 291–304.

Tate, B. (2005), 'The NGO Environment in Samoa: A Case Study of the Socio–Political Environment's Impact on Local NGOs', unpublished Masters Thesis, Victoria University.

UN Millennium Project (2005), *Investing in Development: A Practical Plan to Achieving the Millennium Development Goals* (New York, London: Earthscan).

UNAIDS (n.d), 'The Impact of HIV', <http://www.unaids.org/en/Issues/Impact_HIV/default.asp>, accessed 25 February 2007.

—— (2004), Oceania: HIV and AIDS statistics and feature, *UNAIDS*, <http://www.unaids.org/wad2004/EPIupdate2004   _html_en/Epi04_10_en.htm>, accessed 13 September 2005.

UNICEF, UNESCAP and ECPAT (2006), *Child Sexual Abuse and Commercial Exploitation of Children in the Pacific: A Regional Report* (Suva: UNICEF).

United Nations (2008), *The Millennium Development Goals Report 2008*, (New York: United Nations).

United Nations General Assembly (2000), United Nations Millennium Declaration, <http://www.un.org/millennium/declaration/ares552e.htm>, accessed 23 September 2007.

United Nations Statistics Division (n.d), 'Millennium Development Goals Indicators: The Official United Nations Site for the MDG Indicators', <http://mdgs.un.org/unsd/mdg/Host.aspx?Content=Indicators/OfficialList.htm>, accessed 23 September 2007.

Vandemoortele, J. (2004), *Can the MDGs Foster a New Partnership for Pro–Poor Policies?* (New York: Poverty Group – United Nations Development Programme).

WHO (n.d), Women and HIV/AIDS, <http://www.who.int/gender/hiv_aids/en/>, accessed 16 March 2008.

Willis, K. (2005), *Theories and Practices of Development* (Oxford: Routledge).

Young Women's Christian Association (1999), 'Pacific Regional Report on Implementation of the Beijing Platform for Action', mimeo, Pacific Regional YWCA, Suva.

Chapter 9

'Trade Driven Development': Contradictions and Insecurity for the Pacific Islands[1]

Jane Kelsey

There is a tendency in contemporary analyses of development and economic globalization to fragment and dissociate the main elements of what is an integrated dynamic. This chapter weaves together diverse questions of development, gender, the Millennium Development Goals (MDGs), trade and security in the context of the South Pacific.

Development rhetoric has become pervasive in the formal rationale and legal texts that advance neoliberal globalization, especially trade liberalization; however, the development priorities of poor countries and their people are rarely perceivable in the practice of its more powerful advocates. When I was researching the origins of the Pacific Agreement on Closer Economic Relations (PACER) in 2003, a New Zealand government representative confirmed what politicians and officials from various of the Pacific Islands had told me: 'When it comes to trade, there is no special relationship with the Pacific. The negotiators do a group hug, then they put their Geneva [WTO] hats on.'

The pursuit of self interest in the name of development is unproblematic for believers in the current ideology of 'trade driven development'. They argue that even small remote and vulnerable Pacific Islands have a potential 'comparative advantage' and will benefit from gradual immersion into a competitive global economy. That same model of market driven development underpins the Poverty Reduction Strategy Papers prepared by the Asian Development Bank (ADB), notionally in partnership with Pacific Islands' governments. These are ostensibly primary vehicles through which the MDGs are to be achieved. 'Trade driven development' is embodied in Goal 8 of the United Nations MDGs:

> Goal 8 Develop a global partnership for development.
> Target 12: Develop further an open, rule–based, predictable, nondiscriminatory trading and financial system (includes a commitment to good governance, development, and poverty reduction – both nationally and internationally).[2]

---

1   A version of this chapter was originally presented in 2005 to the 40th Otago Foreign Policy School *Human Security and Development: Meeting the Millennium Development Goals?*

2   See also 'Target 13: Address the special needs of the least developed countries (includes tariff– and quota–free access for exports)' and 'Target 14: Address the special

It also underpins the policy of donor governments, where 'coherency' between aid, finance, trade and governance now drives the aid agenda – most explicitly with the European Union (EU) under the Cotonou Agreement 2000.

This hegemonic market model of development is deeply worrying to those who believe that its theoretical premises are deeply flawed and that the real world impacts of this agenda are anti–development. If countries that are already vulnerable are encouraged or required to adopt and implement a trade led policy agenda that is inappropriate to their economic, social and political circumstances, there is a heightened risk of economic, social and political instability. These risks are borne primarily by the people and governments of those countries; but they also affect regional security and stability.

Despite the public embrace of the globalization agenda by Pacific leaders, a number of Pacific Island governments seem to share this concern. Their reticence is evidenced by foot–dragging in the implementation of existing agreements among themselves, notably the Pacific Island Countries Trade Agreement (PICTA) and the Melanesian Spearhead Group Trade Agreement, in their choice of defensive positions on the Economic Partnership Agreement (EPA) negotiations with the EU, and their attempts to delay engaging in negotiations towards a Pacific economic community with Australia and New Zealand under PACER.

I am not opposed, in principle, to measures that promote regional integration if they have been carefully considered, openly debated and enjoy the support of the people whose lives they will affect. However, I am sceptical that there is genuine endorsement of trade driven integration in various Pacific Islands and am deeply concerned at the absence of genuinely participatory debate among Pacific peoples. I am also not suggesting that the Pacific Islands should turn from the changing world. There is a risk that urging governments to challenge the globalization agenda could become a recipe for doing nothing. It is always much easier to stonewall than it is to debate alternatives, especially where governments lack confidence and expertise and where the voices of NGOs and trade unions are weak. Intransigent defence of the status quo in favour of local interests can also inhibit the consideration of sensible ways to achieve productive efficiencies and lower prices for consumers.[3] The challenge is to move beyond the binaries of global evangelism and intransigent protectionism to find a more Pacific way to move forward. The lead must come from Pacific people to promote a new development agenda that can realistically address their challenges and which their

---

needs of landlocked countries and small island developing states', through the *Program of Action for the Sustainable Development of Small Island Developing States* and 22nd General Assembly provisions <http://www.ddp-ext.worldbank.org/ext/MDG/homePages.do>.

3   That attitude was apparent in the standoff between Vanuatu and Fiji over imported biscuits, involving a breach of the MSG Trade Agreement. In 2004 and 2005 Vanuatu banned imported biscuits manufactured in Fiji to protect its sole local biscuit producer, causing job losses at the biscuit manufacturer in Fiji. In response, Fiji eventually banned the import of *kava* from Vanuatu. After much diplomatic wrangling the bans were lifted.

governments might engage with. The task for outsiders who are concerned about development, human rights, social justice and security in the Pacific is to find ways to support that process.

The context[4]

The Pacific Islands face a huge dilemma. They remain heavily dependent on former colonial powers, especially Australia, New Zealand, the United Kingdom and the United States (US), for export markets, imports, investment and aid. These economic relationships have been sustained historically through a number of preferential and non–reciprocal agreements that provide a lifeline for their limited range of commodity exports. Since the mid–1990s and the creation of the World Trade Organization (WTO) these arrangements have been under concerted attack. In a Green Paper in 1996 the EU signalled to the African Caribbean and Pacific (ACP) countries its intention to replace preferences under the Lomé Convention with WTO–compatible reciprocal agreements, negotiated on a regional basis (European Commission 1996). The ruling of the WTO Dispute Settlement Body in 1997 against the preferential regime for imports of bananas from ACP countries into the EU gave impetus to that process (Report of the WTO Panel 1997).

The Pacific Island Forum Economic Ministers discussed these developments at their annual meeting in July 1997 and resolved 'to pursue a common goal of free and open trade and investment, allowing for the special circumstances of smaller states with few exports' (Pacific Islands Forum Press Release 1997). They mandated a study of the options for implementing a free trade area among themselves. At the inaugural meeting of Forum Trade Ministers in 1998, the Forum's Secretary General Noel Levi acknowledged that people would ask 'why do this?' when the Islands had almost nothing to trade and most of their products were similar. Levi said that this assessment was 'not exactly true': there might be some immediate welfare gains from lower tariffs and prices, and longer term business opportunities that were not currently obvious might emerge in another ten or twenty years. He conceded that the real objective of regional integration was for the Pacific Islands to create a critical mass, politically and economically, in response to the new global trade environment. Levi endorsed the trade led development strategy with a sense of resignation:

> We must prepare ourselves for the changes in global trade now underway. These changes are inevitable as is the need for us to respond or else we get left further behind. We are mostly small and isolated and lack any influence as individual countries. A free trade area creates a larger economic unit or bloc that gives us a stronger foundation for responding to globalization and universal trade

---

4   The next two sections have previously been published in Kelsey 2005a.

liberalization…Many of the changes have to happen as the world moves towards greater trade liberalization. This process is not of our making but we cannot sit there and do nothing while the foundations of our economies are being removed (Levi 1999).

This was, and remains, the centre of policy advice from the Pacific Islands to the International Monetary Fund (IMF), World Bank and ADB and a series of reports from trade economists that were commissioned by the Forum Secretariat. The Island governments remained cautious. They opted for a 'stepping stone' approach that began with a free trade area among themselves – the Pacific Island Countries Trade Agreement (PICTA) – expected to lay the economic and political foundations for the renegotiation of their preferential trade arrangements with the EU, as required by the Cotonou Agreement 2000,[5] and with Australia and New Zealand as mandated by PACER.[6] The expectation of gradualism has been rapidly overtaken by developments that are interlocked and externally driven. The Pacific Islands have been submerged in a complex array of simultaneous WTO–compatible obligations and negotiations:

- The multifaceted Doha Round of multilateral trade negotiations for current WTO members (Fiji, Papua New Guinea and the Solomon Islands) began in 2001, with a seemingly indeterminate deadline;[7]
- A prolonged WTO accession process involving multilateral and bilateral phases for Vanuatu since 1996, Tonga from 1996 to 2005, and since 1998 for Samoa;[8]
- A regional Economic Partnership Agreement (EPA) with the EU for all fourteen Pacific Island members of the ACP grouping, with a deadline of December 2007 (Kelsey 2005a);
- Implementation of the Melanesian Spearhead Group Trade Agreement between Fiji, Vanuatu, Papua New Guinea and the Solomon Islands;
- Implementation of the PICTA in relation to goods among the Forum Island Countries, including domestic legislation to amend tariff schedules, its proposed expansion to the US Compact States (Palau, Marshall Islands and Federated States of Micronesia), and its extension to cover services;

---

5   Partnership Agreement Between the Members of the African, Caribbean and Pacific Group of States of the One Part, and the European Community and its Members States, of the Other Part (23 June 2000), ACP–EC, pt. 3, tit. II, ch. 1, art. 34.

6   See generally *Pacific Agreement on Closer Economic Relations* (2001).

7   For a detailed discussion of issues arising from the WTO Doha round and WTO accessions see Kelsey (2005b, 247). States engaged in the accession process are observers to the Doha negotiations.

8   Tonga completed its WTO accession in 2005 and eventually ratified the accession in July 2007, a year later than expected.

- An obligation to 'consult with a view to negotiations' for a regional economic integration arrangement with Australia and New Zealand under the PACER, to begin at the latest in 2011, or earlier if triggered by the EPA negotiations with the EU, which Australia and New Zealand insisted had occurred by 2003 (Kelsey 2004);
- The revision of Compacts of Free Association with the United States for the Federated States of Micronesia and the Marshall Islands in 2003 and scheduled for Palau in 2009.

On top of this came the Pacific Plan (Pacific Islands Forum Secretariat 2004), which has regional integration at its core.[9]

The Pacific Island governments have very limited control over most of this agenda. They also face severe problems of capacity: some of the Islands have only one or two people with limited experience or expertise to cover all these negotiations and often depend on external consultants and advisers. At a deeper level, these negotiations have the potential to reshape economic and social life in the Pacific Islands and close off the policy space available to governments to pursue any model for development other than market driven globalization.

Contrasting economic development models

There is growing disagreement, even among economists, about the appropriateness of the trade driven agenda for the Pacific. The international financial institutions and donor countries insist there is no alternative. A classic example is a report published by the World Bank in 2002, entitled *Embarking on a Global Voyage: Trade Liberalization and Complementary Reforms in the Pacific*, in which Ron Duncan and others (World Bank 2002) drew on dynamic econometric modelling to claim that the larger and more comprehensive the liberalization, the greater the aggregate welfare gains for the Islands. They applauded the requirements under Cotonou and PACER for the Pacific Islands to negotiate reciprocal free trade arrangements, because that made liberalization beyond PICTA inevitable: 'Only the timing, extent and benefits are uncertain' (World Bank 2002, 23). This report claimed that broader and deeper trade agreements offered the prospect of technology transfer and cheaper inputs and would lock in free market reforms. There were also downsides: these agreements carried risks of inefficiencies and revenue loss through trade diversion, and a 'hub–and–spoke' effect if production became concentrated in Australia and New Zealand. Larger states could also be expected to protect their own interests during negotiations at the expense of the Pacific Islands.

Rather than reconsidering the formula, the 2002 World Bank report suggested that those drawbacks, and the high transaction costs of multiple negotiations,

---

9   For a discussion of Pacific regionalism see Bryant–Tokalau and Frazer (2006).

could be avoided if the Islands provided every country with the same treatment. This might be achieved by accession to the WTO. Again, the authors conceded that the potential benefits of WTO membership, by way of financial and technical assistance and access to the dispute settlement system, could be outweighed by the transaction costs. Their optimal solution was for the Islands to lower their trade barriers, primarily their tariffs, unilaterally to the rest of the world.

Likewise, Rolf Langhammer and Matthias Lücke (2000) argued for Pacific Islands' membership of the WTO from the premise that: 'In an integrating world economy, sustainable economic growth in vulnerable economies (if and when it occurs) will be accompanied by growing exports of processed commodities or manufactures.' The WTO would provide secure market access and access to the Dispute Settlement Mechanism. Langhammer and Lücke conceded that the gains from WTO membership seem small in terms of increased market access for traditional exports from the Pacific, but they projected five additional benefits: binding governments to (neoliberal) reforms in all trade related policies; access to sizeable technical assistance to build institutional infrastructure and anchor property rights; providing shelter from unilateral pressure by more powerful countries through the ability to publicize such conflicts at the WTO; encouraging the opening of markets through a period of 'free riding', to promote greater efficiency in the allocation of scarce resources, and lower prices for consumers and input costs for exporters; and improved attractiveness to foreign investors.

A contrasting empirically based perspective was offered by Vanuatu's former economic adviser Daniel Gay (2004), who reflected on that country's experience of the ADB's Comprehensive Reform Programme, including trade liberalization and WTO accession. Gay insisted that small vulnerable countries should maintain policy space and genuine flexibility when developing their economic strategies. He reiterated that some factors affecting the Pacific Islands, such as propensity to natural disasters and remoteness, are fixed. It is not inevitable that these countries must rely on a small number of low added–value agricultural commodities whose prices fluctuate widely, even if this is theoretically their 'comparative advantage'. Achieving greater diversification requires long term programmes that are designed to boost export–oriented sectors, provide access to credit for local entrepreneurs and develop potential in services like tourism. The protection that is necessary to encourage local producers and domestic competition is often incompatible with external liberalization. Insisting on trade liberalization can also have perverse results of promoting private sector monopolies in very small markets. Roman Grynberg (undated) also highlighted the risk of inappropriate trade liberalization for the Pacific Islands and questioned whether they are stable or strong enough to weather the severe political and economic consequences of the very long and difficult transitions that neoliberal policies would require.[10]

---

10   This paper was written when Grynberg was Multilateral Trade Policy Adviser at the Forum Secretariat. In 2006 he was appointed the Director of Trade Policy at the Pacific Island Forum Secretariat.

Gay (2004, 36) makes a second, related observation based on Vanuatu's experience: 'Even if the [ADB's Comprehensive Reform] programme had been technically successful there is a moral angle too: a critical mass of country inhabitants must *own* a reform package rather than having it foisted upon them.' A theoretically driven policy template that has been devised from outside, ignores the realities of the country and is implemented at a culturally alien speed, is bound to be sabotaged and fail. Governments become resistant to change and the costs are then borne by their people. Gay's critique highlights the thorny problem of reconciling economic policies with both culture and lifestyle aspirations. How should governments respond if they recognize that competitive markets and export led growth are inappropriate or unachievable, but their people nevertheless want access to imported consumer goods and technologically advanced services? Can dual economies continue to operate where one part of a country's economic, social, cultural and political life, including land ownership, is marketized and the rest is not? Managed temporary migration programmes into Australia and New Zealand to generate remittances and skills have been promoted as economic lifelincs – but is this a genuine development strategy, and is it likely to be sustainable given the history of political and economic expediency in policies on Pacific immigration?

The following three examples on food, employment and migration flesh out the tensions between trade liberalization and development, and the contradictions that are embedded in the MDGs, with particular reference to New Zealand and Australia. Equally important questions about the notion of 'development' arise under the Cotonou Agreement – for example, the interrelationship between the pursuit of MDG 7 (Ensure Environmental Sustainability) through the combination of the EU Water Facility for ACP countries (European Commission 2004), the interests of Europe's dominant transnational water companies, the EU's requests on environmental services during trade negotiations and the promotion of water privatization by the international financial institutions (Corporate Europe Observatory 2007).

Who needs more mutton flaps?

Two World Health Organization reports in 2001 and 2002 drew explicit links between Tonga's dependence on imported foods, especially mutton flaps, diet related disease and trade liberalization (Evans, Sinclair, Fusimalohi and Liava'a 2001; also Evans Sinclair, Fusimalohi and Liava'a 2002). They concluded that people were making conscious decisions to eat less healthy foods because they were cheap and available:

> One effect of globalization has been to increase reliance on imported foods, rather than traditional foods. Imported high fat–content meats, especially corned beef, mutton flaps, and chicken parts, are among the main causes of the rising rates of noncommunicable diseases. Although educational programmes have

increased awareness about healthy diets and nutritional foods, people in the Pacific nonetheless choose to consume less–healthy foods because of cost and availability (i.e. they make economically rational, but nutritionally detrimental decisions to consume certain foods). Thus, poor diet is not simply a health or health–education issue, it is also economic. It appears that the solution to diet–related non–communicable diseases in Tonga cannot be based solely on nutritional education. Both the problem and the solution appear to involve economics. One possible answer would be to follow the example of Fiji and ban the importation of fatty foods. Other policy alternatives would promote the development of sustainable indigenous fishing and farming industries that could make the preferred and healthier traditional foods readily available at a reduced cost. However both these solution could run afoul of the GATT and WTO [and therefore WTO–compatible arrangements like PACER]…It behoves national policy–makers to be aware of the health impact of 'commodities of doubtful benefit', and of the role of trade in the health of the population (Evans, Sinclair, Fusimalohi and Liava'a 2001, 856).

The Tongan government urged its New Zealand counterpart to end mutton flap exports and encourage a return to healthier traditional diets, such as fish, organic chicken and taro that cannot compete in Tonga's small domestic market. The opposite was likely to result from Tonga's accession to the WTO (Working Party on the Accession of the Kingdom of Tonga 2004). During the tortuous nine year accession process, the Tongan government made commitments that have the potential to cripple its economy, entrench the dominance of the elite through private sector monopolies and fuel political instability. New Zealand's trade negotiators followed their standard approach to WTO accessions by demanding commitments that would create precedents for New Zealand's strategic objectives in agriculture and by refusing concessions that might undermine its hard line approach with more significant acceding countries, like Russia.

In April 2004, New Zealand's Trade Minister Jim Sutton (2004) hailed the completion of Tonga's bilateral accession negotiations as 'saving' New Zealand exporters $6 million in tariffs. That meant Tonga, which then drew over 40 per cent of government revenue from border duties, would need to make up a $6 million fall in revenue from elsewhere. The options were a combination of user charges, broader sales tax and consumption tax – in a country where 80 per cent of the people are subsistence farmers and whose cash income comes largely from remittances. Reports suggest that similar demands were made of Samoa in its WTO accession negotiations (*Sunline* 2004). Samoan representatives have been especially critical of New Zealand's behaviour and demands (*Sunline* 2004). It is worth noting that New Zealand has systematically refused to address the special needs of least developed countries and small island developing states in accession negotiations, anticipated in Targets 12 and 13 of MDG 8.

New Zealand supplies around one third of Tonga's imports. About one third of that is foodstuffs, including a large proportion of a fatty waste product known as 'mutton flaps'. According to trade theory, consumers will benefit by lower prices once tariffs are removed. This is not necessarily so; experience suggests that the exporters and distributors tend to increase their prices almost back to the previous level. Aside from that possibility, there are sound health and development reasons, evidenced by the WHO reports, for hoping that prices for meat imports from New Zealand do not fall.[11] Far from accepting responsibility to address this issue, former Labour Member of Parliament Philip Taito Field argued it was the right of Tongan businesses to decide what to import (quoted in Choudry 2002).

Faced with contradictions between health objectives and trade obligations, Pacific Island governments have a difficult choice. Fiji, a WTO Member, did impose a ban on mutton flaps, claiming there are proven links to obesity (Government of Fiji 2001). New Zealand threatened retaliation at the WTO, but backed off doing so. It is unclear whether that reflected a legal assessment of the merits of the case, or fear of being exposed to accusations that it knowingly dumps unhealthy waste products on the Pacific Islands while NZAID funds health education programmes to promote awareness of the health risks of consuming those products.

Garments

Fiji's two major commodity export industries are sugar and garments. Both have been under threat from the loss or erosion of historic trade preferences provided under the Lomé Agreement with the EU, South Pacific Trade and Economic Cooperation Agreement (SPARTECA) with Australia and New Zealand, and with the US under the WTO's Agreement on Textiles.[12] Ironically Fiji had been encouraged to build the garment sector to take advantage of those preferences. Trade liberalization in Fiji's major markets has progressively reduced the value of garment exports. With preferences now also spreading across more countries, new competitors are undercutting Fiji's 'comparative advantage' of cheap labour and incentives for foreign firms. That trend will intensify as Australia and New Zealand conclude free trade agreements with China and other garment exporting countries, such as the Association of South East Asian Nations (ASEAN), that

---

11   Paradoxically, New Zealand's mutton flap exports to the Pacific may fall as other export markets emerge; levels have fluctuated since access to China's market opened in 2002. Exports to China were: 2000: 10,044 tonnes; 2001: 11,059 tonnes; 2002: 10,864 tonnes; 2003: 12,932 tonnes; 2004: 9,633 tonnes (this is considered a most unreliable figure); in 2003 this trade was worth around NZ$22.5 million. Comparable figures for the Pacific were 2000: 9,560 tonnes; 2001: 7,450 tonnes; 2002: 6,011 tonnes; 2003: 6,092 tonnes; 2004: 7,901 tonnes; in 2004 this trade was worth roughly NZ $14.5 million. Figures courtesy of Brian Lynch, former Chair of the New Zealand Meat Board.

12   The expiry of quota restrictions under the WTO Agreement on Textiles and Clothing in December 2004 at the end of a ten year phase–out period allowed equal access for products from other countries, notably China, into Fiji's major markets.

expedite the removal of remaining tariffs on Textiles, Clothing and Footwear (TCF). The continued loss of jobs and potential closure of more firms will have a huge economic, social and political impact in Fiji[13] and also affect Samoa.

After the 1987 coup, the military government led by Sitiveni Rabuka, established Free Trade Zones in an attempt to attract investors back to Fiji.[14] Foreign factory owners were enticed by a special lower minimum wage for garment workers, nonunionized workplaces and a reservoir of unemployed desperate for jobs. New Zealand factories were the first to move from Fiji, after the government began radically reducing tariffs in 1987. Australian factories soon became the mainstay of Fiji's new low skilled and low technology Cut Make and Trim operations. In addition to lowering its domestic tariffs, the Australian government introduced a self–serving Import Credit Scheme. This allowed Fiji to include fabric sourced from Australia, but made elsewhere, as local content to satisfy SPARTECA's Rules of Origin. By 1999 Australia was taking 70 per cent of Fiji's total textile exports. The Import Credit Scheme ran foul of WTO rules and was replaced in 2001 by the SPARTECA (TCF Provisions) scheme. A complex formula gave Fijian exporters new ways to manipulate the calculation of local content, but this proved difficult to implement in practice and offered little to Australian producers. SPARTECA–TCF was due to expire in late 2004 but following a review Australia announced it would be extended for seven more years (until 2011, coincidentally when negotiations under PACER are required to begin), with a further review after three years (Customs Tariff Amendment Bill (No. 1) 2005).

Garment imports are an intensely political issue in Australia, where employment in the TCF industry has fallen but remains significant. China is the domestic industry's prime competitor, but Fiji remains a significant player so long as tariffs and the SPARTECA–TCF arrangement are in place. The Australian government's policies target support to Australian owned garment companies, textile manufacturers and brand name retailers. The cost of that policy has been borne within Australia by over 57,500, mainly women workers who have lost their jobs in three waves of tariff cuts since 1986 as Australian factories relocated to Fiji or Asia, and an estimated 300,000 homeworkers who were reported in 2004 to work up to 18–hour six or seven day weeks for $2 to $3 an hour (see Delaney 2004; Textile, Clothing and Footwear Union of Australia 1995; Webber and Weller 2001). A Productivity Commission inquiry into the industry's future in 2003 led to a tariff pause (Australian Productivity Commission 2003), with renewed cuts in 2010 to reach a 5 per cent tariff level in 2015, plus a ten–year restructuring

---

13   According to The Fiji Islands Bureau of Statistics production in Fiji's garment and footwear industry fell 55 per cent in 2005 compared to 2004, the largest decline since 1997. 'Fiji Garment Industry Takes 55 Percent Plunge', *Fiji Times*, 5 April 2006 <http://archives. pireport.org/archive/2006/april/04-06-09.htm>.

14   Most of the following discussion on the Fiji garment industry is drawn from DFAT Economic Analytical Unit (2003).

package that focused on design, strong brands and new technology (Department of Industry, Tourism and Resources 2004). However, this implied there would be fewer, more highly skilled jobs, which many existing workers are not equipped to fill. That strategy ran in tandem with negotiations between China and Australia for a free trade agreement that was expected to cover textiles.[15]

The story in New Zealand was both similar and different. The garment industry had barely survived repeated rounds of tariff cuts in the 1980s and 1990s, which saw clothing factories close or move offshore. Initially the threat to vulnerable Maori, Pacific Islands and Asian women workers came from Fiji. By the mid–1990s this was overtaken by imports from China, where exploitation of low–cost labour made garments even cheaper. New Zealand factories tried to compete by using labour market deregulation to cut real wages and deunionize the workforce. By 1999 tariffs had been abolished on everything except for TCF, which retained average applied tariffs at 19 per cent due to a campaign led by unions with small town mayors and local factory owners. In 2003, the Labour government proposed abolishing all tariffs by 2010 to meet APEC's voluntary free trade deadline. Unions attacked the hypocrisy of a Labour government whose industry strategy was to produce high value outdoor clothing and chic fashion for niche export markets, both of which require a critical mass of producers and skilled workers, while simultaneously seeking to strip out the remaining 18,000 jobs and infrastructure of the industry (Kelsey 1999, 212–17). The compromise – ten per cent tariffs by 2009 and another review – offered false security. Negotiations for a free trade deal with Hong Kong stalled once it became clear this would provide back–door entry for Chinese garments, but the conclusion of a free trade agreement with China signalled the final surrender of the clothing industry.[16]

These developments have had huge implications for Fiji. The garment industry initially boomed, overtaking sugar as the main export earner by 1997. In 2000 it exported F$200 million in garments to Australia, New Zealand, US and Europe. Almost two thirds of factories were foreign owned, and many of these investors left after the 2000 coup. A longer term threat came from cheaper competition from China and East Asia, and New Zealand's decision in 2000 to remove tariffs on imports from all Least Development Countries, including garment producing Bangladesh. Although garments were still 33 per cent of Fiji's total exports and 6.2 per cent of GDP in 2002, output dropped by 20 per cent (DFAT 2003). Competitive pressure once more fell on women workers. A production cost of US$5 and a sale price of US$50 in 2003 reflected wages that were below the poverty line. These

---

15   The negotiations began in 2005 but became stalled over China's offer on access for agricultural products.

16   The NZ China FTA was sweetened by a 2016 deadline for phasing out tariffs on garments, resulting in a two year freeze on the tariff cuts that had previously been expected in July 2009. This was still too late to foreclose industry closures and job losses at iconic New Zealand garment firms. 'Textile Union Welcomes Tariff Freeze', <http://www.bilaterals.org/article.php3?id_article=12071>.

often (but not always) existed alongside demeaning workplace practices, other kinds of abuse, anti–family work hours, health and safety violations, and threats to union members (Oxfam 2004). It was then estimated that 15,000 women garment workers depended on these low quality non–agriculture jobs to provide direct and indirect support for one fifth of Fiji's urban, and many rural families. In addition, some employers came to prefer immigrant women from outside as a higher skilled, productive and docile workforce, although entry rules were subsequently tightened.

Fijian garment producers argued that the future of the industry hinged upon reducing the local content requirement of the rules of origin under SPARTECA–TCF from 50 per cent to 30 per cent (see e.g., DFAT 2003). This would enable some factories to continue producing higher quality, short run, quick turnaround garments to Australia and New Zealand, and service the niche market tourist sector under PICTA. By sourcing fabric from elsewhere they could also reduce the loss of orders to Asia that resulted from the restrictive rules of origin. The Textile and Fashion Industry of Australia vigorously opposed the proposal (Durutalo 2007). Even if the Australians had agreed, the 'best case scenario' would have required fewer and more highly skilled workers. A majority of garment workers would still become unemployed. Fiji's garment manufacturers used the prospect of closures and job losses to resist moves to alleviate wage poverty of garment workers.[17] Many of those who depended on the dwindling jobs in the garment industry were Indo Fijian women at a time when Indo Fijian men were losing jobs on sugar plantations and the number of families squatting in urban slums was growing dramatically. The cumulative effect of industry decline and job losses in Fiji's fragile economy, especially after the 2006 coup, has potentially serious implications for social and political stability.

This example exposes direct contradictions between MDG 8 and MDG 3 on gender equality, which is to be measured partly through the 'share of women in wage employment in the non–agriculture sector'. MDG 3 aims to promote gender equality and the equitable employment of women through non–agricultural waged labour. However, it says nothing about the quality of that employment in an era that is driven by competitive deregulation, especially of wages and conditions for women workers. Equally, the 'trade driven development' model avoids addressing the consequence of pursuing MDG 3 through the MDG 8 strategy of unilateral liberalization and free trade treaties, and the prospect that it will deepen, rather than reduce, gendered exploitation, insecurity and poverty.

---

17   The Textile Clothing and Footwear Council of Fiji blamed a 20 per cent increase in the minimum wage for garment workers from $1.25 to $150 an hour or $1.48 to $178 an hour for 300 job losses in the industry and warned of 1,000 more to follow. 'Fiji Garment Industry: Wage Increase Threatens Jobs', *Fijilive* 16 February 2009 <http://pidp. eastwestcenter.org/pireport/2009/February/02-17-02.htm>.

Trade in people

The third example involves temporary migration of workers in service sectors. Pacific Islands' governments want to increase the number of their people who are allowed to work temporarily in other countries, especially Australia and New Zealand (Grynberg 2002). They see this as a way to increase remittances as a partial substitute for revenue lost to the country through tariff cuts, earn foreign exchange, soak up unemployment and develop their national skill base. By presenting this as a trade liberalization measure that will enhance their 'comparative advantage', they hope to circumvent the political sensitivity and racism that surrounds short term migration from the Pacific.

The temporary presence of foreign personnel has been defined in the General Agreement on Trade in Services (GATS) as 'Mode 4' of supplying services (Kelsey 2008 189–206). To date, almost all commitments that countries have made to liberalize the international movement of service labour in the GATS and bilateral agreements have been limited to executives, professionals and technical specialists. What rich countries portray as a 'trade' issue when it involves the professionals and executives of transnational companies reverts to being an immigration issue when it involves lesser skilled workers, primarily from the global South.

India has insisted that expanding the categories to include a wider range of skilled workers, technicians and independent contractors is a prerequisite for any deal in the Doha round of WTO negotiations. Richer countries, especially the US, have remained resistant to make such binding commitments. Poorer countries are making similar requests regarding less skilled workers, but they have much less leverage than India. The idea that they could secure binding rights of entry for less skilled services workers is almost inconceivable.

Developed countries are quite content with the current hierarchical brain drain: the richest countries recruit the nurses, teachers and skilled technicians trained in countries like Australia and New Zealand, who in turn lure ready–trained replacements from poorer countries, such as the Pacific Islands, who cannot provide comparable wages, conditions and facilities. Nevertheless, the Pacific Islands governments and advisers promote Mode 4 as the one area where they can potentially gain from through trade negotiations (Pacific Islands Forum Secretariat 2004). The Melanesian Spearhead Group proposed that the EU should accept a guaranteed quota of Pacific Islands services workers in tourism, security and seasonal agriculture on a temporary basis as part of the EPA. The training they received could be used to build up the country's services when they returned home. Remittances would help replace the lost income to the country from tariffs on imports. The Melanesian Spearhead Group conceded that their main objective was not access to the EU, which is a relatively unattractive destination for Pacific people because of distance, language and lack of family ties. They wanted leverage for a future deal with Australia and New Zealand under PACER, either as a stand–alone agreement or as a trade–off for other parts of a free trade pact. The Vanuatu government, which would be hardest hit by the loss of tariffs, calculated the precise number of temporary migrants whose remittances would compensate from the loss of revenue under both a Pacific EPA and PACER. This calculation assumed that people would continue to send back a quarter of their salary for up to 20 years, and noted that their proposal was for a much shorter period.[18]

Fiji economist Wadan Narsey has also strongly advocated for Mode 4 (Narsey undated). He criticized Australia and New Zealand for draining the Pacific's skilled and professional workforce, while shutting their doors to the small number of unskilled workers who want to come from the Islands to do the work that their own people are not interested in. Narsey has argued for

> specific programmes of development co–operation that will result in enhanced levels of investment (both domestic and foreign), higher rates of sustainable economic growth, and most importantly, retention of skilled persons in the FICs, and the regulated access of FIC unskilled labour to the labour markets of Australia and NZ (Narsey 2003, 45).

Narsey proposed a flexible system of permanent residence for skilled and professional workers that would allow them to come and go freely from the Islands. A second scheme for unskilled labour would provide lower cost workers for unattractive jobs, thereby reducing unemployment pressures in the Pacific and providing remittances. According to Narsey, this concrete benefit that ordinary people could obtain would far outweigh any abstract concerns about the broader loss of sovereignty from the trade agreements.

Narsey rejected fears that people would overstay, saying the option of earning better money offshore and then returning home would be much more attractive than emigrating permanently. That is debatable. Such schemes would also only be possible with the support of Australian and New Zealand trade unions. The unions are genuinely concerned about the potential exploitation of Pacific migrant workers. This already occurs in low skilled service industries, such as cleaning, where the transnational firms that control these contracts pay the minimum wage for unregulated work hours and poor conditions, and are consistently hostile to unions. Those workers struggle to meet their living costs, pay church tithes and remit money home. At the same time, the unions are concerned that cheap migrant labour will be used to drive down wages and deunionize in already vulnerable occupations.[19] These concerns are heightened by Narsey's suggestion that temporary migrants might be paid less than local workers (Narsey undated).

New Zealand's Recognised Seasonal Employer programme, introduced in 2007, and the Australian three year trial guest worker programme that began in

---

18   Information provided to the author by Vanuatu trade officials on a visit to Port Vila in 2003.

19   'Australia's Pacific guest workers scheme' ABC Radio 9 September 2008, <http://www.radioaustralia.net.au/news/features/s2359609.htm>

2009, were responses to the pressure to increase temporary access for Pacific workers. Yet both governments retained the discretion to determine the numbers of workers, select participating countries and be able to unilaterally terminate the schemes.

The Commonwealth Secretariat has promoted a more structured proposal to train nurses explicitly for export.[20] The notion of 'managed temporary migration' was based on a scheme for training nurses in the Caribbean. It was argued that the Pacific Islands are already losing large numbers of professionals to out–migration. Australia and New Zealand suck out nurses trained at the Islands' expense without taking any responsibility for the resulting brain drain. As demand for nurses and caregivers continues to rise, the sustainability of local Pacific services will be jeopardized. Yet Pacific Islands' governments maintain that the decision to migrate is a matter of people's choice. A managed approach would provide a means to balance national needs and the desire to emigrate with incentives for skilled workers to return.

The proposal involved Australian or New Zealand universities delivering their accredited health care qualifications in the Pacific, in return for incentives and tax write–offs, guaranteed work permits and remittance of profits. This would operate as a commercial enterprise that catered to full fee–paying Pacific students and to Australian and New Zealand students who could not gain entry to the course at the home campus. A quota of nurses with appropriate levels of experience would be guaranteed entry to Australia and New Zealand each year. They would be selected by lottery, with no guaranteed job on their return home. Others who chose to stay in their home country would receive assistance through land grants, training benefits and tax incentives. The Pacific Island governments would be responsible for maintaining the regulatory framework and policing a Code of Conduct that dealt with certification, length of stay, years of service before eligibility and reintegration arrangements.

This proposal has its attractions. Accepting a limited number of specially trained workers could ensure that good labour laws protect migrant and local workers. There are also significant downsides for other aspects of development. A study of a Caribbean model predicts that the cost of nurse training will rise, and over time it will be viewed as a purely commercial enterprise (Thomas, Hosein and Yan 2005). Even in a mixed system of full fee–paying and subsidized students, it is difficult to maintain a balance between public services and commercial objectives. There could also be a corresponding marketization of

---

20   'Outcomes Document. Framework of Action for a Programme of Temporary Movement of Agreed at the Caribbean Conference on Temporary Movement: Towards a Trade and Development Approach, 30–31 March 2005, Barbados', in 'Migration in the Caribbean: What do we know?' Expert Group Meeting on International Migration and Development in Latin America and the Caribbean, November–December 2005 Port of Spain, Annex 2, <http://www.un.org/esa/population/meetings/IttMigLAC/P09_ECLAC(Port%20of%20Spain).pdf>.

health care where people's access to, and use of, more expensive professional services reflects their ability to pay. The for–profit health care sector would have incentives to engage in skimming off the most qualified staff and lucrative services, which would seriously undermine the public health system. Local cultural dimensions of nurse training would also be eroded by foreign courses that might be based on an imported curriculum.

There are other downsides in the Pacific context. The proposal assumes a level of regulatory sophistication that does not currently exist in any of the Pacific Island source countries. The nurses, primarily women, would face risks of exploitation by their home government, recruiters and employers. There is already evidence that Filipino nurses in New Zealand face insecure contractual employment, racism in the workplace, and hostility from local workers (Manchester 2005). Larger scale temporary migration has additional social, gender and cultural implications for the Pacific. The absence of adult women for several years at a time can contribute to family breakdown, disrupt village and community relationships, and alter traditional cultural values and roles. None of these are recognized, let alone addressed, within the 'trade' discourse.

The pretence that this is a trade issue removes the onus from governments to explore the potential costs and benefits of managed migration as a development strategy. Uncritically pursuing mode 4 carries additional risks that governments will commit themselves to further liberalization that compounds the push factors behind migration for remittances. That would increase dependency on remittances in a vicious cycle that erodes the potential for adopting more socially responsible development strategies (Kelsey 2008, 213–20).

Putting people back into development

These examples reveal some of the economic, social and cultural implications of 'trade driven' development. They are development issues; yet they are being dealt with in the secretive arena of trade negotiations, whose ideology and processes does not allow for open, critical debate and a consideration of alternatives. The current paradigm is supported by reports from economic consultants that are routinely based on econometric modelling and crude proliberalization assumptions (e.g., Scollay 2002). That advice is often kept secret, even after decisions have been made, so there is no opportunity for critical peer review. Pacific Islands ministers and officials are therefore denied the breadth of advice that is necessary to inform their decisions.

This practice has been strongly criticized by regional NGOs. In response to NGO criticisms of PICTA and PACER the Forum Secretariat commissioned a 'social impact assessment' on PICTA in 2001. The consultants argued that the agreement would have little economic impact, so its social impacts would also be negligible (Forsyth and Plange 2001). If there were to be impacts, economic theory told them that PICTA would produce lower unemployment, rising incomes, better living standards and improve the status of women. The Forum Trade Ministers simply noted the report at the same meeting as they signed both agreements. The ministers also asked the Forum Secretariat to convene a regional workshop on training and preparations to establish a framework to monitor PICTA, but did not allocate the resources to do so. Three years later the Secretariat finally contracted two regional women's organizations – the Pacific Foundation for the Advancement of Women (PACFAW) and the United Nations Development Fund for Women (UNIFEM) to work alongside to provide training in implementing a module on social impact assessment that had been prepared by an outside consultant. One stated goal of the training was to convince participants of the value of social impact assessments. The first assessment would not be conducted until at least 2006, and would be solely about PICTA – the agreement that would have the least impact on the Pacific Islands.

Some Pacific governments have recognized this concern. The negotiating strategy of the Vanuatu government on the Pacific EPA acknowledged how little research had been done on social impacts and that none had assessed the social meaning of an EPA. Although a social impact study was beyond the terms of reference and role of Department of Trade, it could help to coordinate a social impact study conducted by a NGO, the Kaljoral Senta (Vanuatu Cultural Centre) or a trade union. That study might include:

- Examination of the likely social impact of tariff reductions on prices of staple products such as rice, tinned fish and kerosene;
- An examination of the tax structure and how possible changes resulting from trade liberalization would affect low income groups, especially if tariff cuts accelerate the need for income tax and lead to a more progressive tax regime;
- An assessment of the impact on employment;
- An analysis of what would happen socially if the service sectors identified by the government were liberalized;
- Social impact of the movement of seasonable agricultural workers overseas, including the possible impact of remittances on community consumption levels; whether the temporary movement of people overseas would erode cultural values; the effect of on–the–job training received abroad; and potential for any brain drain.[21]

The Vanuatu government appears not to have pursued that proposal. As a result of continued criticism, several Social Impact Assessments and similar reports commissioned by the Pacific Islands Forum Secretariat have been published more widely (e.g., Nathan Associates 2007), and one was even contracted to a consortium led by a regional NGO (Pacific Network on Globalisation 2008).

---

21   *Vanuatu's Negotiating Position for the Economic Partnership Agreements with the European Union*, November 2004. On file with author.

However, the narrow terms of reference for these studies continue to constrain the potential for critique, let alone the exploration of alternatives to the trade driven paradigm of development.

The closure of debate around trade negotiations exposes a serious constitutional dilemma. Trade agreements increasingly usurp the normal democratic and legislative processes of governments in a wide range of areas. Yet most governments seem reluctant to expose their trade negotiating proposals to scrutiny, not simply because it would undermine their bargaining position but also perhaps because they do not always understand their implications, lack the resources to engage in public debate and ultimately enjoy the opportunity to exercise unfettered executive power.

As the trade liberalization carousel spins ever faster, most Pacific Islands governments seem to feel they cannot afford to say no to their more powerful donors.[22] The EU brought unconscionable pressure to bear on Pacific ACP countries during the EPA negotiations. Australia and New Zealand have insisted that those negotiations have triggered the obligations of the Forum Island countries to negotiate even broader concessions under PACER. The impact on government revenue, local businesses and jobs in the Pacific of a reciprocal free trade agreement that deals only with goods could be devastating; even more so if its coverage was extended to services and foreign investment. Yet Australia and New Zealand, like the EU, maintain the pretence that their self interested ideological, economic and trade objectives are really about development (see Kelsey 2003). The challenge facing critics of the 'trade driven development' paradigm is to create enough breathing space for the people and governments of the Pacific to explore alternative models that reflect their own aspirations for development.

References

Australian Productivity Commission (2003), Review *of TCF Assistance – Inquiry Report* (Report No. 26).

Bryant–Tokalau, J. and Frazer, I. (eds) (2006), *Redefining the Pacific? Regionalism Past, Present and Future* (Aldershot and Burlington: Ashgate).

Choudry, A. (2002), 'Killing me Softly', ZNET Commentary, 3 August 2002, <www.arena.org.nz/azpacfod.htm>, accessed 4 September 2004.

Customs Tariff Amendment Bill (No. 1) 2005.

Corporate Europe Observatory (2007), *WTO and Water. The EU's Crusade for Corporate Expansion*, <www.corporateeurope.org/water/infobrief3.htm>.

Delaney, A. (2004), *Campaigning At Work; A Guide to Campaigning for Homeworker Organizations, Unions, Campaign Groups and Activists* (London: Homeworkers Worldwide).

---

22   For accounts of the pressure exerted on Pacific Islands governments see <http://www.pang.org.fj/>.

Department of Industry, Tourism and Resources (27 May 2004), 'Textile, Clothing and Footwear Industry Fact Sheet', <www.industry.gov.au/industry>, accessed 5 August 2004.

DFAT Economic Analytical Unit (2003), *Future Directions for Fiji's Garment Industry: Scoping Study* (Canberra: DFAT), <www.dfat.gov.au/publications/catalogue/fiji_garment_industry_paper.pdf>, accessed 5 August 2004.

Durutalo, A.L. (2007), 'Melanesia in Review: Issues and Events, 2006: Fiji', *The Contemporary Pacific* 19:2, 578–82.

European Commission (1996), *Green Paper on Relations Between the European Union and the ACP Countries on the Eve of the 21st Century – Challenges and Options for a New Partnership* (Brussels: European Commission).

—— (January 2004), 'Establishment of a European Water Facility for ACP Countries', <http://europa.eu.int/scadplus/leg/en/lvb/r12531.htm>, accessed 5 August 2005.

Evans, M., Sinclair, R.C., Fusimalohi, C. and Liava'a, V. (2001), 'Globalization, Diet and Health: An Example from Tonga', *Bulletin of the World Health Organization* 79:9, 856–62.

—— (2002), 'Diet, Health and the Nutrition Transition. Some Impacts of Economic and Socio–economic Factors on Food Consumption Patterns in the Kingdom of Tonga', *Public Health Dialogue* 9:2, 309–15.

Forsyth, D. and Plange, N.–K. (2001), *Social Impact Assessment of Membership of the Pacific Free Trade Area* (Suva: USP).

Gay, D. (2004), 'The Emperor's Tailor: An Assessment of Vanuatu's Comprehensive Reform Programme', *Pacific Economic Bulletin* 19:3, 22–39.

Government of Fiji (2001), 'Health of Fijians More Important than NZ Threats', Press Release, 15 March 2001, <www.fiji.gov.fj/press/2001_03/2001_03_15-01.shtml>, accessed 29 July 2003.

Grynberg, R. (undated), 'The Pacific Island States and the WTO; Towards a Post Seattle Agenda for the Small Vulnerable States'. Mimeo.

—— (2002), 'Liberalising Global Labour Markets: Recent Developments at the WTO', *Estey Centre Journal of International Law and Trade Policy* 3:1, 62–81.

Sunline (April 2004), Interview with Tuala Falani Chan Tung.

Kelsey, J. (1999), *Reclaiming the Future. New Zealand and the Global Economy* (Wellington: Bridget Williams Books).

—— (2003), *Big Brothers Behaving Badly. The Implications for the Pacific Islands of the Pacific Agreement on Closer Economic Relations* (Interim Report) (Suva: Pacific Network on Globalization).

—— (2004), *A People's Guide to PACER. The Implications for the Pacific Islands of the Pacific Agreement on Closer Economic Relations* (Suva: Pacific Network on Globalization).

—— (2005a), *A People's Guide to the Pacific's Economic Partnership Agreement. Negotiations between the Pacific Islands and the European Union Pursuant to the Cotonou Agreement 2000* (Suva: World Council of Churches Office in the Pacific).

—— (2005b), 'World Trade and Small Nations in the South Pacific Region', *Kansas Journal of Law and Public Policy* 14: 2, 247–306.

—— (2008), *Serving Whose Interests? The Political Economy of Trade in Services Agreements* (Abingdon UK: Routledge Cavendish).

Langhammer, R.J. and Lücke, M. (2000), *WTO Negotiations and Accession Issues for Vulnerable Economies* (Kiel Institute of World Economies: Working Paper No. 990, 1).

Levi, N. (1999), *Question and Answer Brief on Free Trade Issues*, Pacific Islands Forum Secretariat, Suva, 21 April 1999 <www.forumsec.org.fj>, accessed 4 June 2004.

Manchester, A. (May 2005), 'Filipino Nurses Suffer', *Kai Tiaki Nursing New Zealand*, 11–12.

Narsey, W. (undated), 'Regional integration or remittances: what options?', <www.fdc.org.au/files/NarseyREMIT.pdf>, accessed 5 August 2005.

—— (2003), 'Towards a Negotiating Framework for the Economic Partnership Agreements with the European Union', report prepared for the PIFS, 45.

Nathan Associates (2007), *Pacific Regional Trade and Economic Cooperation Study – Joint Baseline and Gap Analysis*, A Report for the Pacific Islands Forum Secretariat, December 2007.

NZCTU Submission on the New Zealand–China Free Trade Agreement August 2004, <http://www.union.org.nz/policy/109407758825419.html>.

'Outcomes Document. Framework of Action for a Programme of Temporary Movement of Nurses Agreed at the Caribbean Conference on Temporary Movement: Towards a Trade and Development Approach, 30–31 March 2005, Barbados'.

Oxfam (2004), *The Fiji Garment Industry* (Auckland: Oxfam).

Pacific Agreement on Closer Economic Relations (PACER) (18 August 2001), <http://www.forumsec.org.fj/division/TID/PACER-PICTA/PACER%20-%20as%20endorsed%20and%20signed%20by%20Forum%20Leaders%20-%2018-8-01.pdf>.

Pacific Islands Forum Press Release (11 July 1997), 'Ministers Adopt Action Plan for Sustained Economic Growth in the Pacific', <www.forumsec.org.fj>, accessed 4 June 2004.

Pacific Islands Forum Secretariat (9 December 2004), 'Working Draft: The Pacific Plan for Strengthening Regional Cooperation and Integration', <http://www.forumsec.org.fj/>.

—— (2004), *The Pacific ACP–EU Partnership. The Way Forward* (Suva: PIFS).

Pacific Network on Globalisation (PANG), 'A Social Impact Assessment of the Economic Partnership Agreement being negotiated between the European Community and the Pacific ACP States', A report for the Pacific Islands Forum Secretariat, 20 March 2008, <http://www.pang.org.fj/doc/EPA_SIA_PANG.pdf>.

Partnership Agreement Between the Members of the African, Caribbean and Pacific Group of States of the One Part, and the European Community and its Members States, of the Other Part. (23 June 2000), ACP–EC, pt. 3, tit. II, ch. 1, art. 34.

Program of Action for the Sustainable Development of Small Island Developing States and 22nd General Assembly provisions <http://www.ddp-ext.worldbank.org/ext/MDG/homePages.do>.

Report of the WTO Panel (22 May 1997), European Communities – Regime for the Importation, Sale and Distribution of Bananas (Complaint by the United States), WT/DS27/R/USA.

Scollay, R. (2002), Impact Assessment of Possible Economic Partnership Agreements (EPAs) with the European Union. A Report for ACP Secretariat and the Pacific ACP States (Suva: PIFS).

Sutton, J. (2004), 'NZ Signs WTO Accession Agreement with Tonga', Press Release, Hon. Jim Sutton, 8 March 2004, <http://www.beehive.govt.nz>, accessed 4 June 2004

TCFC Partnership (September 2002), *The Way Ahead: Industry and Government TCFC Partnership. A draft strategy for the textile, clothing, footwear and carpet industries.*

Textile, Clothing and Footwear Union of Australia (1995), *The Hidden Cost of Fashion* (Melbourne: TCFUA).

Thomas, C., Hosein, R. and Yan, J. (2005), 'Assessing the Export of Nursing Services as a Diversification Option for CARICOM Economies', extract from *The Report Prepared for the Caribbean Commission on Health and Development*, January 2005, <www.cpc.paho.org/%5CFiles%5CDocFiles%5C 59_107.pdf>, accessed 5 August 2005.

Vanuatu's Negotiating Position for the Economic Partnership Agreements with the European Union, November 2004.

Webber, M. and Weller, S. (2001), *Refashioning the Rag Trade: Internationalising Australia's Textile, Clothing and Footwear Industries* (Sydney: UNSW Press).

Working Party on the Accession of the Kingdom of Tonga (4 May 2004), *Draft Report of the Working Party on the Accession of the Kingdom of Tonga* (WT/ACC/SPEC/TON/4/Rev.2).

World Bank (2002) *Embarking on a Global Voyage: Trade Liberalisation and Complementary Reforms in the Pacific*. Pacific Islands Regional Economic Report, No. 24417–EAP. Poverty Reduction and Economic Management Unit, East Asia and Pacific Region.

Chapter 10

Reformasi, Environmental Security and Development in Indonesia

Budy P. Resosudarmo

For a natural resource rich country such as Indonesia, being able to properly manage its natural resources is crucial in eradicating extreme poverty and hunger and ensuring environmental security. The fall of President Soeharto in 1998 provided the opportunity for Indonesia to rapidly move from an authoritarian society to a more democratic one (often referred to as *reformasi*), and to conduct a 'big bang' transformation from a highly centralized towards a much more decentralized system of government. It was suggested in the early process of these transformations that this would offer the prospect for Indonesia to better manage its natural resources, and achieve a long–term development path that embraced environmental security, equity and alleviated significant rural poverty. This chapter conducts an overview of whether these predictions have begun to materialize. The findings of this chapter suggest that these the radical changes have instead created an environment of political uncertainty, inconsistent laws and regulations, weak law enforcement, a weak governmental system and insecurity of land tenure, with the result that 'the management of natural resources in the country may not have worsened, but neither has it improved' (Resosudarmo 2005, 1) at least in the short and medium term.

The setting

Indonesia is the largest archipelago in the world with approximately 17,000 islands stretching along the equator for about 6,000 kilometres between the Indian and Pacific oceans, and linking the continents of Asia and Australia. The country covers approximately 7.9 million km² (including the Exclusive Economic Zone area), of which only approximately 1.9 million km² is land. The main islands are Sumatra, Kalimantan, Sulawesi, Papua, and Java. Indonesia shares the islands of Kalimantan with Malaysia, and Papua with Papua New Guinea (Resosudarmo, Subiman and Rahayu 2000).

The country is diversified, both in terms of its population and its natural resources. In 2006, the population reached approximately 240 million, consisting of around 350 ethnic groups. Most of these have their own languages and customary (*adat*) laws, regulations and norms. The two largest ethnic groups are the Javanese

(45 per cent of the population) and the Sundanese (14 per cent). The population is growing at an annual rate of about 1.5 per cent. The majority of Indonesians – 61 per cent – live in Java and Bali, which together have a land area comprising only around 7 per cent of Indonesia. Another 21 per cent live in Sumatra (27 per cent of Indonesia), while the remaining 18 per cent inhabit Sulawesi, Kalimantan, Nusa Tenggara, Maluku and Papua – comprising the greater part of Indonesia in terms of land area. The majority of the population is Muslim (88 per cent). Nevertheless, other religions and denominations are represented; Protestants comprise 5 per cent of the population, Catholics 3 per cent and Hindus 2 per cent.

Indonesia has long been considered to have abundant natural resources, such as oil, gas and minerals as well as rich and very biodiversified forest and marine resources. For example, oil and gas are found in Aceh, Riau, South Sumatra and East Kalimantan. Mineral ores such as copper and gold are abundant in Papua, coal in most of Kalimantan and West Sumatra, tin on Bangka island, and nickel in South Sulawesi and North Maluku. Indonesia's vast rainforests account for over 50 per cent of the tropical forests in the Southeast Asian region and more than 10 per cent of the world's tropical forests (Barbier 1998). In terms of area, the country's tropical forests are third only to those of Brazil and Democratic Republic of the Congo (Zaire). Extremely diverse flora and fauna with abundant nutrients and untapped medicinal potential are found within these forests. Indonesia also carries the world's largest remaining mangrove forests and has the largest area of coral reefs of any country. Indonesia's waters are among the most productive of all tropical seas. The Banda–Flores Sea lies at the heart of global marine biodiversity; nowhere else on earth is there a comparable diversity of marine resources (Dutton, Hidayat, Gunawan, Sondita, Steffen, Storey, Merrill and Sylvianita 2001; Dutton 2005).

Forest and marine resources have always been important for Indonesia. At least 20 million Indonesians depend on the forests for their livelihood (Sunderlin, Resosudarmo, Rianto and Angelsen 2000). Similarly, millions of Indonesians have been, and continue to be, dependent on marine resources. Fish stocks in Indonesian waters provide a source of income and livelihood for more than five million fishermen. Fish provides more than 60 per cent of the animal protein intake of the average Indonesian and is the only affordable source of protein for the majority of the population (Bailey 1988; Dutton 2005). Indonesian women, though mostly do not take part actively in the commercial extraction of natural resources (except fuel wood extraction), have been significantly active in the processing activities of natural resources, such as fish processing, plywood as well as pulp and paper industries.

Ironically, despite these forest and marine territories being rich in resources, most people whose livelihood primarily depends on them are among the poorest. Table 10.1 shows estimated numbers of poor people by major island groups in 2004. The majority of rural poor in Eastern Indonesia, Sulawesi and Kalimantan, as well as significant numbers of rural poor in Sumatra and Java–Bali, depend on forest, marine and mining resources for their livelihood.

Table 10.1   Estimated numbers of total and poor population by major island group in Indonesia, 2004

Island groups	Urban		Rural	
	Total	Poor	Total	Poor
Sumatra	15.7*	2.2	30	5.7
		14%		19%
Java–Bali	65.0	7.8	64.5	12.9
		12%		20%
Kalimantan	3.8	0.3	7.7	1
		8%		13%
Sulawesi	5.0	0.4	11.5	2.3
		8%		20%
Eastern Indonesia	6.7	0.8	9.4	2.9
		12%		31%
Indonesia	96.1	11.5	123.0	24.8
		12%		20%

Notes: * = Numbers shown are in millions.

In general poor people in this table are those who are living below Rp 150,000 (US$15) per month in urban areas and below Rp 125,000 (US$12.5) per month in rural areas. The percentage number shows the percentage of poor population from the total urban or rural population in the island group.

Source: Statistics Indonesia (2005).

Indonesia's natural resources have been exploited for many centuries, including prior to the colonial period. This exploitation intensified with colonialism, particularly in Java, but it became worse and involved the whole country after President Soeharto came to power in 1966–67. He was quick to realize the potential of the country's abundant forests, oil, gas and minerals for development. Realizing that large scale resource extraction could be performed only with the involvement of foreign investments, Soeharto enacted three important laws in the first year of his presidency. Law 1/1967 on foreign investment provided clear procedures for foreign operations in Indonesia along with generous tax concessions for foreign companies; Law 5/1967 on forestry, placed all forests under the control of the state; and Law 11/1967 on mining, inferred that all lands within the Republic of Indonesia could be used for mining. These three laws made all of the country's natural resources available for extraction by large scale operations with a foreign investment component (Resosudarmo and Kuncoro 2006; Gellert 2005).[1]

---

1   The Basic Agrarian Law No. 5/1960 also worked toward Soeharto's interests on large–scale natural resource exploitation. This law clearly defined that in cases of

Within the first few years of Soeharto's presidency several multinational companies started natural resource extraction throughout Indonesia. Their operations were protected by Soeharto's regime, which was then virtually unchallenged politically. During the 1970s, several major foreign companies became involved in oil extraction, particularly in Aceh, Riau, South Sumatra and East Kalimantan. During this period, oil became Indonesia's main export commodity and the country's major source of government revenue. In the 1980s, the role of oil in the Indonesian economy declined, but remained important, while that of other natural resource products, such as liquefied natural gas, copper, gold and timber, increased. By the mid–1990s, Indonesia had become the world's largest exporter of liquefied natural gas (Barnes 1995) and hardwood plywood,[2] the second largest producer of tin (after China), the third largest exporter of thermal coal (after Australia and South Africa) and the third largest exporter of copper (after the United States and Chile).[3] It also produced significant quantities of gold, nickel and other forest products.

Natural resource revenues were the main engine of economic growth in Indonesia during the 1970s, and remain of critical importance to the Indonesian economy. During the 1990s, oil and gas still contributed approximately 30 per cent of the country's total exports (Resosudarmo and Kuncoro 2006), minerals and related products 19 per cent and forest products 10 per cent (Simangunsong 2004). However, since the 1980s the non natural resource based sector, particularly the labour intensive, export oriented industry, has taken over as the main generator of economic growth. The overall performance of the Indonesian economy from the early 1970s to the mid 1990s was remarkable. The economy grew at an annual rate of about 7 per cent, while the number of people living below the poverty line declined from around 40 per cent in the early 1970s to below 15 per cent in the mid–1990s.

The massive and widespread exploitation of natural resources created problems, particularly since the granting of rights to exploit natural resources was not based on considerations of resource sustainability. Neither did it convey fair and equitable benefits to the public. Extraction rights were mainly given to individuals or companies that were close to Soeharto and played a key role in strengthening his regime (Gellert 2005; Seda 2005) and mainly had the objective to generate cash incomes for the regime as soon as possible (Resosudarmo and Kuncoro 2006; Seda 2005). The two main problems of natural resource extractions were, first, a sharp acceleration in cases of environmental degradation and, second, the skewed distribution of benefits from natural resource extractions. For example, although local resources and local land were being exploited, local communities received little or no benefit from these activities (Resosudarmo, Subiman and Rahayu 2000; Resosudarmo and Subiman 2003; Colfer and Resosudarmo 2002; Azis and Salim 2005; Dutton 2005). By the mid–1990s, the two major problems with regard to

conflicts over land use between the state and local people, priority should be given to national interests.

2   World Forest Institute available at <http://www.worldforestry.org/wfi/trade-5.htm>.
3   Global InfoMine available at <http://www.infomine.com/countries/indonesia.asp>.

natural resource extraction had reached their peak among the general public. Many stakeholders believed that as long as Soeharto remained in power and as long as Indonesia was unable to move to a more democratic society, these problems of natural resource management would persist.

The 1997 East Asian economic crisis hit Indonesia devastatingly hard, causing severe disruption to the country's economic activities, so that in 1998 the economic output had contracted by about minus 14 per cent and inflation reached approximately 57 per cent. The crisis also induced a volatile political situation, forcing Soeharto to step down from the presidency on May 1998 after 32 years in power. The fall of Soeharto provided impetus for the transformation from an authoritarian society to a more democratic one in Indonesia, and for the move from a highly centralized towards a much more decentralized system of government. These transformations were thought to offer the prospect that Indonesia would be better able to manage its natural resources, and achieve a long term development path including environmental security. Environmental security in this chapter is generally defined as a sustainable environmental condition maximizing the benefits, which are accessible, by members of the society in an equitable way (see also Agrawal and Ribot 1999; Crook and Manor 1998; Maxhood 1983; Smoke 2001; Uphoff and Erman 1974). Improvement in managing Indonesia's natural resources should alleviate poverty, since most people whose livelihood primarily depends on natural resources are among the poorest. This chapter considers whether or not such expectations have begun to materialize.

Political and economic development

During his presidency, Soeharto adopted an authoritarian rule. He did not permit any individual or organizations, including the military, to challenge this. Besides his own party, Golkar, Soeharto only allowed the existence of two other parties, the Indonesian Islamic Party and the Indonesian Nationalist Party. He intervened to a great extent in their activities, even in the choice of the parties' leadership. In the last four elections during Soeharto's era, Golkar won more than 50 per cent of the seats in parliament [4]

In 1999, a year after Soeharto stepped down, the parliament enacted two laws related to political parties and elections. The first was Law No. 2/1999, allowing the establishment of new political parties that had clearly defined rights to compete in elections. The second law was Law No. 3/1999, paving the way for a considerably more democratic election that was held in 1999. During this election the media, with much greater freedom than in Soeharto's era, played an important role in reporting political debates. The establishment of a new democratic environment with freedom to speak and to choose had not only made the election successful,

---

4   In the last election of Soeharto's era, 1997, Golkar gained 73 per cent of the seats in parliament.

but also made it very similar to election situations in developed countries. This process of moving from an authoritarian to a much more democratic political condition was called *reformasi* by Indonesians.

Two years later, Laws No. 31/2002 and 12/2003, respectively, amended Law No. 2/1999 and No. 3/1999, aiming to establish an even better democratic political system in the country. In 2004, Indonesia conducted its second democratic election. These elections were conducted remarkably smoothly, with relatively few cases of violence or electoral fraud. In the April 2004 general election, 11 of the 24 participating parties succeeded in gaining seats in parliament for their candidates. Later in the same year, Indonesians elected their president and vice president directly for the first time. The two rounds of presidential elections held in July and September 2004 went extremely well, with Susilo Bambang Yudhoyono and Yusuf Kalla being elected president and vice president. More importantly, a balance of political power was achieved between the president and parliament and among political parties. This balance had been lacking under Soeharto (Aspinall 2005) and in this sense, *reformasi* has certainly induced a much better political environment compared to that during Soeharto's era.

The euphoria of *reformasi* also inspired society to push parliament to enact various new laws. This situation benefited the majority of Indonesians, since there were laws established during Soeharto's era, particularly relating to land and natural resource utilization that needed to be amended. However, in many cases the newly enacted laws conflicted with other laws and created various problems and ambiguities. Take, for example, the case of mining in protected forests. Until the enactment of the new forestry law, Law No. 41/1999, there was no law explicitly prohibiting open pit mining activities in protected forests. Implementation of this new law prohibited operations intended by 150 mineral and coalmining companies. The affected mining companies argued that they should be allowed to continue their operations in the protected forests because they were granted their permits or contracts before the issuance of the new forestry law. Meanwhile Non Governmental Organizations (NGOs) and the Department of Forestry argued the need to maintain the quality of protected forest. Although finally President Megawati Soekarnoputri approved Perpu (government regulation in lieu of regulation) No. 1/2004, which exempts all mining permits or contracts granted before the issuance of Law 41/1999 from the prohibition, the conflict has promoted an unstable business climate and created disincentives for future business investment.

Another major change occurred in the governmental system. During Soeharto's era, the governmental system was very centralized. First, almost all decisions at the local level were decided or strongly influenced by the central government. Regional governments had little input about policies in their own regions. Secondly, most revenues from economic activities in the regions, particularly from natural resource extractive industries, were collected by the central government. Although the central government distributed some of these revenues to regional governments, resource rich regions, particularly, considered that they should obtain much more than the amount redistributed to them.

After Soeharto stepped down, Indonesia rapidly moved towards a much more decentralized system of government. This was achieved through the enactment of Law 22/1999 on local government and Law 25/1999 on fiscal balancing between the central and regional governments. In 2001 authority for all but a few areas of governance was transferred from the central government to districts and municipalities, including authority for agriculture, industry, trade and investment, education, health and natural resource management (Alm, Aten and Bahl 2001). The main goal of the decentralization policy was to give the regions a greater say in the development and growth of their own localities, so that regions could grow according to their potencies and capacities and allow locals to enjoy much greater benefits from this economic growth. The new policy also sought to resolve the longstanding tensions between some regions and the central government over the unfair distribution of benefits from natural resource extraction, by giving resource rich regions a greater share of the revenue generated by their own natural resources.

The implementation of the two decentralization laws provided local people and local governments with input in the development and management of natural resources within their areas. These also created an environment to enable the exposure of conflicts and mismanagement of natural resources through various media and debates within parliament. The decentralization laws ultimately established more equal natural resource revenue sharing arrangements between local and national governments as a way to ensure that local people could enjoy a higher portion of the benefits of natural resource extraction.

However, the implementation of these two decentralization laws also increased conflict among various levels of government, particularly in cases where related laws and regulations were unclear. These conflicts typically occurred over trans– or near–boundary economic activities. In the spirit of resolving this problem, in 2004, both decentralization laws were amended by Law No. 32/2004 on local government and No. 33/2004 on fiscal balancing between the central and regional governments.

Meanwhile by 2005, the Indonesian economy began to recover from the 1997 crisis. Economic output grew at the annual rate of approximately 4.8 per cent, so that in 2004 the gross domestic product (GDP) returned to the pre–crisis level of 1997, though the per capita income was still 4 per cent below that in 1997, as a result of the increasing population. The inflation rate decreased from about 15 per cent in early 2002 to below 5 per cent in February 2004. International reserves grew steadily, while fiscal policy was considered relatively prudent. This improvement in economic performance has not been without challenges, particularly since the level of investment did not bounce back to the pre–crisis rate. One of the main reasons for this low investment is that *reformasi* and decentralization also created a very uncertain business climate in the country (McLeod 2005). There are at least three major explanations for this uncertain business climate. First, as mentioned, various levels of government faced increasing conflict over authority to produce permits for doing business in a particular region. These conflicts also often involved local people, particularly when the economic activities utilized local land areas. Business communities became confused over who they should approach for the appropriate permit to establish a new economic activity. Second, there was a strong temptation for local governments to create new local nuisance taxes to increase their own local revenues. The main reason for this tax creation was that local governments faced increasing expenditure responsibilities. Although local governments were happy with *reformasi* and decentralization, they were also overwhelmed when their responsibilities increased due to the transfer of several central government functions, such as payment of all civil servant salaries (including those of several thousand central government employees reassigned to regional level jobs), and providing full public services previously performed by the central government, such as primary and secondary education, health clinics, local and regional roads, water supply and sewerage systems. Third, there was a change in the nature of corruption within Indonesia. The era of centralized political systems had ended and was replaced by a system where power and authority were more diffused. The nature of centralized corruption had also gone, replaced by a more fragmented bribe collection system where ministerial and local government officials, military, police and legislative members, both at the national and local level, demanded bribes. While in other countries decentralization may have nothing to do with corrupt behaviour, in Indonesia, already burdened with a corruption problem from Soeharto's era, decentralization further fragmented corruption (Resosudarmo and Kuncoro 2006; Kuncoro 2004).

Although the global economy may have positively affected Indonesia it has also created three major challenges. The first is the impact of the increasing and highly volatile world price of oil. To keep domestic prices of fuel stable and low, the government subsidized these prices. This policy puts severe pressure on the country's fiscal position and reduces the incentive to improve efficiency in fuel use. If this policy is maintained, domestic demand for fuel will keep increasing rapidly, escalating Indonesia's emissions of carbon dioxide (McKibbin 2005). The rapid increase in domestic demand for fuel also reduces Indonesia's net gain from oil exports (Resosudarmo and Tanujaya 2002). The second challenge is the impact of China's high growth and rapid expansion in world trade in the new millennium. While the rapid pace of development in China is threatening because China and Indonesia compete in the same export markets, it is also promising because China is also increasing its imports, providing an opportunity for Indonesia to export more of its products, particularly primary products, to China. Indonesia can therefore expect to experience negative terms of trade effect for manufacturing and positive terms of trade effect for primary sectors such as forest products, including logs, lumber and woodchips (Coxhead 2005). If Indonesia is not cautious, the increased pressure on its natural resources caused by demand from China will lead to unsustainable levels of extraction.

The third global challenge to Indonesia is the world recession of 2009. Slowly but persistently, it is slowing Indonesian exports, that causes export oriented industries to lay–off a significant number of workers. Without strong government social safety net programmes, the number of unemployed and poor people in the country is likely to significantly increase and drive those unemployed and the poor, particularly those in rural areas, into natural resource extraction activities such as cutting forests, mining and fishing; and so creating a higher pressure on the environment.

Natural resource management

Reformasi and the implementation of decentralization often emphasized the need for local initiatives in shaping the vision and future actions of local authorities. Such initiatives have indeed occurred. In relation to natural resource management, these initiatives have produced a diversity of procedures for exploiting local resources to increase revenues and for safeguarding valuable sources of revenue from exploitation by others. Most of these initiatives have been based on expectations to gain immediate local revenues, but a few, in the spirit of *reformasi*, truly mean to improve the management of natural resources. These initiatives have produced new challenges in the management of natural resources that have long been problematic.

Forestry

The major challenges in the forestry sector related to the *reformasi* movement and the implementation of decentralization are the allocation of forest extraction rights, redistribution of forest revenue from the centre to local governments, illegal logging, and deforestation.

The allocation of forest extraction rights continued to be contentious with decentralization. With the spirit to empower local communities, in January 1999 the government enacted a regulation (PP No. 6/1999) to allow districts to produce small scale logging permits (up to 100 hectares for a short duration, typically one year) and to grant these permits to local communities. District governments, particularly in Kalimantan and Papua, realized this was an opportunity to raise local revenues and so swiftly produced many types of this license in their regions. Communities, but lacking capital, also reacted quickly by finding business partners to conduct the logging activities. All activities were typically conducted by the business partners, while the communities, since they usually are at a disadvantage during negotiation, received marginal fees from their partners.

These small scale logging licenses created two main problems. First, these permits caused an increasing number of conflicts among communities, typically over local rights to the areas associated with the logging permits. Secondly, the regulations for these small scale logging permits did not contain any requirement for replanting or systematic felling. There was no incentive for loggers to follow any measures for sustainable forest management. After the government recognized the problems caused by these small scale licenses, it cancelled the authority of district governments to produce these in June 2002 (PP No. 34/2002). Some districts quickly obeyed this new regulation, but in many cases it was not easy for the central government to enforce this (Colfer and Resosudarmo 2002; Fox, Adhuri and Resosudarmo 2005).

Several issues concerned the redistribution of forest revenue from the central to local governments. District governments complained to the central government that the timing of the redistribution of these revenues had been uncertain and the calculation to redistribute these revenues was not transparent. The latter problem usually arose because only the central government knew how much forest revenue had been collected, while some the rules for distribution were unclear. For example, the rules to distribute the reforestation fund stated it should go to 'producing regions'. District governments interpreted 'producing regions' as producing districts, while the centre defined 'producing regions' as producing provinces. The unclear timing of distribution and the lack of transparent calculation of the amount distributed made it difficult for district governments to estimate their revenues, and ultimately to plan their spending. Further complications have occurred since many district governments have asked logging companies to directly pay their taxes to district governments (Fox, Adhuri and Resosudarmo 2005).

The combination of confusing laws and regulations with other dynamics at the local level, increased conflict among communities, between communities and the authorities, and among levels of authorities. This also decreased the power of the centre at the local level, which created an incentive to local communities to reclaim their lands previously taken by Soeharto's government with unfair or no compensation. The magnitude of 'illegal' logging activities also increased.[5] Local communities and governments saw these activities as a way to increase their revenues, and became involved or even instigated these activities. Local government then taxed these activities, one of the mechanisms being the issuing of small scale logging permits, hence 'legalizing' the activities of these illegal loggers (Casson and Obidzinski 2002).

Not only small scale loggers have conducted illegal logging, but also large logging companies have done so for many years, by logging outside their concession areas, cutting trees of less than the allowable diameter, and under reporting their production. There are an increasing number of cases where large logging companies have also bought the products of small scale illegal loggers as cheap inputs to their companies emerged after *reformasi*. Clearly many parties benefit in the short run from these illegal activities (Obidzinski 2005).

This illegal logging and the large amount of small scale logging activities, combined with continuing activities of the usual logging companies and land clearing for plantations, continuing occurrences of forest fires, as well as the increasing demand for forest products from China, have doubled the rate of forest clearing in Indonesia from approximately one million to two million hectares per year during

---

5	The definition of illegal logging here is broad, basically contravening any forest regulations.

the period of the *reformasi* and decentralization (Fox, Adhuri and Resosudarmo 2005). From this perspective, the ongoing *reformasi* and decentralization era has not yet produced better management of Indonesia's forests.

Fisheries

One institutional change after the *reformasi* in fisheries was the establishment of the Ministry of Marine Affairs and Fisheries (MMAF). This accorded the issues of coastal and marine management a higher profile, symbolized an increased level of political recognition of the significance of the country's seas,[6] and created the opportunity to conduct an integrated approach in managing fishery–related marine issues for the first time in the country's history (Dutton 2005). Since its establishment, the MMAF has been conducting a comprehensive review of fishery and coastal development policies and has been proposing various management reforms.

Marine captured fisheries in Indonesia can be divided into offshore and inshore fishing. Offshore fishing is conducted by large boats, over 30 Gross Tonnes (GT) and often foreign owned, operated beyond 12 nautical miles from the coast, between the islands and out to the 200 nautical mile limit of Indonesia's EEZ. Meanwhile, inshore fishing is conducted by domestic subsistence and artisanal fishers using small boats and gears, up to 30 GT, operated up to 12 nautical miles from the coast. Under the decentralization policies, jurisdiction over inshore fishing is partly under district (*kabupaten*) governments, from shore to 4 nautical miles, and the rest on the hand of provincial government, from 4 up to 12 nautical miles. The central government retains jurisdiction over the offshore fishing. The size of vessels, the nationality, wealth and political influence of their owners differs between inshore and offshore fishers and presents different challenges to fisheries' management (Fegan 2003; Fox, Adhuri and Resosudarmo 2005).

For offshore fishing, approximately more than 9,000 fish and shrimp trawlers operate in Indonesian waters, plus a large proportion of pelagic purse seine and pole and line vessels and their motherships and reefers (international frozen cargo carriers). The majority of these vessels are owned by companies in China, Thailand, Taiwan, South Korea, the Philippines and Japan (Fegan 2003). Most of these vessels conduct illegal fishing in Indonesian waters; fishing without proper licenses, under reporting, or using destructive fishing techniques. In 2003, the MMAF indicated that about 7,000 vessels or about 85 per cent of all modern vessels above 50 GT have been operating in Indonesia without proper licenses (*Kompas*, 9 June 2003). A significant number of these vessels operate without any license, some use duplicate licenses for other vessels, some use expired licenses, some use invalid licenses and some operate outside the permitted zone. The majority of these are vessels reflagged as 'Indonesian' by registering them as owned in joint venture

---

6   Fishery issues used to be the responsibility of the Directorate–General for Fisheries under the Ministry of Agriculture.

or chartered, under the name of a local company that provides only the vessel and fishing licences and in some cases, port services. The Indonesian company receives a fee to arrange papers for the vessel and crew, arranges supplies of fuel at the domestic price that is much lower than the world price, supplies water and food and deals with officials. It has no ownership in the vessel, gear or catch and no share in the profit or loss. These foreign vessels underreport their catches by only reporting approximately 30 per cent (Fegan 2003).

After the decentralization period, many of these joint venture vessels asked regional governments for licenses. In many cases, to obtain licenses from regional governments, vessel owners lie by stating that the GT of their vessels is less than it actually is. After receiving these licenses, these vessels can operate anywhere they want, including outside the areas stated in the licenses. Meanwhile regional governments are often eager to produce these licenses in an effort to increase their local government revenues as well as their personal incomes. Regional governments do not have any incentive to keep these vessels operating only in their sea territories since the higher these vessels' production, the higher the expected incomes for regional governments.

The MMAF estimated that the total loss of revenues to Indonesia from illegal fishing in 2003 was around US$2,136 million, or almost equal to the total export value of Indonesian fish products, comprising US$1,200 million in the value of fish captured from the Indonesia EEZ and exported,[7] US$574 million in lost licensing fees, US$240 million in unwarranted fuel subsidy, and US$122 million in loss of royalty and other fees (*Tempo Interaktif*, 19 February 2003). Additionally, illegal ships employ foreign crew, which represent a lost employment opportunity valued at approximately $780 million (*Media Indonesia*, 29 April 2002). It is expected that the amount of illegal fishing will continue to increase, since conducting surveillance activities in Indonesia's huge water territory is very expensive. There is a strong incentive for regional governments to produce licenses, although these are not always the proper ones and collusive behaviour from some authority officials is difficult to detect. Consequently, over–fishing occurs almost everywhere in Indonesian waters (MMAF 2001).

For inshore fishing, district governments have the right to produce licenses for boats between 5 to 10 GT, which are expected to operate within a 4 nautical mile limit. Provincial governments can offer fishing licences to boats between 10 to 30 GT, that are expected to operate between 4 and 12 nautical miles. 'Traditional fishing' or boats using less than 5 GT have not been regulated. All coastal regions are therefore open to exploitation by this simple method.

Meanwhile, after the *reformasi* and decentralization era, there has been a strong call for local community involvement in surveillance of local resources, including marine resources. The uncertainty of area restriction for the use of small fishing boats as well as local community involvement in surveillance created increasing

---

7   Representing an estimated theft of 1 to 1.5 million tons per year (*Jakarta Post*, 15 August 2002).

conflict within local community fishing. A typical case would be where fishermen from one district are caught by local fishermen in another district for fishing in their waters. For example in 2000, around seven boats from Pati and Tegal in Central Java were burned by local Masalembo fishers in East Java. Fishers from Brebes and Tegal in Central Java took Maduranese fishers from East Java captive for fishing in their waters. In many cases, these conflicts induced violent confrontations. Some cases cannot easily be resolved but others can be solved by the establishment of local fishing agreements (Fox, Adhuri and Resosudarmo 2005).

Mining

The utilization of mining resources also involves similar issues of ambiguity over jurisdiction and levels of authority as were encountered in the forestry and marine sectors. Unclear guidance to calculate and distribute revenues from mining operations to regional and local governments is also the source of disputes among regional and local governments and the centre. The Ministry of Finance determines the allocation of funds to each province; each province then becomes the distributor to its regions. In this process, provinces usually claim not to have received their right share from the central government and regions within provinces often also claim that their appropriations were inappropriate. Furthermore, subdistricts and villages, the areas immediately affected by mining operations, are the least likely to receive a fair share from these mining operations (Fox, Adhuri and Resosudarmo 2005).

The uncertainty as to how much total revenue is generated by the centre, the unclear guidance as to the distribution of this revenue to local regions, and the excessively long chain of revenue distribution to local levels make it difficult for local people to receive benefits from mining operations. Therefore local frustrations often induce land disputes between local and mining companies, and destructive activities over mining operation (Fox, Adhuri and Resosudarmo 2005).

During the Soeharto era, mining activities were regulated by individual Contracts of Work directly between the central government and the companies, typically under close supervision by Soeharto and his regime. These arrangements never included explicit contractual benefits to local people. There were companies that offered some assistance to local people affected by their operations, but these were usually as goodwill rather than as part of their contracts. Mining operations also typically brought in better skilled workers from outside the regions. Local communities certainly had reasons for feeling ignored in mining activities. However, since Soeharto and his regime used the military to guard these mining operations, local people were afraid to demand any compensation.

In the *reformasi* era, high level coverage in the media of human rights violations by the military and their ruthless business activities weakened their position in the regions. This gave locals the opportunity to reclaim their lands that were utilized by mining companies and demand compensation, and for illegal miners, often directly or indirectly involving local people, to operate in the areas of mining companies.

Cases of land disputes between local people and large mining companies as well as the amount of illegal mining increased significantly in the few years just after the fall of Soeharto (Erman 2005).

The implementation of decentralization laws, as mentioned, provided strong incentive for regions to raise their own revenues. In regions where mining operations were dominant, regional (district and provincial) governments quickly issued a variety of taxes and levies on mining companies. In several cases, regional governments tried to obtain revenues from illegal mining activities, such as in the case of developing and coordinating a village cooperation unit for illegal miners in West Sumatra, making these activities 'legal' (Erman 2005).

These taxes and levies imposed by regional governments, in addition to those specified in individual Contracts of Work; the activities of illegal mining as well as land disputes, have been regarded by mining companies as an increasing cost and arbitrary burden. Mining companies have responded to this situation by suggesting two possible options: either that regional governments become parties to the next generation of Contracts of Work or, that these remain as bilateral contracts between central government and companies but contain shares of taxes and royalties for regional governments.

Further complications occurred when a new Forestry law (Law No. 41/1999) was implemented. This law explicitly prohibited open–pit mining activities in protected forests for the first time. Approximately 150 mineral and coalmining companies were no longer able to carry out their operations.

In 2001, for the case of oil and gas, the central government enacted a new mining law (Law No. 22/2001) confirming the right of the central government to award mining contracts and to set the terms of these agreements, including the way in which profits, royalties and fees are determined and distributed. In 2004, the central government produced a government regulation in lieu of regulation (Perpu No. 1/2004), which exempted all mining permits or contracts granted before the issuance of Law 41/1999 from the prohibition.

The conflicts, uncertainty and confusions have induced an unstable business climate in the mining sector and created disincentives for future mining investments. However, in the case of marine and forestry resources, exploitation appears to have increased after the *reformasi* and decentralization era, the reverse seems to be the case for the mining sector (Fox, Adhuri and Resosudarmo 2005). Hundreds of exploration projects in Indonesia have been suspended, withdrawn or remain currently inactive and investment in the mining sector has been very low up until now.

Conclusion

Reformasi and the implementation of decentralization have provided the opportunities and challenges for Indonesia to respond to natural resource related utilization issues. Unfortunately, the transition period brought a situation of conflicting laws and regulations, weak law enforcement, a weak governmental system, and insecurity of land tenure. This created several problems. First, instances of conflict among various levels of government have increased. Conflicts between central and regional governments particularly occur in cases where the centre wishes to assert its dominance. Conflicts among regional governments typically are jurisdictional disputes over natural resources that lie on provincial or district borders. Second, cases of disputes involving local communities over the right to exploit natural resources have also increased. These disputes tend to be between local communities and the state or a large natural resource company concerning a piece of land occupied by the state or the company but claimed by locals as theirs, based on their *adat* (customary) law, and among local communities themselves. Third, the nature of corruption has moved from a centralized type to a more fragmented bribe collection system, in which government officials, military, police and members of the legislatures, both in the centre and regions, are all demanding bribes. Fourth, the number of local nuisance taxes and natural resource extraction licences established by regional governments to increase their own revenues has increased. These local taxes and levies have increased the cost of doing business in the country, creating slow growth and low investment.

Despite these challenges, the ability of Indonesia to carry out such ambitious *reformasi* and decentralization programme within such a short period of time without incurring any significant social or political costs was an important achievement. In a short period of time, new laws and regulations related to natural resource management have been enacted, and though not perfect, they are an improvement over the old laws and regulations. Local communities as well as local and regional governments now have a greater say in the management of natural resources in their areas. Media and parliaments have the opportunity to conduct debates openly on conflicts and mismanagement of natural resources. A fairer system for the sharing of natural resource revenue between the central and local governments is now in place.

There are also some signs that *reformasi* and decentralization policy will eventually lead to a better Indonesia. In 2004, as previously mentioned, to address some of the problems associated with the implementation of decentralization, the national parliament enacted two new decentralization laws, Law No. 32/2004 on regional autonomy to replace Law No. 22/1999, and Law No. 33/2004 on regional finance to replace Law No. 25/1999. If implemented properly, these new laws should soften the conflict between the central government and regional governments over authority for several key areas of responsibility (particularly those related to natural resources), result in a better distribution of the central to regional financial transfers and place some much needed controls on the number and type of local taxes.

An investment climate survey conducted by LPEM–UI (2005) indicates that, in time, the process of decentralization would itself contribute to an improvement in government performance and a reduction in corruption in the regions. The authors argue that as regional governments come to terms with their new responsibilities under decentralization and are held directly accountable by their constituents, this would create an incentive for an improvement in regional government performance – one aspect of which is a reduced prevalence of corrupt behaviour. Local governments that appreciate the importance of attracting business and investment to their regions will also understand that business people and investors will be reluctant to commit themselves to regions in which the quality of public services is poor and corrupt officials are likely to impose heavy costs on their operations. Competition among Indonesia's several hundred local governments to attract business and investment may well prove an effective means of improving the quality of public services and discouraging corrupt behaviour. In the end, better quality of public services and significant reduction of corrupt behaviour should significantly contribute to better management of natural resources in the country.

Finally, it may be concluded that, although *reformasi* and decentralization hold promises for better management of Indonesia's natural resources, it will take a longer horizon for these promises to materialize. It remains to be seen whether or not Indonesia is able to secure its natural resources and environment for the benefits of the majority of Indonesian people.

References

Agrawal, A. and Ribot, J. (1999), 'Accountability in Decentralization: A Framework with South Asian and African Cases', *Journal of Developing Areas* 33, 473–502.

Alm, J., Aten, R.H. and Bahl, R. (2001), 'Can Indonesia Decentralise Successfully? Plans, Problems, and Prospects', *Bulletin of Indonesian Economic Studies* 37:1, 83–102.

Aspinall, E. (2005), 'The Politics: Indonesia's Year of Elections and the End of the Political Transition', in B.P. Resosudarmo (ed.), *The Politics and Economics of Indonesia's Natural Resources* (Singapore: ISEAS), 13–52.

Azis, I.J. and Salim, E. (2005), 'Development Performance and Future Scenarios in the Context of Sustainable Utilisation of Natural Resources', in B.P. Resosudarmo (ed.), *The Politics and Economics of Indonesia's Natural Resources* (Singapore: ISEAS), 125–144.

Bailey, C. (1988), 'The Political Economy of Marine Fisheries Development in Indonesia', *Indonesia* 46 (October), 25–38.

Barbier, E.B. (1998), *The Economics of Environment and Development: Selected Essays* (Cheltenham: Edward Elgar).

Barnes, P. (1995), *Indonesia: The Political Economy of Energy* (Oxford: Oxford Institute for Energy Resources).

Casson, A. and Obidzinski, K. (2002), 'From New Order to Regional Autonomy: Shifting Dynamics of "Illegal" Logging in Kalimantan, Indonesia', *World Development* 30, 2133–2151.

Colfer, C.J.P. and Resosudarmo, I.A.P. (eds) (2002), *Which Way Forward? People, Forests, and Policymaking in Indonesia* (Washington, D.C.: Resources for the Future).

Coxhead, I. (2005), 'International Trade and the Natural Resource "Curse" in B.P. Resosudarmo' (ed.), *The Politics and Economics of Indonesia's Natural Resources* (Singapore: ISEAS), 71–91.

Crook, R.C. and Manor, J. (1998), *Democracy and Decentralization in South–East Asia and West Africa: Participation, Accountability and Performance* (Cambridge: Cambridge University Press).

Dutton, I.M. (2005), 'If Only Fish Could Vote: the Enduring Challenges of Coastal and Marine Resources Management in Post–*reformasi* Indonesia', in B.P. Resosudarmo (ed.), *The Politics and Economics of Indonesia's Natural Resources* (Singapore: ISEAS), 162–178.

Dutton, I.M., Hidayat, K., Gunawan, T., Sondita, F., Steffen, J., Storey, D., Merrill, R. and Sylvianita, D. (2001), 'Sikap dan Persepsi Masyarakat Mengenai Sumberdaya Pesisir dan Laut di Indonesia', *Pesisir dan Lautan* 3:3, 46–52.

Erman, E. (2005), 'Illegal Coal Mining in West Sumatra: Access and Actors in the Post–Soeharto Era', in B.P. Resosudarmo (ed.), *The Politics and Economics of Indonesia's Natural Resources* (Singapore: ISEAS), 206–215.

Fegan, B. (2003), 'Plundering the Sea', *Inside Indonesia*, No. 73, January–March.

Fox, J.J., Adhuri, D.S. and Resosudarmo, I.A.P. (2005), 'Unfinished Edifice or Pandora's Box? Decentralisation and Resource Management in Indonesia', in B.P. Resosudarmo (ed.), *The Politics and Economics of Indonesia's Natural Resources* (Singapore: ISEAS), 92–108.

Gellert, P.K. (2005), 'Oligarchy in the Timber Markets of Indonesia: From Apkindo to IBRA to the Future of the Forests', in B.P. Resosudarmo (ed.), *The Politics and Economics of Indonesia's Natural Resources* (Singapore: ISEAS), 145–161.

Kompas, 9 June 2003.

Kuncoro, A. (2004), 'Bribery in Indonesia: Some Evidence from Micro–level Data', *Bulletin of Indonesian Economic Studies* 40:3: 329–354.

LPEM–UI (Institute of Economic and Social Research, University of Indonesia) (2005), *Monitoring Investment Climate in Indonesia: A Report from the Mid 2005 Survey* (Jakarta: LPEM–UI report in collaboration with the World Bank).

Maxhood, P. (1983), *Local Government in Third World* (Chichester: John Wiley).

McKibbin, W.J. (2005), 'Indonesia in a Changing Global Environment', in B.P. Resosudarmo (ed.), *The Politics and Economics of Indonesia's Natural Resources* (Singapore: ISEAS), 53–70.

McLeod, R.H. (2005), 'The Economy: High Growth Remains Elusive', in B.P. Resosudarmo (ed.), *The Politics and Economics of Indonesia's Natural Resources* (Singapore: ISEAS), 31–52.

Media Indonesia, 29 April 2002.

Ministry of Marine Affairs and Fisheries (MMAF) (2001), *Pengkajian Stok Ikan di Perairan Indonesia* (Jakarta).

Obidzinski, K. (2005), 'Illegal Logging in Indonesia: Myth and Reality', in B.P. Resosudarmo (ed.), *The Politics and Economics of Indonesia's Natural Resources* (Singapore: ISEAS), 193–205.

Resosudarmo, B.P. (ed.) (2005), *The Politics and Economics of Indonesia's Natural Resources* (Singapore: ISEAS).

Resosudarmo, B.P. and Kuncoro, A. (2006), 'The Political Economy of Indonesian Economic Reform: 1983–2000', *Oxford Development Studies* 34:3, 341–355.

Resosudarmo, B.P. and Subiman, N.I. (2003), 'The Management of Biodiversity in Indonesia at a Sustainable Level', *Indonesian Quarterly* 31:1, 73–87.

Resosudarmo, B.P., Subiman, N.I. and Rahayu, B. (2000), 'The Indonesian Marine Resources: An Overview of Their Problems and Challenges', *Indonesian Quarterly* 28:3, 336–355.

Resosudarmo, B.P. and Tanujaya, O. (2002), 'Energy Demand in Indonesia: Past and Future Trend', *Indonesian Quarterly* 30:2, 158–174.

Seda, F.S.S.E. (2005), 'Petroleum Paradox: The Politics of Oil and Gas', in B.P. Resosudarmo (ed.), *The Politics and Economics of Indonesia's Natural Resources* (Singapore: ISEAS), 179–192.

Simangunsong, B.C.H. (2004), 'The Economic Performance of Indonesia's Forest Sector in the Period 1980–2002', *GTZ–SMCP Briefing Paper 4*, Jakarta, July.

Smoke, P. (2001), 'Fiscal Decentralization in Developing Countries: A Review of Current Concepts and Practice', Programme Paper Number 2, *Democracy, Governance and Human Rights* (Geneva: United Nations Research Institute for Social Development).

Statistics Indonesia (2005), *Statistical Yearbook of Indonesia 2004* (Jakarta: Statistics Indonesia).

Sunderlin, W.D., Resosudarmo, I.A.P., Rianto, E. and Angelsen, A. (2000), 'The Effect of Indonesia's Economic Crisis on Small Farmers and Natural Forest Cover in the Outer Islands', *CIFOR Occasional Paper. No. 28(E)* (Bogor: Center for International Forestry Research).

Tempo Interaktif, 19 February 2003.

Uphoff, N.T. and Erman, M.J. (1974), *Local Organization for Rural Development: Analysis of Asian Experience*, Special Series on Rural Local Government Paper No. 19, Rural Development Committee (Ithaca, NY: Cornell University).

Chapter 11

Mexico's Commitment to Development and Human Security in the New Millennium

María Angélica Arce Mora[1]

It is important to underline Mexico's deep commitment to multilateralism, which it has demonstrated through its active participation in the negotiations for the Millennium Declaration, adopted by the United Nations General Assembly in September 2000. This was also the first year of the administration of President Vincente Fox in Mexico, when the country took a step further towards democracy.

In order to inform the national and international public about the Mexican Government's progress in the implementation of the Millennium goals, on 20 April 2005 President Fox presented the document, 'Mexico's Millennium Development Goals – Preliminary Report 2005', which is the result of the combined efforts of different federal government bodies, Non Governmental Organizations, academic institutions and representatives of the main multilateral organizations with a focus on development.[2] Most of the information in this chapter is derived from this report. This details Mexico's achievements by 2005 and the challenges as it endeavours to move forward with social development policies aimed at diminishing the inequalities within the population and improving living conditions for the most vulnerable. These are the indigenous peoples, those living in rural areas or in poor urban settlements and the migrant population.

The most fundamental way to tackle this topic is to discuss the advances and challenges with respect to each of the eight major MDGs, including the 18 targets and 48 indicators. It should be emphasized that Mexico has set itself some additional targets, particularly where goals had already been achieved, to take into account the situation in which the country finds itself. The frame of reference, which dictates the actions of the Mexican Government in this area, is the National Development Plan 2001–2006, as it includes a strategy for human and social development.

---

1 This chapter was originally presented as a paper, 'Mexico's Commitment to the Implementation of the Millennium Development Goals.' to the 2005 Otago Foreign Policy School, when the author was the Mexican Ambassador to New Zealand. The chapter complements Phil Goff's chapter to provide an official perspective on internal issues of development and human security in 2005.

2 See Gabinete de Desarrollo Humano y Social (2005).

Eradicating extreme poverty and hunger

In Mexico, the first of the targets of the first MDG has already been met, since between 1989 and 2002, extreme poverty was more than halved, with the proportion of the population with an income of less than a dollar a day dropping from 10.8 per cent to 4.1 per cent. This was primarily the result of three factors: an increase in the salaries of unskilled workers, an increase in government expenditure for the poorest sectors of the population and control of inflation.

The second target of the first MDG has also been met by the Mexican Government as between 1988 and 1999, national nutrition surveys indicated that the prevalence of underweight children under five years of age was reduced from 14.2 per cent to 7.6 per cent. The majority of child malnutrition is concentrated in localities with fewer than 2,500 inhabitants, that is, in rural areas. Similarly, between 1999 and 2002, the proportion of the population below the minimum level of dietary energy consumption was reduced from 2.5 per cent to 2.1 per cent.

These improvements were achieved through the enormous contribution of official programmes with an integral focus on human and social development and on poverty as a multidimensional reality that must be addressed, both in terms of its causes and its effects.

With the government programme, 'Opportunities', five million undernourished and underachieving families have benefited through payments provided on the condition that the parents keep their children within the school system, attend talks providing information on health and nutrition and regularly take their children to health centres on a regular basis. Monetary grants are also made directly to the mothers so that they can improve the family diet. Through the Social Milk Supply Programme, 5.2 million people now receive fortified milk and the Food Support Programme is working to help poor families in remote areas.

Taking into account that 20 per cent of Mexicans have nowhere to live, the 'Your House' programme provides federal, state and municipal subsidies to poor households for the building and purchase of homes. The Programme of Direct Support for Rural Areas gives direct assistance to farmers by means of a subsidy that the Federal Government grants per hectare, reaching almost 40 per cent of those working on the land. The Business Development Programme promotes the creation of micro, small and medium enterprises, thereby contributing to the creation of permanent employment and regional development.

In addition, in 2003 the Social Security Health Scheme was established and it will eventually be extended to the 48 million Mexicans who currently lack social security cover. The financing of this scheme is tripartite: one part from the central government, a second from the state government and a third from the family, taking into account the amount they are able to pay. A Single Registry of Beneficiaries is also being drawn up, bringing together all the Government's social programmes to avoid duplication and to better target social spending. A further determining factor in President Fox's administration was the passing, in December 2003, of the General Law of Social Development which guarantees that increases in social spending are at least as great as the increase in gross domestic product (GDP). Since 2001, the proportion of public spending put aside for social development projects and for combating poverty has been more than 60.8 of total budget expenditure, which counts for almost 16 per cent of GDP.

Despite these measures, by 2002, 20.3 per cent of Mexico's population was suffering from food poverty (defined as the inability to cover the dietary needs of a family), though this figure had reduced by 35.5 per cent since 1989; 26.5 per cent from underachievement (which is food poverty associated with limited access to health and education services) which in turn has been reduced by 28.9 per cent since 1989 and 51.7 per cent from inadequate income (when personal earnings are not sufficient to cover the costs of food, health, education, clothing, footwear, accommodation and public transport) which decreased by 13.3 per cent over the same period.

Although there has been significant economic growth, the social and economic inequalities existing in Mexican society are so great that government policies have been insufficient to rectify the situation. By 2002, the richest 10 per cent of the population gained 35.6 per cent of GDP, while the poorest 10 per cent only earned 1.6 per cent. Poor families are characterized by high dependency rates, low rates of economic participation, subsistence incomes and a high placing in the informal economy. This inequality also has a geographical dimension and the poorest places are generally rural, marginalized localities spread over a large area with difficult access, mainly in the southern part of the country. According to the Human Development Index of the United Nations Development Programme, the figures for Mexico in 2002 indicate that the Mexican capital has a similar Human Development Index level to that of Portugal (0.89), while the level for the State of Chiapas is comparable to that of Equatorial Guinea (0.70).

The impact of poverty on Mexican women is generally greater than that on men. This is due to several factors, which can include inequality of pay for similar work, too few opportunities in the labour market because of discriminatory practices and the lack of accommodation and of access to credit facilities, preventing women from purchasing essential personal assets on which to build a livelihood.

A significant factor, which exacerbates inequality in income, is the pervasiveness of the informal economy. In Mexico the informal sector is very large and concentrated in micro business with approximately 21 million jobs (according to 2004 figures), characterized by low income, poor work conditions and no social security. Looking at the whole social spectrum, it is estimated that 42.8 per cent of Mexicans have no social security.

Therefore to go beyond the targets of MDG1, the Mexican Government established two additional targets. The first was to reduce poverty in half by 2015. The starting point was the official food poverty line, which would lower the figure to 15.7 per cent of the total population (17.8 per cent in rural areas and 6.7 per cent in urban areas). The second additional target was to halve the percentage of the population below the minimum level of protein consumption and reduce this to 1.2 per cent by 2015.

Achieving universal primary education

By 2003 Mexico had already achieved the target of an almost universal net enrolment ratio at primary level (99.4 per cent) and literacy rate of those between 15 and 24 years of age (97.3 per cent). However, the most vulnerable groups of indigenous people, peasants and migrants still lag behind. Gender constitutes an additional dimension, with women especially disadvantaged in access to education, within these vulnerable groups.

Twenty–one per cent of the indigenous population is monolingual, speaking only an indigenous language, and within this group 39 per cent of those between 5 and 24 years of age do not attend school. There are 62 indigenous languages in Mexico. In response, the Mexican Government set itself additional targets to extend beyond the MDGs. First, to ensure that by 2015 all children between three and five years of age receive preschool education and they should complete this within the standard time of three years. By 2004, the net enrolment ratio within this was 63.1 per cent. Second, the Mexican Government made a commitment that by 2015 all children aged twelve years should be enrolled in secondary education and that 90 per cent of these students should complete their studies within the standard period of three years. In 2004, the net ratio of new enrolments at the secondary level was 56 per cent, with 79.7 per cent of these completing their courses within the recommended time frame. Mexico's third target was to ensure that a significant majority of primary and secondary students would reach satisfactory levels in language skills and mathematics. By 2005 the gross ratio of coverage of basic education as a whole, in the three levels described above, was 84.1 per cent. Mexico is committed to raising this rate to 100 per cent by 2015.

The Mexican Government has faced other challenges in the field of education. These include increasing enrolment in '*telesecundaria*', which is distance education provided through television broadcasts for remote rural areas (currently one fifth of Mexican children take advantage of this programme), facilitating that more women, indigenous peoples, migrants and young workers are involved in educational programmes. There is the need to increase the student option, address the problem of student failure and leaving school early and improving teacher training and secondary education reform.

The promotion of gender equality and the empowerment of women

Mexico has virtually achieved this target. Figures for the 2003–2004 school year for enrolments are positive: 98.2 girls for every 100 boys of preschool age; 95.4 girls for every 100 boys at primary level; 98.1 female pupils for every 100 male pupils at secondary level; 104.2 young women for every 100 young men at the subsequent level of education (ages 15 to 18) and 99.8 women for every 100 men in tertiary education.

The gender disparity in access to education is more obvious in the rural female population. The causes are manifold. Sometimes the families of these women prevent them from attending classes, as their assistance is required for domestic duties. Some leave school before the legal age due to economic pressures and therefore need to seek work. Teenage pregnancy and early marriage compound the problems. By 2005, 2.6 per cent of women in Mexico aged between 15 and 24 could neither read nor write.

Women's involvement in the Mexican economy has increased significantly. In 2004, 37.5 per cent of women of over 12 years of age had links with the labour market. Among these 63.1 per cent had received some tertiary education, but 27.6 per cent had no schooling as they were predominately working in the informal sector for example, as street vendors or domestic workers. The median female income represents, on average, 83.5 per cent of the male income.

Despite a decision in Mexico in 1996 that political parties would specify in their statutes that candidacies for deputies and senators must not exceed 70 per cent of one gender, during 2003–2006, participation of women in the national Parliament was only 18.8 per cent in the Senate and 22.6 per cent in the Chamber of Deputies. Nonetheless, female participation in public servant positions helps to put discussion on the gender theme and the promotion of laws on issues of particular importance to women on the political table.

One of the most distressing illustrations of gender inequality is violence against women. According to the information available for Mexico in 2003, 35.4 per cent of women over 15 years of age were subjected to mental cruelty by their partners, 27.3 per cent to financial deprivation, 9.3 per cent to physical violence and 7.8 per cent to sexual violence. These are only the official statistics.

The principal challenge facing the Mexican Government regarding the MDG to promote gender equality and empowerment of women is to ensure that women who live in rural areas and indigenous women are provided with educational opportunities up to a basic level and that they remain in the school system. It is also important to stop all women from pulling out of school early, to boost programmes on sexual and reproductive health so as to bring down the numbers of unwanted teenage pregnancies and to attend to the situation of women who are working without social security benefits.

Regarding political participation and with the aim of complying with the United Nations standard of having women in 30 per cent of public servant positions, it is necessary to consolidate the increased political involvement of Mexican women, as well as to continue to work on the root of the problem of gender inequality so as to eradicate violence against women. On this final point, 27 of the 32 Mexican states already have laws to prevent family violence and to take appropriate legal action when it does occur. Legislation is also being drafted to bring national legislation into line with international agreements and treaties concerning women's rights.

Reducing child mortality

By 2005 Mexico was in the fifteenth place in the Latin American and the Caribbean region regarding levels of child mortality under five years of age. Between 1990 and 2003, infant mortality in the country decreased by 43.4 per cent, with 25 deaths for every 1,000 births in 2003. Mexico has already met the target of reducing infant and child mortality under age five by at least a third by 2006 and aims to achieve a 50 per cent reduction by 2010.

These advances have been made by steps taken to prevent and control diseases through immunization (including the Universal Vaccination Programme, eradication of polio, diphtheria, neonatal tetanus and measles), acute respiratory infections (reduced by more than 70 per cent) and illnesses involving diarrhoea (an 84 per cent reduction). Infant mortality still represents 9.5 per cent of all mortality in Mexico. The highest rates are found in the most marginalized and poorest areas. Therefore the Mexican Government has added three indicators to those drawn up in the MDGs, to eradicate infant mortality. In 2003 full vaccination cover was given to 95.3 per cent of children by one year of age. The mortality rate for illnesses involving diarrhoea for children aged less than five years in 2003 was 24.9 deaths for every 100,000 children in this age group. The mortality rate for acute respiratory infections for under–fives was 42 deaths among 100,000 children in this age group.

The government's priorities include an improvement in quality of care for newborns, guaranteeing full immunization for 95 per cent of children below one year of age (10 vaccines), having three national immunization weeks each year, improving training of all the technical operational staff of the Infant Health Care Programme, reducing mortality from respiratory infections and diarrhoea, introducing an influenza vaccine for those between 6 and 23 months of age and lowering neonatal mortality.

Maternal health: Improvements?

Mexican women have a 65 per cent lower chance of dying through complications of maternity than the Latin American average. Between 1990 and 2003, maternal mortality was reduced by 26.7 per cent to 65.2 deaths within 100,000 births. Despite this, 76 per cent of the total number of maternal deaths in Mexico occurs in twelve states, with the highest levels in the central and southeastern areas of the country. These areas also have higher rates of marginalization and lower rates of contraceptive use and of provision of care during pregnancy and labour by qualified personnel. In rural areas, within the indigenous community and the more marginalized areas there are higher levels of maternal mortality; constituting a fourth cause of death amongst women of childbearing age.

To fulfil MDG5 it is necessary to enhance the coverage and quality of antenatal care, labour and puerperium services, especially in rural and highly marginalized areas; bolster the structure of hospitals; increase the coverage of family planning services with an emphasis on the adolescent population and on vulnerable groups, while according full respect to the sexual and reproductive rights of each individual; improve women's nutrition in rural and indigenous areas and ensure the provision of skilled care 24 hours a day by trained personnel. A decrease in maternal mortality requires the combined efforts of women, families, communities, NGOs and governments.

Combating HIV/AIDS, malaria and other diseases

In 2005 it was estimated that Mexico had the fourth highest level of people living with HIV in Latin America and the Caribbean (and approximately 94,000 cases of AIDS were reported by December 2004) but it is one of the countries with the lowest HIV/AIDS rates in the adult population (0.3 per cent). Sexual transmission is the cause of 90.8 per cent of all AIDS cases (55.8 per cent of these relating to men having sex with other men and 44.2 per cent to heterosexuals), 6.9 per cent of cases were transmitted through blood (70.2 per cent of these by blood transfusions) and 1.9 per cent were perinatal cases. The HIV/AIDS epidemic is concentrated in urban areas and the most densely populated cities. From 2000 the spread of the disease appeared to level off and was set to decrease during the coming years. The target set for 2015 is to maintain this indicator at between five and seven new cases for 100,000 inhabitants and the forecast is for mortality to decrease to 3.5 deaths among 100,000 people, which will involve extensive efforts being made towards prevention.

Combating HIV/AIDS is one of the health priorities of the Government of Mexico, so it is endeavouring to ensure universal treatment with antiretroviral drugs, especially for those without social security. Between 2000 and 2004, official budget resources increased by more than 14 times for the purchase of these medicines. The Action Programme for the Prevention and Control of HIV/AIDS, which resulted from national public consultations carried out in 2001, has led to projects being implemented with the following objectives: to increase the use of preventative measures in the at–risk population; to lower rates of sexual and blood transmissions; to bring an end to perinatal transmission of HIV and of syphilis and to ensure that comprehensive detection, treatment and monitoring services are universally available. Joint strategies are also in place to control tuberculosis for those who are HIV positive.

The Mexican Government has brought into effect the Federal Law for Prevention and Elimination of Discrimination, in part to defend the rights of those with HIV/AIDS. NGOs have also played an important role in the fight against the epidemic, mainly by endeavouring to overcome stigmatization and discrimination, develop preventative programmes, provide adequate medical services and increase access to medicines. In summary, the priorities for Mexico are to prevent the AIDS epidemic spreading to the general population and to reduce the prevalence of HIV in the most affected groups, as well as to strengthen programmes for the adolescent population, antenatal control and family planning.

Mexico has virtually met the Millennium target of halting and reversing the incidence of malaria. In 2003 there were only 3.7 cases for every 100,000 inhabitants and there have been no deaths from malaria since 1982. Malaria is only found in ten per cent of Mexican territory in some of the rural localities in the southeastern states with poor access and with a population dispersed over a large area. The Mexican Government has made a commitment to keep the incidence of malaria below three cases for every 100,000 inhabitants. Particular attention is being given to the Southern Frontier Programme focussed on the route often used by illegal migrants from Central America so that serious cases of malaria being brought into the country can be detected and treated early.

The target of halting and reversing the incidence of tuberculosis has already been reached. In the six years after 1997 there was a drop of 32.7 per cent to 16.7 cases for every 100,000 inhabitants in 2003. With the Mexico Free From Tuberculosis Programme, the country hopes once again to surpass the Millennium target by lowering this number still further to 5.5 cases for every 100,000 inhabitants by 2015. Work will therefore continue to reach universal coverage in priority areas, with efforts being stepped up for vulnerable groups (migrants, agricultural day workers, indigenous peoples and those with HIV/AIDS) and to provide sufficient care to the prison population. It is also necessary to train and retain enough technical personnel, as well as to continue with the Binational Health Card project being undertaken with the United States to ensure that migrants with tuberculosis receive treatment in both countries.

Environmental sustainability

Mexico's results in relation to this target are mixed. Clear gains have been made in conservation policies, management of natural resources and energy use but negative trends also persist such as a reduction in forested areas. These decreased from 36.6 to 33.4 per cent of Mexico's total land area between 1993 and 2002.

For many years environmental issues were sidelined in decisions concerning economic policy. It was only when the National Development Plan for 2001 to 2006 was adopted, that sustainability was established, as a fundamental principle for development, which protects the present and safeguards the future. There is now an integral focus incorporating the environmental dimension in decision making in economic and social matters. Thanks to this development, priority is now being given to incorporating environmental costs into economic activity, improving environmental infrastructure, promoting clean industry, working towards saving and efficiently using energy, reducing emissions of greenhouse gases and producing cleaner fuel.

Land use is also being regulated and in 2001 protection and sustainable exploitation of water and forests were declared national security issues. Deforestation is being reversed through rural reforestation using native Mexican trees and soil degradation due to overgrazing and poor agricultural practices are being addressed. The use of coal or wood for fuel, used in 19.8 per cent of private homes in 2000 (particularly in rural or indigenous areas) has also decreased. Though Mexico's total emissions of greenhouse gases are greater than those of other Latin American countries and they represent almost 2 per cent of global emissions, in the period from 1990 to 2002 there was a decrease of almost 85 per cent in per capita consumption of substances that deplete the ozone layer due to the increased use of alternatives. Mexico is committed to continue this trend so as to reach the levels established in the Montreal Protocol.

The challenge for Mexico is to bring into practice the transversal agenda and to ensure that all official activities take place in a framework of sustainability so as to halt and reverse the deterioration of ecosystems and natural resources. Information systems must also be strengthened and the country must ensure that the desire to satisfy economic or social requirements does not lead to even greater environmental degradation. It is also important to apply legislation when environmental crimes are committed.

By 2003 Mexico had already halved the proportion of the population that had been without drinking water in 1990 and provided 89.4 per cent of its people with this service. Drainage systems had also been put in place for 77.3 per cent of the total population. However, the rural areas continue to fall behind with drainage provided to only 70.5 per cent of homes. More work is critical to tackle the problem of river pollution and improve sewerage treatment, since figures for 2004 show that only 29.7 per cent of all sewerage was collected and treated. The 2004 National Waters Law incorporates the principles of 'user pays' and 'polluter pays' and aims to promote the reuse of water, as well as to apportion blame for environmental damage.

In Mexico there is not enough information to determine the exact pattern of property ownership in urban areas, which is why the first census of illegal settlements in cities will be held. Two thirds of the population live in 364 cities and metropolitan areas. The rapid growth of cities goes a long way towards explaining the urbanization of poverty, since the illegal settlements lack essential services resulting in illness and higher levels of insecurity and violence. It is estimated that in 2002 more than half of the Mexican population below the poverty line (26.2 million) lived in cities and metropolitan areas. To address this problem, the Mexican Government is strengthening town planning and disaster prevention programmes while improving infrastructure and basic services. Social policies to cater to the needs of marginalized groups continue and a national programme for the purchase or improvement of housing has been instigated.

Developing a global partnership for development

Mexico is a country that supports multilateralism and promotes international cooperation and the United Nations reform process is a priority of Mexico's foreign policy. Because of this, Mexico proposed the creation of the Group of Friends for the Reform of the United Nations in March 2004 and 15 countries now belong to this group: Algeria, Australia, Canada, Chile, Colombia, Germany, Japan, Kenya, Mexico, the Netherlands, New Zealand, Pakistan, Singapore, Spain and Sweden.

This group presented 14 substantive documents, one of which contains proposals to monitor the Millennium Declaration as well as the Monterrey Consensus on Financing for Development and the Doha and Johannesburg Declarations. It stressed that countries must continue their efforts towards international development, mobilizing resources to stimulate growth in the least developed countries and strengthening dialogue between the UN and multilateral financial institutions, NGOs and the private sector.

Mexico is a prominent player in the APEC Ministerial process, the G20, the OECD and other international financial fora. It takes an active role in the World Trade Organisation; supporting international standards in financial matters, appropriate reforms for each country, initiatives for cooperation and exchange of information and a reduction in trade barriers. Mexico supports programmes aimed at promoting development for the least developed countries and the small island states, as well as the reduction or cancellation of external debt for emerging economies. It is an active participant in the Programme of Energy Cooperation with the Countries of Central America and the Caribbean (San Jose Pact) through the supply of petroleum and financial assistance for commercial exchanges and the carrying out of public and private sector projects. In 2001 it launched the Puebla–Panama Plan to give a boost to social and economic development in the Central American isthmus and Mexico's nine southeastern states.

Conclusion

To conclude, I stress that the challenge for Mexico is to redouble its efforts to better direct social spending, to generate income opportunities for the disadvantaged strata of the population and to maintain a stable macroeconomic environment and low inflation. Mexico must also continue with programmes focused on rural, remote communities and on solo mothers and strive towards attaining better coordination between social and economic policy with the creation of formal employment, while also tackling the problems within the informal economy. Resources must be channelled to make the most of the 'demographic bonus' (between 2005 and

2030 the percentage of children and the elderly compared to those of working age will decrease significantly). The Mexican Government must also improve childcare programmes and facilities, increase pensions, strengthen environmental protection policies and ensure that all official programmes are correctly evaluated and monitored.

Reference

Gabinete de Desarrollo Humano y Social (2005), 'Los Objectvos de Desarrollos del Milenio en México: Informe de Avance 2005' (Planta Baja Colonia Juárez) <http://www.undg.org/archive_docs/5932-Mexico_MDG_Report.pdf>.

PART IV
Reflections

Chapter 12
Trade, Aid or What?
Reflections on Development and Security

Jenny Bryant–Tokalau

Come on Laugh
Come on laugh
　　　　　Make us laugh
Think ——
　　　　　Make us think
Do not cry ——
　　　　　Don't make us cry
Trust ——
　　　　　Be trustworthy
Achieve (Accomplish)
　　　　　That you will do something
　　　　　We trust and we wait
　　　　　　　　　(Sreedevi 2005)

Introduction

On 26 December 2004 a tsunami struck the coasts of countries bordering the Indian Ocean. Thailand, Indonesia, Sri Lanka and India were the hardest hit. The result of a massive underground earthquake centred near Sumatra, waves of up to 30 metres high were responsible for the deaths of more than 200,000 people and an almost incalculable loss of property and livelihoods. Global response to the 'Boxing Day Tsunami' was large in terms of money pledged, and many countries provided immediate assistance of basic supplies and medical aid. Some of the countries themselves were initially overwhelmed by the extent of the tragedy and assistance such as burying the dead and access to fresh water and shelter were seen as urgent and immediate priorities.

Assistance to survivors came from international organizations, governments and Non Governmental Organizations. While such aid is imperative in response to a massive humanitarian tragedy, it brings with it several conflicts and concerns. Attitudes of donors towards recipients, appreciation of local cultures, willingness to listen, an understanding of gender roles, village politics, and sensitivity towards religious practices are just some of the ways in which donors, whether formal, governmental, institutional or individual, need to understand the situation in which they are working, and to be 'sensitized' (see Rossi 2006, 27–49).

In a panel discussion entitled 'Trade, Aid or What?' at the 40th Otago Foreign Policy School in 2005 issues of the dilemmas of development assistance were addressed using recent humanitarian and developmental tragedies as examples while searching for 'workable approaches' such as trade and participatory approaches. The panel was made up of an eclectic group, including an academic economist, Stephen Knowles, examining issues of trade and investment, Chris Mahony, a student recently returned from Sierra Leone who discussed issues of child soldiers, Cedric Simpson, a member of Amnesty International and Jubilee Rajiah, a psychiatrist.

Panellists were given a broad brief and asked to address issues relating trade, security and human rights, the right to a better standard of living and the contradictions of 'development', human security and culture. Coming towards the end of the school with lively discussion on the nature of poverty and human rights, the key focus of the panel quickly became the issue of how trade can enhance or hinder human rights. The relative roles of Non Governmental Organizations (NGOs), humanitarian aid and issues of red tape and bureaucracy of aid provided extensive of debate and profoundly illustrated increasing weariness with donor aid, and the real challenges of not only 'dealing with disasters' but also of becoming engaged with donor agencies and their frequent lack of understanding of the situation on the ground.

The panel was very honest in challenging unspoken reasons for both trade and aid when they utilized case studies from Sierra Leone and South India. In her critique of humanitarian aid in South India, Dr Rajiah presented poems written by young female survivors of the 2004 'Boxing Day Tsunami' and their confusion and weariness about non governmental assistance. Sreedevi's poem 'Come on Laugh' illustrates this confusion and the cynicism that develops when people who have suffered massive tragedy see both conflict and confusion amongst donors as well as being forced to 'trust' and 'wait' for assistance which theoretically should be easy to provide.

The Millennium Development Goals

The 'Boxing Day Tsunami' and the other humanitarian tragedies debated at the Foreign Policy School occurred after the setting in 2000 by the United Nations of its 'Millennium Development Goals'. The eight MDGs, to be achieved by 2015, are one way of measuring progress towards poverty alleviation and are aimed at the world's greatest development challenges – specifically to eradicate poverty and hunger, improve health, broaden access to education, achieve environmental sustainability, promote gender equality and to develop global partnerships. It became clear shortly after the establishment of the goals that even partial achievement would happen only by involving a range of organizations and partners, particularly with the involvement of civil society in what is sometimes referred to as 'multi–stakeholder engagement' (see Tuomioja 2005, xii).

The Millennium Declaration, committed to by 147 heads of states and governments in September 2000, declared that by 2015 the number of people living on less than US$1 per day would be halved (Millennium Development Goals 2008). By 2004, half of the population living in developing countries lived on less than US$2 per day and thus disillusionment about achieving the goals remains, unless finance, governance and security can be dealt with as essentially linked towards achieving the MDGs (see Cheru and Bradford 2005, 1–7). By 2008, during a global economic crisis, UNDP stated that 'the proportion of people in sub–Saharan Africa living on less than $1 dollar a day is unlikely to be reduced by the target of one–half' (United Nations 2008, 4). In the current economic downturn the increase in fuel and thus food prices as well as costs of education and health are having a direct effect on the poor. Currently the UN suggests that food prices especially could push as many as '100 million into poverty', mostly in sub–Saharan Africa and in Southern Asia (United Nations 2008, 6).

In the panel discussion at the Otago School, Knowles commented that if using such UN measures, many of the MDGs might be met in Asia and Latin America by 2015, but not in sub–Saharan Africa where extreme poverty remains (measured in this case as people earning the equivalent of less that US$1 per day). Knowles outlined the obvious failures of foreign aid, and its stated intention of poverty reduction, as well as the fact that development assistance is frequently given for political purposes and more especially to help broker investment and trade arrangements. Clearly, how the goals are achieved will depend not only on local commitment, national ownership and funding, but also on how countries participate in the setting of the global economic agenda (Bradford and Cheru 2005, 225). In an analysis of the MDGs and how resources can be raised in order to tackle issues of poverty Cheru and Bradford, with authors such as Vayrynen attempted to locate questions of economic inequality, poverty and marginalization within the broader global frameworks of for example better redistribution of resources (Vayrynen 2005, 21–23). It remains to be seen how this can be carried out (for example through trade, taxation and political commitment). What is becoming obvious however, is that no matter how poverty and resource distribution are measured, the gaps between rich, super–rich, poor and those in extreme poverty continue to grow.

Measurements of poverty and inequality and the global list of MDGs remain anathema to those living in conditions of hardship or poverty. Global and local statistics may demonstrate improvements in living conditions, access to water, sanitation, mortality and education for women in poorer countries but conditions for these women still remain inadequate. In 2008 for example more than 500,000 prospective mothers in developing countries died during childbirth or pregnancy complications (United Nations 2008, 4). Writing on gender and development and the difficulties that still remain in incorporating gender analysis into development analysis, Ruth Pearson (2005, 169–170) noted how armed conflict and war was absent from much of the earlier development literature. Although gender became 'mainstreamed', for example, into DfID (United Kingdom Department for International Development) responses to humanitarian disasters, there is little evidence that gender is acknowledged in practice. The consequence is that MDG targets cannot be achieved, as evidenced by, for example, statistics on access to fresh water. Rossi commented that with aid policies in Niger:

> …everyone working for the project thought that Niger's poverty was the outcome of environmental factors [desertification]…water scarcity is perceived by all the inhabitants of the Ader as the major obstacle to their well–being. Many development workers…recognize erosion and famine as one of the country's main problems and have internalized a belief in the superiority in foreign, technical solutions (Rossi 2006, 40).

Further, much money provided as aid goes towards debt servicing, as in Malawi, where instead of funds being committed to improve maternal mortality, infant health, drinking water or education, aid simply services debt while destroying basic social services (Raffer 2005, 168). Raffer illustrated this with the case of Malawi being forced to sell maize from its food reserve in order to pay off loans. People were left short of food after the 2002 drought demonstrating the 'priority of creditor interest over survival' (Raffer, 167). Raffer argues that such sales should be impossible if the life and human dignity of people is to be respected no matter where they live.

These situations also fail to demonstrate the impact of ignoring basic needs such as water and sanitation on women. Tipping, Adom and Tibaijuka have addressed the role of women in poor households, where they constitute around 70 per cent, and found these women pay a 'heavy price' for lack of access to basic services. Access to water is a key indicator of woman's privacy and dignity because difficult access implies long hours collecting and carrying water. Unless that access can be improved women have an arduous and difficult burden (Tipping, Adom and Tibaijuka 2005, 192). Maternal deaths throughout sub–Saharan Africa are 'indirectly related to the water carrying burden and exposure to waterborne disease when collecting water' (Tipping, Adom and Tibaijuka 2005, 192–3; Zwarteveen 1997). In the Pacific the situation is similar and deteriorating when in times of stress, such as the severe droughts in Papua New Guinea during 1997 people had to carry water for greater distances, putting the health of women and children at risk (Allen and Bourke 1997). By 2005 (the latest data available) maternal deaths per 100,000 live births for Oceania numbered 430, barely lower than for South Asia at 490 (United Nations 2008, 25).

Responses to disasters

Kothari (2005, 50) argues that we need to 'be wary of…attempt[s] to create distinct and artificial boundaries between the exploitation of empire and the humanitarianism of development.' She disagrees with views (e.g., Goldsmith 1997) that development assistance merely perpetuates early ideas of colonial expansionism and argues that humanitarianism and moral responsibility continue in contemporary development agendas.

Distinctions between humanitarian aid and development assistance were made in the panel discussion at the Otago Foreign Policy School where it was argued that links between trade and human rights, and differing definitions of human security[1] needed to be taken into account in any discussion on development assistance. Of key concern was the right to a better standard of living and that trade arrangements and indeed humanitarian aid can compromise and hinder human rights because peoples' livelihoods can be taken away through both good intentions and pragmatic decision making. Much humanitarian aid is given without full appreciation of local conditions but also on the assumption, for example, that Non Governmental Organizations will always do a better job than government agencies (even if they know and understand nothing of local conditions) and that trade will *always* bring long term development benefits for all when most often they are designed as arrangements to suit trading partners, again without an understanding of local conditions and livelihoods. One example of such trade agreements could be regional trade arrangements, which could be viewed both as 'building blocks or stumbling blocks for developing countries' (Narsey 2006, 77, quoting Bhagwati 1991).

Just as humanitarian aid and development assistance are negotiated for very different reasons, so too are trade agreements and fair trade practices. Opportunities for greater social responsibility are also possible however and although such practices are at early stages, fair trade advocates see possibilities for shaping policy that is both moral and fair (see for example Luetchford 2006, 143–144).

1　Definitions of human security vary. Largely the definition tends to be associated with threats related to war, genocide and population displacement. It differs from national security (defence of a country) and is more about 'protecting individuals and communities from any form of political violence' (Human Security Report, 2008, 2) but there is debate over the nature of the threats. These can include poverty, poor governance and inequality and inequity. This was the prevailing view of the Otago Foreign Policy School in 2005.

> The Development Set is bright and noble
> Our thoughts are deep and our vision global;
> Although we move with the better classes
> Our thoughts are always with the masses.
>
> (Ross Coggins)[2]

The 2004 'Boxing Day Tsunami' that swept through the Indian Ocean killed more than 275,000, largely poor, people in 14 countries. Apart from loss of life, loss of homes and livelihoods was massive and reconstruction continues. Humanitarian assistance was immediate with more than US$14 billion pledged or raised internationally (www.tsunami-evaluation.org) – the scale of which had not been seen before. Despite the public response, not all of this assistance was well placed or practical. In some cases the 'flood' of people wanting to assist was too much for small and distraught communities to handle, some donor behaviour was inappropriate, and not all the money pledged reached those most in need.

Jubilee Rajiah provided an excellent reminder of the failure of humanitarian aid based on personal experience of working in five small villages in southeast coastal India affected by the tsunami. In these villages, with banners on trucks announcing their presence, NGOs responded to calls for assistance. They described themselves as having 'adopted' villages and according to Rajiah, were working in a 'carnival atmosphere' within areas where devastation had been great. Villagers however, saw little evidence of viable humanitarian assistance on the ground. Many non government workers were present, but little changed for the people most affected. There was still no shelter, water or food, or even medical relief some weeks after the tsunami, and the people whose livelihoods based around fishing had been swept away were now in the situation of having to wait for assistance, without basic needs such as food, health, employment and education as well as being left to deal with red tape and bureaucracy. Alongside the tragedy of being without basic needs the survivors also had to cope with contradictory agendas and inappropriate responses such as donations of warm clothing, where more urgent needs were water and medical supplies. Although it was recognized that many of the aid workers had 'good intentions', very little of practical use was done and questions surrounding the apparent lack of targeted assistance were left unanswered.

How does an environmental catastrophe relate to human insecurity? Initially the government of India refused all assistance, and the governor of Thailand's tourism authority noted that the garbage had been swept away and that areas of Phuket's ocean were 'the clearest they have been in twenty years' (Roberts 2005 quoted in Keys, Masterman–Smith and Cottle 2006, 202). In some areas women

---

2   This is from the poem, 'The Development Set' by Coggins. It was originally published in *Adult Education and Development,* September 1976 and reproduced in the journal's 1988 issue (volume 30, page 56). It has been extensively reproduced in publications and on the internet but we were unable to trace copyright.

were raped in refugee camps, child trafficking increased in Indonesia (also noted by Rajiah in the Indian villages). Women comprised the majority of deaths in the wider tsunami afflicted area, since they were likely to be home at the time it struck (Keys, Masterman–Smith and Cottle 2006).

Such commentaries reiterate the necessity to scrutinize not only government and intergovernmental institutions in their response to development needs and humanitarian disasters, but also the intentions and practices of Non Governmental Organizations. Although the positioning of many NGOs as being on the side of the 'other' is laudable, there is also a need to be aware of the dangers of lack of 'sensitization' (Rossi 2006) and 'disregard of difference' (Shrestha 2006, 201). Celayne Heaton Shrestha, when relating a story of fieldworker morality in Nepal notes that workers in the field are subject to constant scrutiny of their behaviour, including professional competence but that equally the fieldworkers face many dilemmas and confusions. Shrestha (2006, 213) reminds us that development work is not simple and cannot be viewed simplistically as 'us' and 'them.' Fieldworkers are not always sensitive to local conditions, but so too are they under great pressure to act correctly in often trying circumstances. It is not surprising that aid, and its delivery, does not always adequately target those most in need.

The confusion felt by the people of Southeast India in the face of the tsunami and also the variety of responses is reflected in the poems of the young women from the area. Their commentaries reflect sadness, loss, anger and hope and challenge the role of women in participating in the development future of their countries. Despite the vision of the MDGs to 'promote gender equality and empower women', 'eradicate extreme poverty and hunger' and develop a 'global partnership for development', young women remain excluded from the process. Although the MDGs are interrelated, with outputs from one (such as education) impacting on another (such as poverty), it is questionable as to how far such goals seem relevant to the young women of South India when faced with an epic human disaster.

The Tsunami
Near the sea, tossing and raging
> Played my little brother

Tossing waves running and playing
> Looked beautiful

Your billows rose higher and nearer
> Why did you come?

To protect him, my little brother thought

And then you buried him in the sand
And when I dug the earth to take him and bury him
Lo there were thousands and thousands of little people
> Lying dead, covered in the sand

You are called the Tsunami
I call you Yemen – the god of death.
> (Sreedevi 2005)

The beautiful lady of charity: 'Unintended' consequences and empowerment

Beauty
She came on the bus – this beautiful lady
> Beautiful not only in looks
> But in her spirit as well

No heart, no place to stay
> She gave us hope and a home
> Not only for me but also for the old
>> (Sreedevi 2005)

In other moving presentations at the Otago Foreign Policy School, Chris Mahoney a law and commerce student, who campaigned for good governance in Sierra Leone, and Cedric Simpson, Director of Amnesty International, commented on levels of corruption in aid, superstitious views prevalent on children's and human rights and reiterated similar tales of both international donor and local aid to those that occurred following the 'Boxing Day Tsunami'. The role of corporations, the lure of great mineral wealth with its links with the black market, child soldiers and corruption have been examined very deeply in Sierra Leone, particularly with the Truth and Reconciliation Commission (2002), which had its origins in the 1999 Lome Peace Agreement between the Government of Sierra Leone and the Revolutionary United Front (RUF) (International Crisis Group, 2002). The desire for human security and development still requires capacity, transparency and good governance – both at local and central government level as well as in communities and charities. Corruption in the aid and charity industries is not limited to aid donors. Politicians of many developing countries see aid as an opportunity to line their own pockets, and in military regimes, 'skimming, delving and leaking' is common (see Hancock 1989, 174–175). Mahoney and Simpson's comments have resonance in recent academic and other popular writing on the aid and charity 'industries' where large, dramatic gestures frequently have no impact on human security, poverty and human rights. Indeed, charity and aid can have unintended consequences leaving countries in a worse situation than previously. Some argue that aid can be 'worse than incompetent and inadvertently destructive' (Maren 1997, 12) leaving local communities and nations seriously undermined in their ability to develop local economies and take an independent stance, for example in trade arrangements (see Naidu 2006, 143, 151). As Vijay Naidu (2006, 153) emphasizes, the reform agendas of OECD countries promote the private sector and the market along with human rights and democracy, but at the same time need to accommodate non government groups such women's and church groups.

Human capacity and the ability to deal with aid and all its repercussions and dimensions are fundamental. In the words of Gina Houng Lee (2006, 235), 'we start with small changes; we start with every day challenges. Our first weapon is education.' Houng Lee demonstrated small changes such as having locally trained officers to work with women to access, for example, maintenance payments or safe drinking water or to participate in village meetings, all within a human rights approach. This can be most effective in empowering people at the grass roots level where this would lead to a situation where people 'can make decisions because they are informed and not because they have to listen and obey' (Houng Lee 2006, 236).

The market, aid and security

Aderinwale (2006, 88–89) challenges the definition of the 'essence of security'. Is this the state or the individual? If security is more than a military approach then it must be viewed as 'multi–dimensional' embracing all aspects of human existence including freedom of choice. Aderinwale is pessimistic about Africa's 'quest' for development and sees threats to security as threats to livelihoods and public order (Aderinwale 2006, 90–1). He identifies conflict as emanating from inequitable access to and distribution of socioeconomic resources but cautions that aid needs to first recognize local interests and should not view countries and regions as homogenous entities (Aderinwale 2006, 105). If this is applied to the South Indian situation where humanitarian aid took on an almost farcical quality, it is questionable how a move from aid to trade as part of a 'global economic' approach in such a situation would benefit those most in need. In New Zealand the mission statement of New Zealand's overseas development assistance is to be changed to 'support sustainable development in developing countries, in order to reduce poverty and to contribute to a more secure, equitable and prosperous world.' The core focus within that goal will be the pursuit of sustainable economic development (New Zealand Government 2009).

The recent move by the National government in New Zealand to subsume NZAID back under the umbrella of the Ministry of Foreign Affairs to remove 'conflicts of interest' and 'seek excellence in aid delivery' (New Zealand Government 2009, para. 6) accentuates debates on humanitarian versus development aid and the respective roles of trade, aid and development. These continue to challenge accepted notions such as trade 'trickling down' to the poorest groups and improving living standards through greater access to economic power. Despite the stated goals of international agencies in 'promoting good governance and market development…to support the rebuilding of societies after war and humanitarian emergencies' (Bryant–Tokalau 1999) towards providing fundamental 'developmental security to the global population' it was clear from the presentations in the panel at the 40th Foreign Policy School that the disadvantaged populations of countries in crisis do not share the views of international agencies. Aid, trade and security remain anathema; best summed up in the words of Sreedevi, the young woman of South India, after the 'Boxing Day Tsunami' when she commented on government officials.

Government Officials
For the loan we took
    The taxes take away our business
What livelihood do we have
    Oh Gandhi Mahatma
    Get ready to come
    We need you urgently
        (Sreedevi 2005)

References

Aderinwale, A. (2006), 'The Securitization of Development Aid' in *The Reality of Aid 2006: An Independent Review of Poverty Reduction and Development Assistance* (Manila: Focus on Conflict, Security and Development), 88–106.

Allen, B.J. and Bourke, M. (1997), *Report of an Assessment of the Impacts of Frost and Drought in Papua New Guinea* (Canberra: Australian Agency for International Development).

Bradford, C. and Cheru, F. (2005), 'A Political Agenda for Global Economic Governance', in F. Cheru and C. Bradford (eds), *The Millennium Development Goals: Raising the Resources to Tackle World Poverty* (London: Zed Books), 211–226.

Bryant–Tokalau, J. (1999), 'Regional Resilience and Regional Cooperation: UNDP in the Pacific' Presentation to Island State Security Conference, Asia–Pacific Center for Security Studies, Honolulu, 22–24 June 1999.

Cheru, F. and Bradford, C. (eds) (2005), *The Millennium Development Goals: Raising the Resources to Tackle World Poverty* (London: Zed Books).

Goldsmith, E. (1997), 'Development as Colonialism', *The Ecologist* 27:2, 69–77.

Hancock, G. (1989), *Lords of Poverty: The Power, Prestige, and Corruption of the International Aid Business* (New York: Atlantic Monthly Press).

Houng Lee, G. (2006), 'Embracing a Culture of Human Rights in the Pacific' in M. Powles (ed.), *Pacific Futures* (Canberra: Pandanus Books), 235– 236.

Human Security Report Project (2008), *Human Security Brief 2007* <http://www. humansecuritybrief.info/>, accessed 8 May 2009.

International Crisis Group: Working Towards Preventing Conflict Worldwide. 'Sierra Leone's Truth and Reconciliation Commission: A Fresh Start?' Africa Briefing No. 12. 20 December 2002 <http://www.crisisgroup.org/home/index. cfm> accessed 1 January 2009.

Keys, A. Masterman–Smith, H. and Cottle, D. (2006), 'The Political Economy of a Natural Disaster: The Boxing Day Tsunami 2004', *Antipode* 38(2), 195–204.

Kothari, U. (ed.) (2005), *A Radical History of Development Studies: Individuals, Institutions and Ideologies* (London: Zed Books).

Leutchford, P. (2006), 'Brokering Fair Trade: Relations Between Coffee Cooperatives and Alternative Trade Organizations – A View from Costa Rica' in D. Lewis and D. Mosse (eds), *Development Brokers and Translators: The Ethnography of Aid and Agencies* (Bloomfield: Kumarian Press), 127–148.

Maren, M. (1997), *The Road to Hell: The Ravaging Effects of Foreign Aid and International Charity* (New York: The Free Press).

Millennium Development Goals (2008), <http:/mdgs.un.org/unsd/mdg/>, accessed 3 December 2008.

Naidu, V. (2006), 'Development Assistance Challenges', in M. Powles (ed.), *Pacific Futures* (Canberra: Pandanus Books), 142–163.

Narsey, W. (2006), 'PICTER, PACER and EPAs: Weaknesses in Current Trade Policies and Alternative Integration Options', in M. Powles (ed.), *Pacific Futures* (Canberra: Pandanus Books), 72–110.

New Zealand Government (2009), Office of the Minister of State Services and Office of the Minister of Foreign Affairs. 'New Zealand Agency for International Development: Institutional Arrangements'. Paper to Cabinet External Relations and Defence Committee. <http://www.nzaid.govt.nz/ library/publications/corporate/docs/cab-paper-2-institutional-arrangements. pdf >, accessed 8 May 2009.

Pearson, R. (2005), 'The Rise and Rise of Gender and Development', in U. Kothari (ed.), *A Radical History of Development Studies: Individuals, Institutions and Ideologies* (London: Zed Books), 157–179.

Raffer, K. (2005), 'Debt Work–Out Mechanisms: Debt Arbitration', in F. Cheru and C. Bradford (eds), *The Millennium Development Goals: Raising the Resources to Tackle World Poverty* (London: Zed Books), 156–180.

Rossi, B. (2006), 'Aid Policies and Recipient Strategies in Niger: Why Donors and Recipients Should not be Compartmentalized into Separate "Worlds Of Knowledge"', in D. Lewis and D. Mosse (eds), *Development Brokers and Translators: The Ethnography of Aid and Agencies* (Bloomfield: Kumarian Press), 27–49.

Shrestha, C.H. (2006), 'They Can't Mix Like We Can: Bracketing Differences and the Professionalization of NGOs in Nepal', in D. Lewis and D. Mosse (eds), *Development Brokers and Translators: The Ethnography of Aid and Agencies* (Bloomfield: Kumarian Press), 195–216.

Tipping, D., Adom, D. and Tibaijuka, A. (2005), 'Achieving Healthy Urban Futures in the Twenty–First Century: New Approaches to Financing Water and Basic Sanitation', in F. Cheru and C. Bradford (eds), *The Millennium Development Goals: Raising the Resources to Tackle World Poverty* (London: Zed Books), 181–210.

'Tsunami evaluation' <www.tsunami–evaluation.org>, accessed 3 December 2008.

Tuomioja, E. (2005), 'Foreword' in F. Cheru and C. Bradford (eds), *The Millennium Development Goals: Raising the Resources to Tackle World Poverty* (London: Zed Books), xi–xii.

United Nations (2008), *The Millennium Development Goals Report 2008* (New York: United Nations), 4–8, 25. <http://www.undp.org/publications/MDG_Report_2008_En.pdf>, accessed 8 May 2009.

Vayrynen, R. (2005), 'Global Inequality, Poverty and Justice: Empirical and Policy Issues', in F. Cheru and C. Bradford (eds), *The Millennium Development Goals: Raising the Resources to Tackle World Poverty* (London: Zed Books), 9–27.

Zwarteveen, M.Z. (1997), 'Water: From Basic Need to Commodity: A Discussion on Gender and Water Rights in the Context of Irrigation', *World Development* (Special section: Gender and Property Rights) 5:8, 1335–1449.

Index

Gender in a Global/Local World

Transnational Ruptures
Gender and Forced Migration
Catherine Nolin
ISBN 978-0-7546-3805-6

'Innocent Women and Children'
Gender, Norms and the Protection of Civilians
R. Charli Carpenter
ISBN 978-0-7546-4745-4

Turkey's Engagement with Global Women's Human Rights
Nüket Kardam
ISBN 978-0-7546-4168-1

(Un)thinking Citizenship
Feminist Debates in Contemporary South Africa
Edited by Amanda Gouws
ISBN 978-0-7546-3878-0

Vulnerable Bodies
Gender, the UN and the Global Refugee Crisis
Erin K. Baines
ISBN 978-0-7546-3734-9

Setting the Agenda for Global Peace
Conflict and Consensus Building
Anna C. Snyder
ISBN 978-0-7546-1933-8